Brave New
Neighborhoods

Brave New Neighborhoods

THE PRIVATIZATION OF PUBLIC SPACE

Margaret Kohn

ROUTLEDGE
NEW YORK AND LONDON

Published in 2004 by
Routledge
29 W 35th Street
New York, NY 10001
www.routledge-ny.com

Published in Great Britain by
Routledge
11 New Fetter Lane
London EC4P 4EE
www.routledge.co.uk

Routledge is an imprint of the Taylor & Francis Group.
Printed in the United States of America on acid-free paper.

10 9 8 7 6 5 4 3 2

Library of Congress Cataloging-in-Publication Data

Kohn, Margaret, 1970–
    Brave new neighborhoods / Margaret Kohn.
        p. cm.
    Includes bibliographical references and index.
    ISBN 0-415-94462-7 (HB : alk. paper)
    ISBN 0-415-94463-5 (PB : alk.paper)
    1. Public spaces—United States. 2. Freedom of speech—United States. 3. Assembly, Right of—United States. 4. Social change—United States. I. Title.
    HT123 .K64 2004
    323.44'3'0973—dc22
                                         2003022339

ACKNOWLEDGMENTS

The research for this book was made possible by an Andrew W. Mellon Fellowship for Junior Faculty from the American Council of Learned Societies and leave time from the University of Florida. I would like to thank the Department of Political Science at the University of Toronto, where I was affiliated during my leave. Members of the Committee for the Study of Political Thought (Toronto) and the Urban Studies Program at York University provided useful feedback on parts of the manuscript. I am particularly grateful to the following people, who commented on individual chapters or drew my attention to interesting illustrations of the privatization of public space: Leslie Paul Thiele, Keally McBride, Joe Carens, Melissa Williams, Simone Chambers, Asma Abbas, Neal Katyal, Ronald Beiner, Stephen Elkin, Patricia Wood, Engin Isin, Dan Smith, Ana Kogl, Patricia Woods, Aida Hozic, and Mark Belnick. The final version owes a lot to Ryan Hurl who read the entire manuscript. This book emerged out of a short article that I wrote for *Dissent* several years ago. Without the interest and support of Eric Nelson, my editor at Routledge, it probably would never have taken the form of a book. I am also grateful to David McBride who took over the project early in the editing stage.

LIST OF ILLUSTRATIONS

TABLE OF CONTENTS

1

INTRODUCTION

On March 3, 2003, a lawyer named Stephen Downs was arrested for trespassing at the Crossgate Mall in Guilderland, New York, a small town near Albany. He did not sneak into the mall after hours or enter some "employees only" part of the property. He was arrested for wearing a T-shirt that he purchased at the mall with the slogan "Give Peace a Chance." On the eve of the war with Iraq, the message was too political for the mall. Security guards ordered Downs to either take off the T-shirt or leave the premises. When he refused, they summoned local police and he was taken away in handcuffs. This was not an isolated incident.[1] Although the charges were later dropped after a local protest and international uproar, the management did not change its official policy against political expression on mall property.[2]

According to Downs, the security guards tried to convince him to comply with their orders, arguing that the mall was "like a private house" and therefore he was acting inappropriately.[3] Downs believed that his right to political expression was protected by the First Amendment to the United States Constitution. His mistake, however, was trying to exercise this right in a privately owned place. In the landmark decision *Lloyd Corp. v. Tanner* (1972), the Supreme Court found that the right to free speech only extends to activity on public not private property.[4] The reason is that the Bill of Rights states that "Congress shall make no law…abridging the freedom of speech…." Over the course of the twentieth century, this provision has been interpreted expansively to apply to all levels of government but the debate about whether to apply the First Amendment to some private entities remains unresolved. In *Lloyd Corp.*, the Supreme Court rejected the argument that shopping malls are the modern equivalents of old town centers and should therefore be treated like public places. But the secu-

1

rity guards were wrong in asserting that the mall was "like a private house." In a subsequent decision, *Pruneyard v. Robbins* (1980), the Supreme Court recognized that a shopping mall, unlike a home or private club, issues an invitation to the general public and therefore opens itself up to certain kinds of regulations.[5] This means that political speech in publicly accessible but privately owned places, although not protected by the United States Constitution, could be protected by state statutes.

The incident at the Crossgate Mall is emblematic of restrictions on political expression proliferating across the United States. It illustrates the political impact of the privatization of public space. If someone cannot wear a T-shirt emblazoned with a Hallmarkesque endorsement of world peace, then it is hard to imagine union picketers or antisweatshop activists being able to target the Nike or Disney stores at the mall. Even activities that do not challenge commercial practices, for example, gathering signatures on behalf of political candidates and ballot initiatives, are routinely forbidden in malls. When private spaces replace public gathering places, the opportunities for political conversation are diminished. Ironically, just as new malls are increasingly designed to recreate the atmosphere of old-fashioned downtowns, they are restricting the civic, political, and religious activity that gave city centers their dynamism and variety.

Mall managers are not the only ones using property rights to limit the circulation of heterodox views. In California, an apartment complex prohibited the tenants' association from distributing a newsletter under the doors of residents (see Chapter 5). In Maryland, the United States Postal Service had members of a political organization arrested for handing out literature on a sidewalk in front of the post office (see Chapter 3).[6] In Utah, Salt Lake City sold a block of the downtown core to the Church of Jesus Christ of Latter-Day Saints, which subsequently banned nonsanctioned political and religious activity on the public–private plaza (see Chapter 6). Each of these cases poses similar questions about the relationship among private ownership, public space, and political activity.

In this book I argue that public life is undermined by the growing phenomenon of private government. Gated communities proliferate in the suburbs and Business Improvement Districts—now numbering over one thousand in the United States alone—create privileged zones within the city. Furthermore, the suburban shopping mall, a private alternative to the marketplace and the town square, has been so successful that it has become the model for retail development in city centers. This book considers how these changes affect democratic politics. It asks what can be done to protect and revitalize public space. There are two different approaches to this question. Some commentators call for more civility and vigorous enforcement of community norms in the form of policing and laws against begging and loitering.[7] Others take the opposite tack, arguing that the vitality of public space comes from its diversity, heterogeneity, and even its disruptive quality.[8] The two opposing views have been forcefully articulated in a series of American and Canadian legal cases that highlight the tensions among private ownership, the public sphere, and "outsider politics."[9] Drawing upon political theory, cultural analysis, and free speech jurisprudence, this book shows why the disappearance of public space has negative consequences for democratic politics. But before delving into the details of this argument, I want to provide an overview of the three themes that link the various examples of privatization.

SPACE, SPEECH, AND DEMOCRACY

This book shows how the privatization of public space undermines the opportunities for free speech.[10] Although there is a fairly strong consensus that opportunities for political criticism, organization, and dissent are vital for a democratic polity, the dependence of free speech upon spatial practices is not always clear. The usual rationale for free speech goes something like this: free speech protects the circulation of dissenting ideas that can challenge orthodoxy and, perhaps, limit the despotic exercise of power. Free speech is crucial because it facilitates exposure to a wide range of arguments and makes it possible for citizens[11] to reach informed decisions about public policy. Furthermore, free speech is essential if the minority is to have the opportunity to convince members of the majority of its dissenting views and build a coalition in favor of change.[12]

Yet the widespread support for free speech in liberal democracies often belies an underlying discomfort with face-to-face politics. We see this every day when the impatient businessman ignores a leafletter or the homemaker peers out the window and decides not to open the door for a campaign volunteer. Overwhelmed by telemarketing, junk mail, and a constant barrage of sales pitches, many citizens have become deeply resistant to political solicitation. Furthermore, a theoretical commitment to protecting free speech can go hand in hand with a desire to avoid exposure to unfamiliar ideas and unwanted responsibilities. The privatization of public space makes it easy to sustain this theoretical commitment to free speech while shielding oneself from political provocation.

The United States Constitution requires careful scrutiny of restrictions on political expression in public places. But this scrutiny only extends to the actions of government actors and state agencies. The Constitution was written at a time when citizens were particularly concerned with the despotic potential of government and less attentive to insidious effects of private power. This means that a private property owner may, under most circumstances, ban political speech or discriminate against certain viewpoints on his property, even if it is open for use by the general public.

These restrictions threaten the variation and diversity of collective life. The loss, however, is political as well as aesthetic. Public sidewalks and streets are practically the only remaining sites for unscripted political activity. They are places where citizens gather signatures for ballot initiatives, workers publicize their grievances, and church groups distribute Bibles. The face-to-face encounters that take place in public are different from interactions via email or the mass media. Face-to-face political debate allows citizens to ask questions and challenge answers. Furthermore, the politics of public space requires few resources and therefore allows marginal viewpoints to be expressed, debated, and, perhaps, refuted.

Our commitment to free speech requires us to reconsider the spatial practices that can either enhance or inhibit that freedom. Most important, a proper understanding of the connection between spatial practices and freedom of speech should alert us to the dangers entailed by the erosion of public space.

PRIVATIZATION AND POLITICAL ACTIVITY

It is practically a truism to say that the disappearance of public space is caused by privatization. But what exactly is privatization? It can involve several related processes. Privatization, in the narrow sense, describes the sale of state-owned assets to individuals or corporations. This happened in Salt Lake City when the municipality sold a block of downtown to the Church of Jesus Christ of Latter-Day Saints (see Chapter 5). Such direct sales, however, are fairly uncommon. Usually, the process is indirect; private ownership comes to predominate as commercial spaces such as shopping malls and theme parks gradually replace public places such as town squares. Some people feel that this change simply reflects consumers' preferences; others suggest that preferences are themselves determined by economic structures. According to this logic, people go to the mall because there is nowhere else to go. Suburban malls proved more profitable than traditional town centers because of cheap land, plentiful parking, and economies of scale. Shopping malls may have survived because they were the "fittest" according to purely economic criteria but that does not mean that they are preferable from a civic or aesthetic point of view.[13]

Regardless of whether one views the malling of America as a cause for celebration or alarm, it is important to recognize that it has distinctive political consequences. Privately owned places—unlike their state-owned equivalents—are not obliged to allow religious activity or political speech. As more of our lives are lived in privately owned places, the opportunity for certain types of political activity decreases.

Commodification is also part of the broader process that I am calling privatization. Commodification occurs when something is turned into an object that can be bought or sold. Most privately owned common spaces are part of profit-making ventures and are therefore treated as commodities; theme parks charge entrance fees and shopping malls carefully calculate how much "public" space is necessary to draw customers into adjacent stores. But state-owned spaces can also be commodified. In June 2003, for example, Toronto inaugurated a new public plaza in the heart of downtown; in order to pay for two 24-hour security guards, city officials decided to rent it out for concerts and other commercial events. Big corporations have paid tens of thousands of dollars to emblazon their logos on Times Square-style digital billboards while citizens were arrested for drawing peace signs in chalk on the plaza.[14] This process is so widespread that commentators have coined the term "café-creep" to describe the way that commercial ventures are gradually taking over more and more public space.

But the profit motive is not the only thing driving the disappearance of public space. Another dimension of privatization is a desire for control that cannot simply be reduced to commodification. An example of this phenomenon is a 1998 United States Postal Service regulation prohibiting citizen groups from gathering signatures for the initiative and referendum process on sidewalks in front of post offices. The Post Office did not need this sidewalk space to sell extra stamps. Nevertheless, it passed a rule forbidding citizens from soliciting signatures and passing out leaflets. Emboldened by a Supreme Court decision limiting expressive conduct in airports, the lower courts have also begun to restrict the use of government property for protest activity. On May 21, 2001 the Hotel Workers Union (HERE) was denied a permit to stage a protest on Lincoln Center Plaza; United States District Judge Kevin Duffy found that "the plaza was not automatically a public forum because of its park designation and physical characteristics as a public congregating area."[15]

Justice Duffy's view, however, is controversial. The courts have developed two opposing approaches to public space. The earlier one assumed that the government in its role as property owner has all of the same rights as any private individual. According to this "property rights" approach, public space is basically private space owned by the government, and therefore the responsible bureaucracy has discretion to regulate or forbid citizens' access. The latter view—the "traditional public forum doctrine"—ostensibly governs today. This doctrine emphasizes the government's responsibility for protecting citizens' access to public places such as parks and street corners that have traditionally been used for political activity. But the influence of the property rights approach is still apparent as judicial decision-makers have narrowed the range of spaces that are protected as public forums.

The example of the postal service regulation is especially sobering because it has serious consequences for one of the few mechanisms of direct democracy: the initiative and referendum process. The regulations target nondisruptive political activity on government property. Before the new rule was passed in 1998, groups petitioning outside the building were already forbidden from disrupting postal service business; the new regulation excluded them altogether. The initiative and referendum process, while hardly the full realization of radical democracy, is an important alternative to the remote processes of representative government.[16] It provides an opportunity to educate voters about issues and to integrate politics into everyday life.

Access to public space is the linchpin of the initiative and referendum process. In an age when many people live in apartment complexes or gated communities where solicitation is prohibited, public space is the only opportunity for encountering campaign workers.[17] Privatization of public space is not only a social or aesthetic issue. Access to public space is important because public forums are used to communicate ideas to allies and adversaries through techniques such as street speaking, demonstrations, picketing, leafletting, and petitioning. The face-to-face politics that takes place in public places requires no resources except perseverance and energy. Although there are many other sources of political information such as television advertisements and direct mail, these other forms of communication do not allow the citizen to answer back, ask a question, or take immediate action. The street-speaker or petitioner may not be as influential as the mass media or back-room power brokers but public space provides a forum for dissenters who would otherwise be silenced.

The post office regulation is emblematic of a widespread tendency for public places to try to mimic the strategies that have made malls and amusement parks so popular. Essentially it reflects the desire to apply the logic of the private sphere—control over access and use—to public space.[18] Privacy involves the ability to regulate access to a space, excluding some and including others. According to modern conceptions of property rights, ownership also implies control over the range of permissible uses. The saying, "My home is my castle," captures this convergence of privacy and sovereignty. The fantasy of the private realm involves intimacy, safety, and control. According to this fantasy, the home is imagined as a place where the unfamiliar is absent and compromise unnecessary.[19] In a private house one can arrange things the way one wants them. In public she is confronted by visible reminders of the fact that others may want different things.

The preoccupation with privacy is captured by the saying, "Good fences make good neighbors." Ironically, this is probably the best-known line from Robert Frost's famous poem "Mending Wall." The poem's message, however, is better captured by the opening: "Something there is that doesn't love a wall." While the neighbor repeats the truism, "Good fences make good neighbors," Frost's narrator muses, "Before I built a wall I'd ask to know/What I was walling in or out." This book is about fences and neighbors. It attempts to answer Robert Frost's question, to think about what we are walling in or out when we build gated communities and fortress-like shopping malls.

SEGREGATION AND PUBLIC SPACE

The second theme that emerges throughout the book is the claim that privatization reinforces existing patterns of segregation. It makes it easier to ensure that business people do not encounter street people, consumers do not confront citizens, and the rich do not see the poor. Public spaces that fulfill the democratic promise of equality are disappearing while privately owned zones of safety and corresponding zones of danger are proliferating.[20] This process is evident in the architecture of fear, a landscape of gated communities and fortress-like malls policed by private security forces (see Chapters 4 and 6).

The design and regulation of the built environment can either reinforce or challenge existing patterns of inclusion or exclusion. By structuring people's perceptions, interactions, and dispositions, spatial practices and architectural markers can mitigate or intensify ingrained social dynamics. One of the purposes of public space is to create a shared set of symbols and experiences that create solidarity between people who are separated by private interests.

The privatization of public space exacerbates the effects of racial and class segregation that already exists in housing patterns. One illustration of this trend is the disappearance of public recreational facilities. New, middle-class housing developments and condos often provide common recreational facilities such as parks and playgrounds. These facilities are private and accessible only to residents. Meanwhile, public alternatives—the places where black and white, working class and middle class used to come together—are closed because of shrinking user fees and weakening taxpayer support.

Segregation is both a moral and a political problem. From a moral perspective, it is unjust because it reinforces certain groups' privileged access to safer neighborhoods with better facilities and services. [21] From a political perspective, the problem is that segregation itself makes it difficult for members of privileged groups to recognize the existence of injustice. [22] It makes the reality of deprivation invisible to those who do not live in zones of danger. Without exposure to deprivation or even difference, the privileged become unable to recognize their own advantages and unlikely to question a system that produces systematic disadvantages.

As long as people live in economically or ethnically homogeneous neighborhoods, it is particularly important to have opportunities for political conversation across existing boundaries. Public space can serve as a site of political debate and informal encounter. In community centers, schoolrooms, and on the street, people from different classes and cultures have the chance to discuss their needs, agitate for their interests, and formulate a concept of the collective good. The disappearance of public space makes political communication between groups more difficult. [23]

Even when members of different groups do not engage in formal political discussion, exposure to others may help offset the mutual fear and suspicion fostered by segregation. It is difficult to feel solidarity with strangers if we never inhabit places that are shared with people who are different. The privatization of public space gradually undermines the feeling that people of different classes and cultures live in the same world. It separates citizens from each other and decreases the opportunities for recognizing commonalities and accepting differences. Public space is made up of more than parks, plazas, and sidewalks; it is a shared world where individuals can identify with one another and see themselves through the eyes of others. Seeing oneself through the other's eyes may be a first step towards recognizing one's own privilege and, perhaps, criticizing structures of systematic privilege and deprivation.

PUBLIC–PRIVATE

The third theme that links these chapters is the attempt to clarify the meaning of the terms "public" and "private." Or to be more precise, this book challenges the adequacy of the intuitive understandings of public and private space that we rely on when thinking about the built environment. Most of the places that we share with strangers are neither public nor private but exist in a gray area between the two.

In the past few years, some of the most thought-provoking critiques of privatization have come from scholars writing about "the commons." The core idea is that citizens collectively own an array of resources that should not be exploited for private gain. The term "commons", a somewhat archaic concept usually associated with precapitalist agriculture in England, is artfully redeployed by these scholars to suggest that there is a populist alternative to the Scylla and Charybdis of big government and corporate control. David Bollier, for example, describes the commons as "the vast range of resources that the American people own."[24] In his book *Silent Theft* he specifies that the commons includes "tangible assets such as public forests and minerals, intangible wealth such as copyrights and patents, critical infrastructure such as the Internet and government research and cultural resources such as the broadcast airwaves and public spaces."[25] Lawrence Lessig defines the commons more broadly as a resource "in joint use or possession to be held or enjoyed equally by a number of persons."[26] The examples that he offers are (public) streets, parks, and beaches; Einstein's theory of relativity; and creative works that are in the public domain.

There are good reasons for adopting the rhetoric of the commons. The term is etymologically related to community, a word with largely positive connotations whereas the alternative—public—is associated in many people's minds with bureaucratic red tape and inadequate government programs (public schools, public assistance, public transit). The rhetoric of the commons also lends itself to a powerful critique of privatization by way of historical analogy with the enclosure movement that transformed English agriculture in the seventeenth and eighteenth centuries. Just as English lords enclosed common lands in order to appropriate the resources for their personal enrichment, contemporary corporations are privatizing common resources (scientific discoveries, natural resources, public spaces) for their exclusive benefit. The rhetoric of the commons also makes it possible to identify the similarities between otherwise unlike things that are all part of our common wealth.

Despite these compelling features, I am hesitant to adopt the term commons and instead want to defend the more familiar (but discredited) concept of the public. The main reason for my choice of terminology is that the term commons can legitimately be applied to forms of joint ownership that are still extremely elitist and exclusive. According to Lessig, "The commons is a resource to which anyone *within the relevant community* has a right without obtaining the permission of anyone else" (my emphasis).[27] Although this definition may initially seem inclusive, it can actually be very exclusive, at least in the cases where residential communities are extremely stratified and segregated. The crucial caveat is that one must be a member of the relevant community. Gated communities and other common interest developments often provide extensive collective amenities for their residents: swimming pools, golf courses, playgrounds, and so on. These amenities are available to all residents without obtaining anyone's permission and therefore meet Lessig's definition of a commons. Yet, as indicated in Chapter 6, these types of commons do not provide an alternative to the balkanization produced by private interests or a solidaristic, egalitarian oasis within the market economy.

The term "commons" also erases the distinction between a number of different kinds of collective property. The commons of a gated community is not the same as the Boston Common. We need a language that helps us distinguish between apparently similar forms of collective ownership that have very different social and political effects.

The term "public", however, is not without problems. Previous commentators have drawn attention to the contradictory dimensions of the term public.[28] Jeff Weintraub has identified four different uses of the public/private distinction that inform and often confuse political and scholarly discussions.[29] (1) In some contexts the terms "public" and "private" suggest the difference between the state and the family, whereas (2) in others they are synonyms for the state and the market economy. (3) Political theorists influenced by Hannah Arendt use "public" to describe the political community that is distinct from the economy, the household, and the administrative apparatus of the state.[30] (4) Finally cultural critics treat the public realm as the arena of sociability, a stage for appearing before others.[31]

The contradictory meanings of *public space* highlight the difficulty of defining the term "public." Intuitively we take public to mean open or accessible, yet many public buildings are not open to all. Bureaucratic headquarters and military installations, for example, are owned by the government but inaccessible to most citizens. These buildings are public in the sense outlined in definitions one and two; they are owned by the state. Yet places that are owned and operated under free market principles are sometimes also labeled "public." For example, the antiquated phrase "public house" refers to a tavern or restaurant, a place that is not owned by the government but is widely accessible to the population at large. Even a tavern, however, is not open to anyone without restrictions. Normally only paying customers may occupy a table or a stool.

Today, the private and public realms are becoming increasingly intertwined. In New York City, zoning laws gave developers of skyscrapers special incentives in exchange for building plazas and arcades. This has created a situation in which much of New York City's public space is privately owned.[32] Conversely, streets in Times Square and in forty neighborhoods throughout the city are now cleaned and policed by private companies.[33] These companies are paid by Business Improvement Districts, private governments that collect property tax-like assessments that are approved by large property owners in elections that exclude tenants. Another example of the hybridization of public and private space is the shopping mall, a place that is privately owned but often uses its architectural vocabulary to suggest that it is an old-fashioned town center. This progressive blurring of the boundaries makes it necessary to develop a flexible definition of public space.[34]

I propose that we treat public space as a cluster concept. By cluster concept I mean a term that has multiple and sometimes contradictory definitions. The only way to approach such a concept is to outline a range of possible meanings or criteria. A subset of these criteria grouped together would then qualify a site as a public space.[35] Failing to meet a single criterion, however, would not necessarily categorize a space as private.

My proposed definition of public space has three core components: ownership, accessibility, and intersubjectivity. In everyday speech a public space usually refers to a place that is owned by the government, accessible to everyone without restriction, and/or fosters communication and interaction. This definition reflects the widely shared intuition that public spaces are the places that facilitate unplanned contacts between people. These unplanned contacts include interactions between strangers as well as chance meetings between friends and acquaintances.

Table 1.1 imperfectly illustrates how difficult it is to categorize a given space as public or private. Even when we start with just two of the three criteria, a complex continuum emerges with plazas at one extreme and private homes at the other. On the public end of the continuum are places such as the ancient agora that meet all three criteria; they owned by the government, generally accessible to everyone, and serve as a stage for political speech and action. On the private end of the continuum are places such as the home that are owned by individuals or groups and accessible only to members. In between, however, are a wide range of hybrid spaces such as the shopping mall and café that meet some but not all of the criteria outlined above. Often these are places that bring people together for the purpose of consumption. I propose that we use the term *social spaces* to describe these public–private hybrids.

Public space plays an important role as a stage for political activity. According to the courts, generally accessible, government-owned places such as city streets, squares, and parks are "traditional public fora." The political importance of such public spaces was encoded in constitutional theory sixty years ago. In *Hague v. CIO* (1939) the Court considered the constitutionality of a Jersey City ordinance requiring a permit for speaking in public places. Writing for the majority, Justice Roberts held that "streets and parks may rest (in governments but) they have immemorially been held in trust for the use of the public and …have been used for purposes of assembly, communicating thoughts between citizens, and discussing public questions. Such use of the streets and public places has, from ancient times, been a part of the privileges, immunities, rights, and liberties of citizens."[36]

Table 1.1 Two Dimensions of Public Space

Accessibility	Unrestricted	Fee for service	Membership
Ownership			
Individual		Café, bar	Home
Corporate (profit/non-profit/cooperative)	Shopping Mall	Theme park, movie theater	Club, church, residential community facilities, office buildings
Government	City streets, plazas and parks	National parks	Bureaucratic headquarters, military bases

The debate about whether to define social spaces as public or private is not merely an academic question. There are important legal consequences. If a privately owned place is the functional equivalent of a traditional public forum, the courts are more likely to compel the owners to protect civil rights and allow political activity. Furthermore, privately owned places may not arbitrarily exclude members of a specific group if they are otherwise open to the general public. This distinction is captured in constitutional jurisprudence by the concept of *invitee*. In *Marsh v. Alabama* (1946) the Supreme Court found that a privately owned company town could not forbid a Jehovah's Witness from passing out religious literature in the downtown central business district.[37] The basis for this decision, and subsequent legislation that prohibited privately owned businesses from discriminating against blacks, was accessibility. As long as access was not limited to members of an identifiable group, then a privately owned place was deemed to play a quasi-public role and could be regulated by the government.

Deciding whether to assign the label "public space" is not as easy as checking to make sure that a given place meets two of the three criteria outlined above. The relative accessibility or exclusiveness of a place can be difficult to assess. Initially, shopping malls, cafés, and movie theaters, for example, seem generally accessible. The only criterion of admission is some sort of modest fee, the price of a ticket or a cup of coffee. In some cases, however, this apparent inclusivity can be based on subtle or invisible forms of exclusion. Private security guards expel political activists and other undesirables who violate a set of often unwritten rules. These rules are flexibly and differentially enforced in order to sustain an illusion of openness while maximizing management's control.[38] Exclusiveness is often achieved through indirect mechanisms (see Chapter 7). One task of critical social theory is to identify these less apparent forms of exclusion so that they can be acknowledged and, perhaps, challenged.

Ownership and accessibility alone, however, cannot fully explain the distinctive quality of public space. A fuller understanding of the concept requires an account of the kind of encounters that a space facilitates.[39] Some places encourage interaction between people whereas others foster a kind of collective isolation by focusing everyone on a central object of attention. Stadiums and theaters, for example, position individuals as members of an audience whereas others—a playing field, a plaza, a meeting room—may position them as co-creators of a shared world. To capture this distinction I have used the term "intersubjectivity."

Movie theaters and sports stadiums do not feel like public places because they do not facilitate interaction between people. They aggregate individuals but they do so in a way that positions them as spectators rather than participants. In *Society of the Spectacle*, Guy Debord explains:

> The spectacle divides the world into two parts, one of which is held up as a self-representation to the world, and is superior to the world. The spectacle is simply the common language that bridges this division. Spectators are linked only by a one-way relationship to the very center that maintains their isolation from one another. The spectacle thus unites what is separate, but it unites it only *in its separateness*.[40]

According to Debord, the togetherness fostered through the spectacle is the opposite of the commonality constituted through dialogue because the latter allows for interaction, response, and change.[41]

CONCLUSION

Municipalities, citizens, consumers, and developers are engaged in a constant struggle to define and control space. Gated communities are manifestations of the desire to turn public space into private space;[42] the popularity of theme parks and their progeny confirms that spectacle has become a way of life. Downtown districts, residential communities, and shopping malls routinely exclude sources of discomfort for their patrons, including panhandlers and homeless people, religious zealots, strikers, and petitioners. This desire to exclude the unsettling and the unattractive is characteristic of a certain mode of spectatorship. It reflects the widely shared expectation that one should not be forced to view the unpleasant consequences of our social system or witness the sufferings of others. But suffering exists even if the privileged do not view it; forcing the downtrodden out of sight, banishing them from the places that the privileged pass in everyday life is not the same as solving social problems, and may make the problems more difficult to solve. As long as social problems such as homelessness, poverty, and *de facto* segregation are only apparent to those who experience them, there will be few programs committed to change. These problems only become legible and soluble if they are visible in public space.

Public space has the potential to facilitate interaction between strangers and acquaintances. Under what conditions will it realize this potential? First, in order to facilitate interaction a space must be widely accessible. Usually this means that it is owned by the government or a nonprofit organization because other proprietors restrict access to members or potential consumers. When looking at accessibility we should consider both the juridical and practical dimensions. A park located in an exclusive neighborhood that is not served by public transportation is not very public. Similarly, a public forum located on the outskirts of town is useless if it does not provide speakers with a realistic opportunity to be heard by strangers. Accessibility and ownership alone, however, do not exhaust the definition of public space. A community center run by a nonprofit organization seems more like a public space than a high school football stadium does. The concepts of "spectacle" and "intersubjectivity" capture this distinction. A community center is a public space because it has rooms that are designed to host meetings and facilitate debates. A high school football stadium, although owned by the government and open to all (at least on game day) brings people together as spectators rather than participants.

These different functions are reflected in the built environment. A plaza may be designed to provide views of military parades or important buildings on the periphery or it can provide intimate spaces for various groups and activities.[43] Linguists have identified the "phatic aspect of speech," in other words, terms like "Hello" or "How are you?" that initiate, maintain, or interrupt contact.[44] Particular spaces serve a similar function. They aggregate or exclude; they encourage or inhibit contact between people; and they determine the form and scope of the contact. These effects may be achieved through physical properties, such as accessibility of a courtyard, the arrangement of benches, or the presence of a stage. Public places such as parks and plazas and social spaces such as community centers can encourage a certain kind of civic conversation. Sometimes this dialogue takes place quite literally, for example, when a street preacher or petitioner engages the interest of someone passing by. But this conversation does not necessarily take place with words. Often the dialogue is the internal kind that is motivated by viewing and reflecting upon a range of people and activities. Public space can incite democratic effects when it positions both subject and object together in a shared and contestable world.

SUMMARY OF THE CHAPTERS

Critiques of privatization often implicitly or explicitly rely on a nostalgic vision of an earlier, more authentic, organic community; Chapter 2 challenges this vision by demonstrating that public space has always been a site of conflict. It analyzes a decisive moment in the early twentieth century when the Wobblies (members of the IWW) began to fight for the right to address workers from soap boxes that they set up on street corners. The IWW was an unlikely protagonist in the fight for free speech, given its anarcho-syndicalist and anti-liberal ideology. The Wobblies challenged the dominant rationale for free speech (which understood it as a way to protect unique individuals from the conformity of the masses) and defended *street speaking*, a tool for political organization. They argued that forbidding political speech in public places was a tactic used to silence workers who did not have access to privileged forums such as the pulpit or lectern. Chapter 2 is both a theoretical and historical account of their distinctive approach to rights, democracy, and public space.

Although the Wobblies were not primarily concerned with legal principles, they articulated the position known today as the "public forum doctrine." According to this doctrine, the courts must carefully scrutinize restrictions that limit free speech and assembly in widely accessible public places because such places play an important role as platforms for dissent and debate. Chapter 3 analyzes the way that the public forum doctrine has been applied to more recent conflicts over political and religious activity in public places such as airports and subways. It emphasizes the value of a vibrant public sphere and criticizes the expansion of the property rights approach, which treats public space as private property owned by the state.

Chapter 4 traces the *de facto* privatization that has occurred over the past twenty years as shopping malls have replaced downtown business districts. It analyzes the logic behind Supreme Court decisions exempting shopping malls from the free speech protections of the Bill of Rights. It argues that the "poorly financed causes of little people" are jeopardized when centrally located places open to political activity disappear. Chapter 4 also notes that the expansion of suburban shopping malls is not the only threat to public space. Business Improvement Districts (BIDs) have been at the forefront of the attempt to apply the logic of the shopping mall to downtown centers.

Commercial development is not the only mechanism for replacing public space with privately owned alternatives. In Salt Lake City, the Church of Jesus Christ of Latter-Day Saints paid over eight million dollars to purchase a block of downtown and turn it into an ecclesiastical plaza. As a condition of the sale, the city retained a guarantee that the plaza would remain accessible and inviting to the general public. When the Latter-Day Saints forbade leafletting or proselytizing by other religious groups, the Unitarian Church challenged the restrictions on First Amendment grounds. Chapter 5 analyzes the theoretical issues raised by this case. It draws upon the history of religious and political communities—groups such as the Shakers, Harmonists, Oneida Perfectionists, Zoar—and their attempts to create perfectionist zones in the United States. It summarizes and challenges a liberal rationale for the position that intentional communities should have considerable latitude in regulating their territories as they see fit, even if their policies violate liberal principles.

Chapter 6 shifts attention to changing patterns of residential life, most notably the rise of gated communities and residential community associations (RCAs) that function as private governments in which citizens (property owners) and subjects (renters) are not protected by constitutional provisions. The case of the Galaxy Towers, a condominium project in New Jersey, illustrates the political impact of this arrangement. The condo association endorsed candidates for local elections and forbid canvassing by the opposing slate. Condo residents, the majority of the electoral district, consistently voted for the association's candidates, even though the rest of the town, which had information from both sides, supported the opposition slate. The architectural structure of the condo made this possible, by creating an entirely self-contained world. The complex was composed of a high-rise building connected to an underground parking garage and a shopping mall, which made it possible for the residents to avoid public space entirely. Increasingly, single-family homes are also located in semi-private communities. Inspired by the theory of the New Urbanism, hundreds of new developments are integrating residential and retail space. The goal is ostensibly to provide more social spaces, however, the effect may sometimes be to cut residents off from public space.

Proponents of residential community associations argue that neighborhood self-government benefits the polity by educating citizens and democratizing the state. But the theorists of local democracy in America, Thomas Jefferson and Alexis de Tocqueville, did not envision exclusive neighborhoods concerned with protecting property values. Chapter 6 explains why modern residential community associations differ from the cross-class municipal institutions that Tocqueville described and demonstrates how they may actually contribute to the conformism and democratic despotism that he feared.

The gated communities proliferating in the suburbs draw attention to their own exclusivity. Their walls and guard booths are permanent visible markers. The social stratification of urban life is sometimes less

transparent. Chapter 7 analyzes Battery Park City, a successful public–private urban development project in New York City. Battery Park
City is well known for the manicured promenade along the waterfront,
but this apparently "public" park serves to mask the exclusive nature of
a government-sponsored, high-end real estate development. The history of Battery Park City illustrates the way that groups come to live on
different sides of enduring lines separating areas of privilege from areas
of deprivation. Chapter 7 argues that such segregation makes it difficult to sustain the communication and mutual recognition needed to
act together as citizens. Progressive era reformers believed that public
space could provide a shared set of symbols, sites, and experiences that
would counterbalance the centrifugal effect of the private priorities.
This animating spirit is violated when the quality of public space is
achieved by excluding pariah peoples.

Chapter 8 focuses on the perception that public space is threatening
because of the presence of the homeless and other "urban pariahs." It
examines Robert Ellickson's argument that cities should adopt a system
of zoning that prohibits behaviors such as chronic bench-squatting and
panhandling in ninety-five percent of downtown and all residential
areas. His model is based on the old skid rows where street people were
confined and tolerated. Chapter 8 explores three approaches that offer
theoretical resources for criticizing Ellickson's proposal: the liberal, the
romantic, and the democratic.

Chapter 9 is a conclusion that summarizes the argument of the book
and offers a theoretical rationale for the provision of public goods in
general and public space in particular.

Chapter 10—The Afterward—considers the objection that physical
space is irrelevant in the age of cyberspace. Cyber-romantics argue that
the Internet facilitates new forms of community and effective alternative forms of communication. After exploring some weaknesses of this
view, I argue that this book's defense of public space has lessons for
debates about the architecture and regulation of cyberspace.

By looking at places such as shopping malls, airports, gated communities, utopian communes, business improvement districts, and urban
redevelopment projects we can see how the privatization of public
space is changing the physical and cultural geography of the industrialized world. Although these processes are particularly advanced in the
United States, similar transformations are taking place in Canada,
Europe, and throughout the world. The concluding chapter reiterates

the argument that public space plays an important role in fostering democracy by preserving opportunities for political speech and dissent and providing a shared world where we can potentially recognize one another as citizens.

ENDNOTES

1. The local press reported that the mall had been asking mall-goers with antiwar T-shirts to leave for weeks. Winnie Hu, "A Message of Peace on 2 Shirts Touches Off Hostilities at a Mall," *New York Times*, March 6, 2003.
2. Anne Miller, "Mall Drops T-shirt Charges," *The Times Union*, March 6, 2003, B1.
3. cnn.com/2003/US/Northeast/03/04/iraq.usa.shirt.reut, March 4, 2003.
4. In *Lloyd Corp. v. Tanner* (407 U.S. 551) the Supreme Court decided that antiwar protesters had no First Amendment right to free speech in a privately owned shopping mall. The legal precedent regarding union picketing of employers is more complex. In *Hudgens v. National Labor Relations Board et al.* (424 U.S. 507), the Supreme Court found that union members had no First Amendment right to enter a shopping mall to advertise a strike against their employers, however, they might have some protection under the National Labor Relations Act. In *National Labor Relations Board et al. v. Baptist Hospital, Inc.* (442 U.S. 773) the Supreme Court vacated a hospital rule banning union solicitation in the areas of the hospital not devoted to patient care (e.g., the cafeteria, lobbies, and gift shop). This suggests that workers have some right to engage in union activity on their employer's property, but this right is limited by competing private property rights. The most recent Supreme Court decision, *Lechmere, Inc. v. NLRB* (502 U.S. 527), found that union organizers had no right to enter the shopping center parking lot in order to distribute pro-union leaflets to employees. See Jamin Raskin, *Overruling Democracy: The Supreme Court Versus the American People* (New York: Routledge, 2003), 169–70. For a fuller discussion of the shopping mall cases, see Chapter 4.
5. *Pruneyard Shopping Center et al. v. Robbins* (1980) 447 U.S. 74.
6. *United States v. Kokinda et al.* (1990) 497 U.S. 720; 110 S. Ct. 3115. See Chapter 3 for more details.
7. Hadley Arkes, *The Philosopher in the City: Moral Dimensions of Urban Politics* (Princeton: Princeton University Press, 1981); Robert Teir, "Maintaining Safety and Civility in Public Spaces: A Constitutional Approach to Aggressive Begging," *Louisiana Law Review* 54 (1993), 285–338; Robert Ellickson, "Controlling Chronic Misconduct in City Spaces: Of Panhandlers, Skid Rows, and Public-Space Zoning," *Yale Law Journal* 105 (March 1996), 1165–1246.
8. Susan Bickford, "Constructing Inequality: City Spaces and the Architecture of Citizenship," *Political Theory* 28, no. 3 (2000), 355–376; Iris Marion Young, "The Ideal of Community and the Politics of Difference," in *Feminism/Postmodernism*, ed. L. Nicholson. (New York: Routledge, 1990); Richard Sennett, *The Uses of Disorder* (New York: Knopf, 1970).

9. For some readers my decision to include examples from Canada might seem puzzling and for others my excessive reliance on the experience of the United States requires explanation. I focus on the United States because it is the country where the process of privatization is most advanced. It is also the country where I live and work, therefore I am particularly interested in deciphering its political and cultural logic. Focusing on a single country allows me to show how similar legal and cultural dynamics affect a range of public spaces (neighborhoods, transportation hubs, shopping, etc.) At the same time, I want to emphasize that these patterns are not exclusive to the United States or even the post-industrial West. There are gated communities throughout Mexico and Latin America and excellent work has been done on the shopping mall in developing countries. See, for example, Mona Abaza, "Shopping Malls, Consumer Culture, and the Reshaping of Public Space in Egypt," *Theory, Culture, and Society* 18, no. 5 (2001), 97–122. Given that my analysis focuses significantly on the legal dimension of privatization, however, it makes sense to supplement my discussion of the United States with the experience of a country with a similar free speech tradition. The Canadian courts draw upon the same logic and some of the same precedents as the American courts, therefore Canada seemed to be an appropriate point of comparison.

10. I use the conventional term "free speech" reluctantly because, of course, speech is never "free" yet the doctrine of "free speech" is worth defending because it is part of a practice that fosters and legitimizes a politically effective culture of dissent. For a more detailed discussion of the distinctive approach to free speech developed in this book, please see Chapter 2.

11. In this book I employ the term "citizens" expansively. It includes not only individuals who enjoy full membership in the political community (a passport and the right to vote) but all residents in their capacity as political beings.

12. In "The First Amendment and Economic Regulation: Away From a General Theory of the First Amendment," Steven Shiffrin criticized the notion of a single theory of free speech. He claimed that speech intersects with reality in too many complex ways to be adequately resolved by a single theory [*Northwestern University Law Review* 78, (1983), 1212]. I am sympathetic to Shiffrin's argument and do not mean to imply that the political dimension exhausts the meaning of the First Amendment; it is simply the most important for a work on political theory.

13. Benjamin Barber, "Malled, Mauled and Overhauled: Arresting Suburban Sprawl by Transforming the Mall into Usable Civic Space," in *Public Space and Democracy*, eds. Marcel Hénaff and Tracy B. Strong (Minneapolis: University of Minnesota Press, 2001). See also ed. David J. Smiley, *Sprawl and Public Space: Redressing the Mall* (New York: Princeton Architectural Press, 2002).

14. Nick McCabe-Lokos, "Councillor Kyle Rae Force Behind Project," *Toronto Star*, May 29, 2003, J10.

15. "Lincoln Center Bans Union Rally," *City Law* 7 (May/June 2001), 68.

16. Daniel Smith, "Special Interests and Direct Democracy: An Historical Glance," in *The Battle over Citizen Lawmaking*, ed. M. Dane Walters (Durham, NC: Carolina Academic Press, 2001).

17. Although the Internet has been trumpeted as a new kind of public forum, research has shown that it actually fosters hyperspecialization and further atomizes the reading public. See Cass Sunstein, *Republic.com* (Princeton, NJ: Princeton University Press, 2001); Darin Barney, *Prometheus Wired: The Hope for Democracy in the Age of Network Technology* (Chicago: University of Chicago Press, 2000). For a more complete discussion, see Chapter 10.

18. Bickford, "Constructing Inequality."

19. Dolores Hayden, *Redesigning the American Dream: The Future of Housing, Work, and Family Life* (New York: Norton, 1986), 101.

20. This phrase comes from Aida Hozic, "Zoning or How to Govern (Cultural) Violence," *Cultural Values* 6, no. 1 (2002), 183–195.

21. Iris Marion Young, "Residential Segregation and Differentiated Citizenship," *Citizenship Studies* 3, no. 2 (1999), 240–242.

22. Young, "Residential Segregation and Differentiated Citizenship," 242.

23. Young makes this same argument in regard to the broader issue of segregation. See "Residential Segregation and Differentiated Citizenship," 243.

24. David Bollier, "Rethinking the Commons," *Boston Review* 27: 3-4 (Summer 2002), 4.

25. David Bollier, *Silent Theft* (New York: Routledge, 2002) 2-3.

26. Lessig, *The Future of Ideas,* 19.

27. Ibid.

28. Jeff Weintraub and Krishan Kumar, *Public and Private in Thought and Practice: Perspectives on a Grand Dichotomy* (Chicago: University of Chicago Press, 1997), 2; Hanna Pitkin, "Justice: On Relating Private and Public," *Political Theory* 9, no. 3 (1981): 327–352; Norberto Bobbio, "The Great Dichotomy: Public/Private," in *Democracy and Dictatorship: The Nature and Limits of State Power* (Oxford: Polity, 1989).

29. Jeff Weintraub, "The Theory and Politics of the Public/Private Distinction," in *Public and Private in Thought and Practice,* 7.

30. Hannah Arendt, *The Human Condition* (Chicago: University of Chicago Press, 1958), 22–78.

31. See, for example, Richard Sennett, *The Fall of Public Man* (New York: Random House, 1976).

32. Jerold Kayden, *Privately Owned Public Spaces: The New York City Experience* (New York: Wiley, 2000).

33. Richard Briffault, "A Government for Our Time? Business Improvement Districts and Urban Governance," *The Columbia Law Review* 99 (1999), 365–477.

34. In the introduction to *Public Space and Democracy,* Tracy Strong and Marcel Hénaff distinguish among public, private, sacred, and common space. A public space is a human construct that facilitates seeing and being seen. For Strong and Hénaff, public space has both a physical and a social dimension. The social dimension is captured by the term "theatrical", which suggests the importance of visibility and self-presentation. A public space also has a distinctive architectural property: openness. Open spaces like the ancient agora and the renaissance piazza are public in a way that back alleys are not. A private space, on the other hand, is characterized by the way individuals or groups can exclude outsiders. Thus private space is not only a matter of ownership but also of regulation and control of access. Common space includes wilderness areas or oceans, areas that are neither privately owned nor sites of sociability.

35. William E. Connolly, *The Terms of Political Discourse* (Lexington, MA: D.C. Heath and Company, 1974), 14.

36. *Hague v. Committee for Industrial Organizations* 307 U.S. 496 (1939).

37. *Marsh v. Alabama* 326 U.S. 501 (1946).

38. A student in my graduate seminar, Cities and Citizenship, wrote a short paper based on participant observation at the Oaks Mall. He witnessed security guards asking a group of black youth to leave the food court because they violated rules against gambling (playing cards). An elderly woman and young child who were playing Go Fish were not asked to leave. A similar incident in St. Petersburg, Florida was reported in the newspapers. A black youth, the son of a local minister, was forced to leave the mall because he was wearing a baseball cap sideways (considered a gang sign) even though white youths were allowed to wear baseball caps. See Rosalind Helderman, "Lawyer Tests Mall Policy on Clothing, Gets Warning," *St. Petersburg Times,* July 25, 2000, 3B.

39. Richard Sennett, *The Uses of Disorder* (New York: Knopf, 1970).

40. Guy Debord, *The Society of the Spectacle* (New York: Zone Books, 1995), 22.

41. Debord, *The Society of the Spectacle*, 17.
42. Sennett, *The Uses of Disorder*.
43. Setha Low, *On the Plaza* (Austin, TX: University of Texas Press, 1999); Whyte, *The Social Life of Small Urban Spaces*.
44. Michel de Certeau, *The Practice of Everyday Life* (Berkeley: University of California, 1988), 99.

2

WEAPONS OF THE WOBBLIES:
THE STREET-SPEAKING FIGHTS

Most introductory textbooks in courses on constitutional law or civil liberties begin their discussion of free speech with a case called *Schenck v. United States*.[1] The case deals with the Espionage Act of 1917, which made it illegal to criticize the war effort. The defendants were jailed for circulating a pamphlet urging conscripted military recruits to refuse to serve. A unanimous Supreme Court upheld the defendants' conviction and found that the act did not violate antiwar protesters' right to free speech. But this unanimity was the legacy of a passing era. In the next challenge to the Espionage Act (*Abrams v. United States*) Justice Holmes wrote a dissenting opinion tentatively defending free speech. One hundred and thirty-six thousand Americans had lost their lives in World War I and in its aftermath people began to wonder whether a fuller debate about American intervention might have been advisable.

It is misleading, however, to portray the free speech movement as a movement that emerged in the aftermath of World War I. This conventional wisdom is the product of the training of lawyers and professors, who tend to focus on the development of the free speech doctrine in Supreme Court decisions. But there were popular struggles over the meaning of the First Amendment in the United States even before a robust right to free speech was enshrined in legal precedent.[2] In the eighteenth and nineteenth centuries the courts (through the British Common Law doctrine of "bad tendency") and the federal government (through the Sedition Act of 1798) demonstrated their willingness to suppress speech critical of the government. But simultaneously, citizens contested these limitations. Abolitionists were particularly important protagonists in the struggle for free speech;[3] in fact, the free speech

23

movement had one of its first martyrs in the figure of Elijah Lovejoy who was shot by a pro-slavery mob while defending his printing press.[4]

In the twentieth century, labor radicals and religious dissenters made significant contributions to the struggle for free speech. They were challenging laws that made it illegal to hold public meetings in parks, to speak on street corners, and to advocate pacifism or revolution. During the interwar period thirty-three states and the federal government passed peacetime sedition laws that were used to prosecute communists, socialists, anarchists, and members of the IWW (Wobblies). In most states it was illegal to even display the red flag.[5]

The IWW's street-speaking fights were pivotal battles in the struggle to entrench the right to popular protest and political dissent. Whereas the nineteenth century abolitionists had fought for the right to publish their newspapers and distribute them through the United States Postal Service, the Wobblies pushed for the right to speak on the street. Between 1906 and 1917, the International Workers of the World (IWW) engaged in dozens of struggles against local ordinances forbidding speaking on the street. These street-speaking fights mobilized thousands of IWW members and fellow-travelers and received considerable attention in the press; thus they are, in a sense, the beginning of our story about the importance of public space for democratic politics.[6]

The prominent role of the IWW in establishing a constitutional right to political dissent, however, is somewhat puzzling, because the IWW was a most unlikely protagonist in the struggle for constitutional rights. The IWW was one of the few associations that fundamentally challenged American institutions, including the much-revered United States Constitution. An anarcho-syndicalist union, it repudiated traditional electioneering in favor of direct industrial action. In other words, the IWW tried to organize workers through their identities as producers rather than to mobilize them as citizens. This tactic was based on the conviction that political institutions merely reflected and reinforced power relations; given this premise, the only way to achieve meaningful change was to acquire power at its source, in the economic arena. Why would an anarcho-syndicalist union be the first important group to fight for free speech?

For the IWW, the right to free speech was not an abstract principle; it was an indispensable precondition to their struggle for radical political and economic change. Reviled by the mainstream press, the IWW relied on street speaking to spread its message. Access to public space was critical because it was the only way the group could circulate its views and reach unorganized workers. The IWW needed public visibility in order to communicate with workers and adversaries. The IWW also distributed its own newspaper but street speaking was a more popular tactic because it reached those who were not interested in buying a newspaper. It confronted "respectable" citizens with a visible reminder (and powerful critique) of poverty and deprivation. IWW orators tried to transform the figure of the hobo from a symbol of moral deprivation into an indictment of the capitalist economy and its exploitation of itinerant workers.

This chapter focuses on the IWW because they were among the first groups to claim that fundamental political rights are endangered when access to public space is restricted. Subsequent chapters investigate the way that the privatization of public space undermines democratic processes, however, this chapter looks at a period in history when the government itself tightly controlled the use of public space for political activity. By revisiting this history we can better understand the reasons why a democratic society requires public forums. Perhaps a monarchy or fascist government can effectively orchestrate ritualistic uses of public space that reflect the existing social order, but a democratic society maintains its legitimacy by incorporating new ideas and demands. In theory, the political system facilitates the competition between groups with different ideas about how to govern. Public space is crucial because it is a stage on which groups can debate alternative views on policy and principle.

Recounting this history also cautions us against a nostalgic approach to history, which contrasts the privatized social spaces of the present with an idealized public space of the past. The experience of the IWW shows that contemporary anxieties about disorder, crime, and dissent are not new. Nor should we make the opposite mistake and assume that the struggle between the government and dissenters is a historical relic. Struggles over the regulation of protest are not a thing of the past. As we will see at the end of the chapter, protest-free zones in city centers and on university campuses are a renewed source of conflict today.

THE WEAPONS OF THE WOBBLIES

The IWW, founded by Bill Haywood in 1905, was a coalition of unions animated by anarchosyndicalist ideology. The early constituency of the IWW was made up of miners working in isolated camps in the western part of the United States. Radicalized by a series of strikes that were brutally crushed, the miners rejected the accommodationist stance of the American Federation of Labor (AFL) and supported a more militant alternative. The Western and rural roots of the IWW are critical in understanding the importance of street speaking for the organization.

Although the IWW organized workers in textiles, service sectors, steel, and transport, its membership was largely composed of miners, lumberjacks, and agricultural workers in the western United States. Many of these sectors relied on seasonal labor and employed an itinerant workforce. The system of labor recruitment was structured to exploit these vulnerable workers. Jobless men concentrated in western cities such as Spokane, Fresno, and Missoula where employment agents (called "sharks") would dispatch them to isolated labor camps in outlying rural areas. These sharks would often require a fee before providing directions to the labor site, which was itself only accessible to those carrying a pass provided by the shark. Upon arriving at the site, workers often found that wages were much lower than promised or the job itself nonexistent, but they had already invested their savings in the fee and travel costs and were left totally indigent.

The immediate goal of the IWW was to break the monopoly of the sharks by setting up alternative labor recruitment centers. In order to accomplish this, however, they had to educate workers who congregated in western cities in the winter before these workers dispersed to isolated camps during the summer. Because the lumber camps and mines housed workers in barracks on private property, labor organizers had no access to them for most of the year. In the off-season there was the chance to educate and organize itinerant workers. In these off-season hubs the IWW began to hold meetings and agitate on the street. Often their speakers stood up on a soap box directly in front of the storefront operations of the employment agents who they were haranguing against. Thus, there was a distinctively spatial logic to their strategy. Far from engaging in a fight for abstract rights or a vindication of the Constitution, the IWW speakers knew that the viability and growth of their organization depended not only on the right to speak but also on the ability to speak on the street corners where their target audience could be reached. As one Wobblie put it, "The master class is aware of the fact that there are thousands of workers who cannot be induced into a hall and they also know that in thousands of instances the workers have not the money to shell out for a hall. They reason that if street speaking can be prohibited, that a great amount of the agitation now going on by the IWW can be throttled and the workers kept in ignorance of economic conditions throughout the country."[7]

In fighting for free speech, the IWW was fighting for its ability to use its core tactics of education and agitation. The experience of the IWW suggests that rights are not necessarily atomizing and individualizing, as Karl Marx and some of his followers had suggested. The IWW did not frame the right to free speech in terms of the individual conscience; instead, it was understood as a key component of labor organization and collective bargaining. Street speaking made it possible to turn a small group of malcontents into a social movement by unifying workers. From the perspective of the IWW, it was the atomized dispersed condition of itinerant workers that the street meetings were supposed to transform.

The IWW was very skeptical that well-meaning elites, be they elected officials or judges, would reach their decisions based on constitutional principles or commitment to democracy. According to the IWW, "the free speech fight is, in the last analysis, the outcome of conflicting interests between labor and capital."[8] In a series of cartoons, the IWW made it clear that they believed that local officials and judges in towns such as Spokane were doing the bidding of local business interests—the sharks and the large mining and lumber industries that patronized them. In one cartoon, the judge says, "It is against the Constitution to talk on the streets! Do you understand?" while behind his back he is taking a fistful of cash from a short man in a bowler hat labeled "employment shark."[9]

Despite this deeply rooted skepticism about the courts, the IWW made arguments that contributed to the doctrinal development of free speech jurisprudence. Most notably, they drew attention to the differential treatment received by religious organizations and labor organizations. The local officials in Spokane, Missoula, Fresno, Vancouver, and Seattle claimed that street speaking blocked traffic, hurt business, and caused a public nuisance. But the Salvation Army, with its blaring brass bands, was allowed to proselytize on the street with impunity. The real reason for selective enforcement against the IWW was that the organization presented a threat to the powerful economic interests dominant in the West. The IWW argued that any restriction on speech must be content neutral.

Another theme in the Wobblie press was that free speech was, in practice if not in theory, a privilege of the wealthy rather than an equal right. The Wobblies claimed that outlawing street speaking effectively meant forbidding free speech to itinerant workers. The argument recalls the famous quotation from Anatole France about "the majestic egalitarianism of the law, which forbids rich and poor alike to sleep under bridges…." The majestic egalitarianism of the law in the United States supposedly forbade both industrialists and workers from discussing politics on the streets. Street corners, however, were one of the only places for poor people to speak to each other, inasmuch as they didn't have access to the university lectern, country club, or church pulpit. According to the *Industrial Worker*, "If only those holding diplomas from some accredited institution of learning are to be allowed to speak we shall have a very quiet time...for...about the only institution in which the majority of us take a post-graduate degree is the school of hard knocks."[10]

The IWW pioneered a legal doctrine that would be known as the "traditional public forum doctrine," which was finally recognized in a 1939 case *Hague v. CIO*. The IWW argued that a meaningful right to free speech required access to public space. According to this principle, public places such as streets and squares are held in trust by the government for the people. The decision acknowledged that streets and squares have traditionally been used by citizens to assemble, to petition the government, and to publicize grievances, and that these functions should be protected by the courts. The *Industrial Worker* explained that

> ...if Spokane can prescribe certain limits where it is a criminal offense for the poor to discuss those questions which vitally concern every citizen of a republic, other city councils could do the same; the limit could be extended until the only place where those holding different views on economics and politics from the governing class would be allowed to exercise the right of free speech would be where there was no possibility of obtaining an audience.[11]

The Wobblie press was forthright in expressing its skepticism about equal protection under the law. One editorial explained,

> We do not delude ourselves into thinking we have any constitutional rights....The free speech joke has been taken to the Supreme Court (so-called) of the State of Washington merely to be ignored. As a final demonstration of the idiocy of the working people expecting anything but kicks from the law, this 'contempt' of the court is an everlasting lesson.[12]

In fact, the Washington State Supreme Court ultimately found in favor of the Wobblies. In November 1909, the Court decided that the Spokane ordinance banning street speaking did violate the constitutional right to free speech and assembly and ordered the release of those still in jail. This decision, however, would not deter Spokane officials from arresting the IWW orators. Just one week after the court decision, the Spokane paper, the *Spokesman Review,* reported,

> In order to place a curb on fire-brand orators of the IWW circles and to prevent temporary leaders from sowing seeds of discontent among foreigners and Americans who attend meetings, four policemen, beginning tonight, will be detailed to attend all meetings with instructions to arrest all speakers giving voice to revolutionary or incendiary or rabid utterances.[13]

And despite the legal ruling, the local authorities in Spokane continued to arrest Wobblies for speaking on the street. They simply charged them with conspiracy to commit a crime, vagrancy, or disorderly conduct. So the IWW continued to fight for free speech but did not rely on the judiciary for protection. According to Wobblie ideology, both local government and the judiciary were basically institutions designed to protect private property and the interests of the capitalist class. In fact, the courts continued to convict Wobblies on conspiracy or disorderly conduct charges even though their only offense was speaking on the street. The Wobblies believed that free speech would never be won by appealing to the conscience or principles of the ruling class. The only viable tactic would be to exert power and the only power that the IWW possessed was manpower. Their strategy was to crowd the jails and overwhelm the resources of localities until they were forced into at least a tacit acceptance of soap box oratory.

The strategy was victorious in Spokane and became a model for dozens of subsequent free speech fights. Whenever the police arrested someone for getting up on a soap box, another supporter from the crowd stood up to replace him or her. Often these inexperienced orators simply climbed up and began to read the United States Constitution, barely completing a few sentences before they were arrested. The first day that this tactic was employed in Spokane, eighty-three men were imprisoned.[14] Five to eight hundred men and women spent time in the Spokane jail, where the battle continued. The IWW accused law enforcement officers of inhumane conditions, including beating prisoners, confining thirty men in an eight-by-six sweat box, housing them in freezing conditions without blankets or cots, and turning cold hoses on them in freezing conditions.[15] In one month 681 men were treated in the emergency rooms for injuries sustained in prison.[16]

Law enforcement hoped that brutal treatment would cow the political activists into submission. Conversely, the IWW wanted to bankrupt the city by forcing them to absorb the heavy costs of trying and jailing so many prisoners. On March 12, 1910, the fight was finally settled when Spokane agreed to honor the IWW's right to freedom of speech, press, and assembly. Although most of the publicity focused on street speaking, the police had also confiscated issues of the *Industrial Worker* and closed their union hall, effectively foreclosing all possible means of communication.[17] The IWW asked for several things: (1) landlords would not be intimidated into not renting meeting space to the IWW; (2) freedom of the press (the right to sell the *Industrial Worker* on the street); (3) release of IWW prisoners from city and county jails; and (4) the use of the streets for public speaking. Spokane's Mayor Pratt agreed to points one, two, and four and promised the gradual release of the remaining IWW prisoners.

Spokane was among the earliest and most successful of the free speech fights. Similar battles flared up in Fresno, Seattle, Wenatchee, Victoria (British Columbia), Kansas City, and San Diego, with varying degrees of success. The most brutal repression took place in San Diego (1912); armed vigilante squads met freedom riders at the train station and escorted them to the edge of town where hundreds were badly beaten, stripped, tarred and feathered, and run out of town.[18] Victories in Missoula, Spokane, and Fresno confirmed the power of passive resistance, but the stinging defeat in San Diego highlighted the limitations of nonviolent tactics in the face of violent repression.

Given the enormous human toll suffered by the Wobblies, why did they make free speech such a priority? There are two possible answers to this question. The Wobblies might have fought for free speech in order to build alliances and gain support from moderate, civil libertarian groups. Alternately, they might have defended street speaking as a fundamental dimension of political dissent and labor organizing. All of the evidence in the two Wobblie newspapers suggests that the latter is the more compelling explanation. The Wobblies did receive support from other groups, including labor unions, socialists, the middle-class Free Speech League, and a few public intellectuals such as Edward Ross, the President of the American Sociological Society, but this never motivated their struggle or influenced their tactics.[19] The Wobblies were ambivalent about support from middle-class groups and rejected coalitions that would compromise their militant stance.

The Wobblies argued that street speaking was the only way that disenfranchised groups could build solidarity and political power. In the May 28, 1909 edition of the *Industrial Worker*, one commentator explained, "Whenever in any society there exists a class who suffers and its members are allowed to get together and freely discuss their grievances it will only be a matter of time, when, having thrashed out every point, they will agree on some plan for bettering their condition. Then they will act. And act with deliberation and wisdom common to large bodies of people."

The use of the term deliberation might suggest an affinity between the Wobblies' position and the contemporary theory of deliberative democracy. In fact, the two positions differ in a key respect. For the Wobblies, deliberation cannot engender consensus when it is based on a conversation between two parties representing fundamentally opposed interests. Labor and capital, for example, cannot come to a mutually satisfying resolution of their conflicting interests. A compromise can be reached, but this will reflect the balance of power between the two parties. According to the Wobblies, deliberation is powerless to do more than clarify the terms of disagreement because the interests of the two sides, at least in a capitalist system, are mutually exclusive.

Deliberation, however, does have a vital political role to play in creating solidarity between isolated individuals with similar (or reconcilable) interests. The speeches of movement leaders like Elizabeth Gurley Flynn helped workers recognize that their individual experiences were not just the results of hard knocks but rather the products of a system that privileged the interests of one group over another. Deliberation was also a way to develop the most effective political tactics. The *Industrial Worker* warned that muzzling workers would not prevent violence; it would probably exacerbate violence because aggrieved workers who did not have the benefit of wise counsel would lash out indiscriminately. Workers who could discuss their grievances and agree upon tactics would be less violent and more effective.[20]

THE IWW AND THE CRITIQUE OF RIGHTS

The IWW developed an approach to rights that helps answer objections from contemporary critics. Critics of rights come from positions across the ideological spectrum.[21] Communitarians and conservatives worry that rights talk can drown out much needed conversations about responsibilities and make consensual compromises harder to reach.[22] Marxists emphasize that rights can be depoliticizing and individualizing and mask the real basis of social power.[23] Critics from both camps were wrong in insisting that political rights are necessarily individualizing. A neo-Marxist might respond that the problem of atomization does not arise from speech itself but rather from the judicialization of dissent. In other words, speech may well create social bonds but the fight for free speech positions each speaker as an individual supplicant before the court. More generally, the judicialization of politics can motivate social movements to hire lawyers and experts instead of devoting resources to popular education and mobilization. If a successful test case before the courts can change the law, then the exhausting process of political participation seems less necessary.

This link between civil rights and the courts is so powerful in contemporary life that both critics and proponents alike take it for granted. It is easy to forget that the link itself was the contingent outcome of political tactics and historical processes. In the early twentieth century it was by no means firmly established that the courts were the best or the only upholders of civil liberties. The goal of the street speaking fights was not victory in the courtroom but rather the diffusion of popular rights consciousness among citizens and local government officials. The IWW emphasized that everybody was responsible for defending civil liberties, not just the courts. When the *Industrial Worker* reported that an ordinance banning street speaking was to be appealed to the State Supreme Court, the paper noted "it matters not to us which way the decision is handed down: whether for us or against us, we shall still uphold our constitutional right of free speech and the right to peaceably assemble for the purpose of discussing our views on the great social problem."[24]

The IWW's defense of free speech, however, was not entirely consistent. Pamphlets and newspapers published during the free speech fights contain at least two opposing rationales. The first rationale is akin to the position taken today by Stanley Fish. According to Fish, "'Free speech' is just the name we give to verbal behavior that serves the substantive agendas that we wish to advance."[25] Because those in power get to decide what speech may be exercised, free speech is a political prize, a privilege of power, not a neutral standard for adjudicating between conflicting claims. This is very similar to a position articulated in the *Industrial Worker*. According to the Wobblies, the "right" to free speech was a political privilege granted to particular groups in accordance with the goals of the government. This implies that the "right" to free speech does not provide a meaningful check on the government because the government retains for itself the privilege of interpreting and applying the law as it sees fit. Emblematic of this position is the following excerpt from the *Industrial Worker*.

> What do you care, workingmen, what the Constitution says? Is it anything to you when you have NO POWER to enforce the

Constitution? The action of petty grafters who fill the Spokane City Hall in repealing the Constitution is all right if they can make it stick…(workingmen) have no rights unless they have the POWER to enforce those rights….[26]

Despite the cynicism about rights throughout the Wobblie press, there were also voices that expressed a view that was more favorable to the emancipatory potential of rights. In many articles, the Constitution or the right to free speech was set up as a standard against which the government could be evaluated. Over and over, the Wobblies criticized elites (especially local elites) for betraying the United States Constitution and violating the right to free speech. This rhetoric reflected a highly developed "rights consciousness" even as it dismissed the courts as the ultimate arbiter of rights.[27]

This rights consciousness was not an intrinsic part of American culture but a norm gradually established through the political work of dissenting groups. The reaction of local officials, mainstream newspapers, and some citizens reveals just how precarious the idea of liberal rights was at the turn of the previous century. Some commentators argued that in a democracy the will of the majority was absolute and free speech extended only to messages that the majority tolerated. A minister in Spokane, for example, claimed that the responsibility of "the minority (to) submit to the majority…is as sacred a principle in our democratic form of government as is the principle of free speech."[28] The *San Diego Sun* endorsed a proposal that the city hold a referendum to decide whether the "streets are to be open for the use of all classes of citizens at all times."[29]

The treatment of rights in the IWW press appears contradictory. There is the constant refrain that the United States Constitution is a sham. On the other hand, the Constitution is figured as a codification of legitimate values that are betrayed by those in power. In some articles the IWW accepts the claim that "might is right" and in others it mobilizes the language of rights in order to challenge power.

This apparent contradiction actually reflects the paradoxical nature of rights. A political document such as the United States Bill of Rights elides the legal and moral dimensions of rights. The Bill of Rights purports to encode pre-existing moral rights, "self-evident truths" that are the basis of legitimate government. However, these rights come into being only insofar as they are recognized and protected by the state. Yet the state cannot fully realize abstract universal principles. There is always a gap between the abstract ideal and the specific laws and institutions that are formulated to protect it. This unbridgeable gap between the legal and moral dimensions of rights can be the basis for a critique of state power. The abstract character of rights makes it possible to challenge the law in the name of the law's motivating purpose.[30]

The contradictions in the IWW's position also reflect the fundamental dilemma of political outsiders. The experience of the disenfranchised suggests that power does not bend to right, but this realization does not make it any easier to gain power. According to IWW ideology, organization is the key to power but organization is only possible if the basic freedoms of association and speech are protected. The alternatives to organization are acquiescence or violent (and probably unsuccessful) revolt. Sporadic violence, however, is not in the interest of the government or dissenters; therefore, it is sometimes possible for the government and dissenting groups to reach a compromise whereby outsiders agree to express their dissent through nonviolent channels and the government promises not to interfere in peaceful political activities such as demonstrations, meetings, and the circulation of newspapers. In theory at least, this is the *modus vivendi* of the liberal state.

The overall experience of the free speech fights, however, suggests that a certain critical distance from the ideology of rights can have a salutary effect. The Wobblie critique of the neutrality of the liberal state motivated the group to carry its challenge much further than anyone had in the past. Deeply cynical about the neutrality of the judiciary, the Wobblies did not rely on protection from the courts. Instead they used the twofold strategy: a combination of civil disobedience and mobilization of public opinion. The experience of the Wobblies suggests that it is possible to combine a deep awareness of the limitations of rights with an active pursuit of equal treatment under the law.

The Wobblies recognized that political and civil rights were usually extended to those groups that agreed to play by the rules of the liberal-democratic polity, rules that they felt were designed to co-opt dissenting groups and contain their revolutionary aspirations. To put it in a more contemporary idiom, they were cognizant of the disciplinary nature of rights and were therefore successfully able to resist their normalizing effects. But this resistance is one reason that they were defeated by the repressive apparatus of the state rather than incorporated into the polity. Groups that are unwilling to be disciplined are often destroyed. Although liberal institutions allow for dissent and change, they do so in return for the guarantee that such change is gradual, negotiated, and moderate.

The experience of the Wobblies should chasten those critics of liberalism who think it desirable to replace a politics of rights with forms of political action that are somehow more authentic or emancipatory. Even the most radical groups have found it necessary to invoke rights, especially those rights that govern access to the public sphere. Without the capacity to speak, meet, argue, and organize, successful collective action is largely impossible. Thus although not logically necessary, it is practically indispensable for a politics of rights to precede and accompany a politics of emancipation and struggle.

This account of the early years of the free speech movement, however, should also make it clear that my understanding of free speech differs from both the libertarian approach and the progressive approach (the assumption that free speech is necessarily a tool of social progress).[31] Proponents of free speech such as John Dewey and John Stuart Mill were optimistic that unfettered discussion would guarantee the discovery and diffusion of general truths and usher in a more rational society. They thought that the marketplace of ideas could counterbalance the reactionary consequences of authoritarianism and tradition. The metaphor of the marketplace, however, reminds us of why we should be cautious about the more optimistic claims that unrestricted communication can lead to truth or consensus. The modern marketplace is dominated by large corporations such as Wal-Mart and Microsoft that can control suppliers and drive out competitors, not necessarily a salutary model for the exchange of ideas.

My agonistic approach to free speech is inspired by the Wobblies and represents a modification of the two most prominent approaches: the progressive and the libertarian. Libertarians emphasize that free speech protects individual autonomy and counterbalances the tendency in mass society to stifle individual greatness. This may be a legitimate reason for protecting expression but it is unable to account for the importance of public space in reaching a particular audience. Unlike the progressive approach, however, my alternative does not justify free speech in terms of consensus, truth, or social progress. Under certain conditions, consensus, truth, and progress can be furthered by free speech but at other times political speech will necessarily function as an unassimilable remainder—and reminder—of endemic conflict.

STREET SPEAKING TODAY

From the perspective of socialist history, the Wobblies won the battle in Spokane but lost the war. Many of their leaders were deported or jailed under criminal syndicalism and sedition laws and the organization was effectively crushed by the 1930s. Other radical organizations fared no better and, until at least the 1960s, individuals were jailed, blacklisted, deported, and denied citizenship because of socialist sympathies. But the Wobblies did win a different war: the war for street speaking. This right was realized by labor unions, antiwar protesters, and civil rights organizations (and famously, the Nazis in Skokie) who challenged permit systems and other restrictions on protest in public space.

The turning point came in 1939 when the Congress for Industrial Organizations (C.I.O.) was prohibited from holding an open-air meeting in a public park in Jersey City. New Jersey had a long history of industrial conflict and the city government was particularly committed to preventing New York-based unions from making inroads. In this context, Jersey City officials, under the direction of Mayor Frank Hague, refused to grant the C.I.O. a permit to use the park on the grounds that such a gathering might lead to "riots, disturbances, or disorderly assemblage."[32] There was no evidence that the C.I.O. itself planned any violence and the danger came from the possibility that bystanders would attack the speakers. In an important reversal of precedent, the Supreme Court decided that preventing a legitimate meeting merely because vigilantes threatened violence would be tantamount to affirming the right to a hecklers' veto. By punishing the peaceful speakers rather than the violent vigilantes, officials in Jersey City violated the fundamental constitutional right to assembly.[33] With this decision, the era of public protest was established.

In the second half of the twentieth century, protest has become a routinized, scripted activity. Since the iconic civil rights march on Washington DC, gun control advocates, antiwar protesters, public housing partisans, and pro-choicers, to name just a few, have gathered in the capital or other civic centers to voice their grievances. They gather together in order to demonstrate their strength to both insiders and outsiders and publicize their agenda to the government and media. These demonstrations often take the form of highly structured parades with permits, designated routes, port-a-potties, and a strong police presence. Typically, protesters gather on the Washington Mall to chant and listen to music and speeches in a festival-like atmosphere. The legal context for adjudicating conflict between local officials and demonstrators has become almost as familiar as the logistics of mass protest. The courts have recognized the legitimacy of time, place, and manner restrictions that allow political speech as long as demonstrations follow certain rules to guarantee safety and protect public order.

Figure 2.1 Demonstration in Central Park. (Courtesy of Project for Public Spaces.)

The goal is to balance free speech rights with the interests of others who use public streets and parks. The courts have found that these time, place, and manner restrictions are acceptable as long as they meet three criteria: they must not discriminate against a particular viewpoint ("content neutrality"); they must be narrowly tailored to serve a significant government interest; and they must leave open ample alternatives for communication.[34]

The truce between demonstrators and local government officials, however, has always been precarious. The second and third criteria open up particularly wide latitude for discretion. What counts as a significant government interest? Public order and safety are always priorities of government, but does that mean they should trump political speech? Are rumors of "anarchist violence" and potential looting reason enough to exclude protesters from the city center? Which alternative places allow dissenters to reach their target audience? If antiglobalization protesters can demonstrate, but not within view of any of the WTO meeting sites, are they able to communicate their message to their target audience? These are similar to the dilemmas faced by government officials a hundred years ago. In the early twentieth century, municipalities such as Spokane did not ban street speaking entirely but only prohibited it from the city centers. Wobblies were free to harangue whoever might be passing by on isolated roads at the periphery of town. Because their goal was to confront the employment sharks, however, such an alternative was ineffectual. The Wobblies, like today's protesters, wanted to speak on the street corners in the most visible locations at the center of town.

Debates about regulating protest have become heated in the wake of the December 1999 demonstrations in Seattle against the WTO. The downtown retailers' association estimated $2.5 million in damage (mostly broken windows and graffiti) and $17 million in lost sales. Six hundred demonstrators were arrested and hundreds complained of police brutality, particularly the use of pepper spray, rubber bullets, and tear gas against peaceful protesters. A handful also made allegations about police brutality in jail. Several journalists brought lawsuits accusing the police of beating or pepperspraying them for photographing within press zones. Police Chief Norm Stamper resigned in the aftermath of the controversy. But different sides drew very different lessons from the Seattle experience. The protesters felt the tactics of the police revealed the repressive nature of the state and concluded that a more robust culture of civil liberties was needed. The other side used the term "riot" and felt that an even tighter security perimeter should be employed at future economic summits, preventing protesters from gaining access to commercial or civic centers. Other localities have followed this advice. Quebec City, site of the Summit of the Americas (April 20–22, 2001), erected a 3.8 meter high (11 foot), 4 kilometer long chain link fence to prevent the estimated 30,000 protesters from entering the downtown area.[35] Although the Seattle police did not build an actual fence, they did prevent protesters from entering a 25 block area of downtown.

Even before the protests began, the ACLU challenged the constitutionality of the 25 block no-protest zone in downtown Seattle. Aaron Caplan, a staff attorney for the ACLU, said it was "completely unacceptable" for police to allow shoppers or workers into an area but to bar those carrying protest signs or wearing anti-WTO slogans.[36] So far this argument has met with mixed results. In Washington, the federal district court rejected the ACLU's petition for an injunction blocking the city from erecting a 25 block no-protest zone. U.S. District Court Judge Barbara Rothstein concluded that "free speech must sometimes bend to public safety."[37] Similarly, Quebec's Superior Court rejected the claim that a four kilometer long fence blocking out protesters violated the Canadian Charter's right to free speech.

Not all courts have upheld the idea of speech-free zones. In July 2000 U.S. District Court Judge Gary A. Feess granted an injunction preventing the local police force from blocking protesters' access to downtown. He struck down a security zone created by the city of Los Angeles that was erected in order to prevent demonstrators from accessing the site of the Democratic National Convention. The security zone was intended to cordon off the entire downtown convention site and several city blocks in each direction. According to Feess, the city "made no attempt to accommodate or balance the free speech interests of the protesters against the need for security at the convention site."[38] While recognizing a compelling state interest in keeping the peace, he concluded that the restrictions were not narrowly tailored to meet that goal and did not provide alternative means whereby protesters could communicate their message to convention delegates. The judge pointed out that Los Angeles was setting a dangerous and constitutionally dubious precedent, by enacting a "prior restraint" on speech based on the mere speculation that violence might occur.

In late August and early September 2001, the debate around security zones re-emerged in Washington, DC, host to meetings of the IMF and World Bank. DC police proposed a plan to erect a nine foot high fence blocking off the White House and other symbolic sites in the center of the city. This same area had been off-limits to protesters during the IMF–World Bank meetings in April 2000 but the addition of the fence would have made even visual contact between protesters and summit participants impossible. In the aftermath of the September 11 terrorist attacks, however, plans for large-scale anti-globalization protests were modified and the fence was not erected. The constitutionality of security perimeters remains unresolved.

FREE SPEECH ZONES AND SPEECH-FREE ZONES ON UNIVERSITY CAMPUSES

The concept of free speech zones, however, is gaining popularity among image-conscious university administrators as well as security-conscious police chiefs. On March 25, 2002 antisweatshop activists at Florida State University (FSU) were arrested by the campus police. They had inadvertently staged their camp-in outside the designated "free-speech zone." They had set up their tents by the fountain on Westcott Plaza, in front of the main administration building, a site particularly suited to reaching their target audience. Their goal was to pressure the university administration to join the Workers Rights Consortium, an organization that monitors the conditions under which university brand-name athletic clothing is produced.[39] Students claimed that FSU receives three million dollars annually from Nike as part of an endorsement contract, which stipulates that all Seminoles (FSU athletes) display the Nike logo on their athletic uniforms.[40] Nike has threatened not to renew endorsement deals with universities that join the Workers Rights Consortium.[41] Student protesters highlighted this issue and hoped to embarrass university President Talbot "Sandy" D'Alemberte into reversing his stance against joining the consortium. The twelve students were arrested, charged with "trespass after warning," and brought to Leon County Jail. The students were released after posting a $500 bond. Six months later the students were brought to trial and acquitted.[42]

After nationwide negative press attention, President D'Alemberte wrote a letter to the *St. Petersburg Times* insisting that there were no free speech zones at FSU. He claimed that students could leaflet in any part of the campus and that the antisweatshop activists were not punished for political speech but rather for obstructing foot traffic. According to D'Alemberte, the student activists set up dozens of tents on Westcott Plaza and some were blocking the paths leading to the administration building, which also contained one of the campus's largest lecture halls.[43] While endorsing the students' right to protest administration policy, he emphasized that the rules applied were eminently reasonable "time, place, and manner" restrictions.

So are there free speech zones at FSU? The contested policy is found in the campus code outlining "Student Rights and Responsibilities." The code explicitly recognizes the right to freedom of speech and assembly, while specifying that such political activity must not "disrupt nor interfere with the operation of the institution nor impede vehicular or foot traffic including ingress and egress from any campus facility." The code also distinguishes between "open platform areas," where students may exercise speech and assembly rights without obtaining a permit (but still governed by the limitations above) and the rest of the campus, where students may assemble only if they receive a permit 24 hours in advance. After the arrests, the antisweatshop protesters relocated to one of the two "open platform" areas: Landis Green, a centrally located area, far from D'Alemberte's office. Shahar Sapir, one of the protest leaders, lamented, "We wanted to be constantly visible to him, in front of his office, and now we're completely invisible out here."[44]

Dozens of public universities have designated specific areas—sometimes obscure corners of campus—as free speech zones.[45] Although many people associate protest with anti-Vietnam War-style leftist activism, the restrictions have also drawn the ire of conservative groups. An anti-abortion group recently challenged the University of

Houston's decision to refuse them a permit to display photos of aborted fetuses in a central location on campus.[46] Other universities have modified their zoning policies under pressure from students and sympathetic faculty. For example, the University of South Florida designated two areas on campus as free speech zones. One required a reservation through the Student Activities Office and the other was available on a first-come, first-served basis. The policy elicited widespread criticism and was quietly abolished.[47]

Are universities obliged to protect free speech on campus? There are two starkly divergent views on the question. One camp emphasizes that a university—even a public one—is essentially private property. Just as a homeowner is not required to allow protesters on her lawn, the administration need not allow students to demonstrate on university plazas. According to this position, the university, like a military installation or administrative office building, is not a public forum but rather a private institution owned by the government. Any activity that the relevant administrators feel disrupts the primary mission can be prohibited at its discretion.

The other side of this debate emphasizes that universities—particularly public universities—were originally founded as schools of citizenship in which students learned to become competent participants in democratic governance.[48] The link between protest activity and university property has a long history dating back to 1765 when Bostonians gathered on Harvard Yard to debate the Stamp Act.[49] Universities in particular have a special obligation to facilitate the free exchange of ideas and to foster critical viewpoints, the argument goes. In a 1957 decision, the United States Supreme Court endorsed the view that free speech on campus contributes to democratic governance, emphasizing that "to impose any straight jacket upon the intellectual leaders in our colleges and universities would imperil the future of the nation."[50] In spite of this holding, public universities still have much latitude to protect their core mission from the disruption of protest. Because the courts have proved a fickle ally, students, like IWW members a century ago, have relied on public opinion to shame administrators into modifying the most restrictive limitations.

ZONING OUT DIFFERENCE

The eleven foot high fence erected in Quebec City to achieve the total insulation of government leaders materializes a social process that is widespread yet often invisible. The proliferation of speech-free zones in civic and commercial centers and on university campuses reflects the same logic that motivated local governments in the early twentieth century to arrest the Wobblie street speakers. Their tactics today have become more refined and more elaborate, but the impetus is the same: to prevent protesters from symbolically appropriating salient sites and to isolate protestors from those whom they might disturb.

This logic culminated in a recent United States Supreme Court decision, *Hill v. Colorado* (2000), which upheld a state statute that made it a crime to "knowingly approach another person within eight feet of such other person, unless such other person consents, for the purpose of passing a leaflet or handbill to, displaying a sign to, or engaging in oral protest, education, counseling with such person in the public way or sidewalk area...."[51] Effectively this statue banned leafleting and face-to-face political speech. Some leftists might be relieved to know that the statute only applies to activities that take place in front of "a health care facility" (read abortion clinic), however, the precedent is still chilling (see Chapter 3 for a fuller discussion of anti-abortion protests). By affirming the constitutionality of a buffer zone between activists and the citizens that they seek to persuade, the decision is a blow to all political speech. If such a statute is constitutional, then there is no reason why labor activists or Green party organizers or political candidates should be able to come within eight feet of pedestrians to ask them to sign a petition or educate them about an issue.

The rationale for the court's decision was particularly troubling. Although stopping short of discovering a constitutional right to be left alone, the majority recognized a compelling interest in avoiding unwanted communication. They felt that this interest outweighed the First Amendment right to free speech. This decision reflects the way in which the values and attitudes of the private realm are transforming the public sphere. The desire to be left alone, to avoid disturbing unfamiliar ideas, experiences, and people is natural. We all need some times and places where our ideas and identities are not challenged. The private realm is the space where we can surround ourselves with symbols that reflect our needs and values and avoid conflict if that is what we choose.[52] The danger arises when these attitudes that are appropriate in private life infect and transform the public arena. The public should be a place where it is possible to encounter different ideas and unsought experiences.

The growing willingness to create buffer zones preventing contact between members of groups with different viewpoints strikes me as unconstitutional, not just in the technical legalistic sense that it violates existing standards of First Amendment jurisprudence. The appeal of such buffer zones reminds us why rights such as free speech and assembly were institutionalized in the first place: to protect ourselves from ourselves. The constitutional protection of free speech is akin to the binding of Ulysses, who had his sailors tie him to a post so that he could hear the seductive sirens' song without jumping to his death. The guarantee of free speech is the inverse; it forces us to hear unappealing sounds: the discordant protests of others that are unpleasant to hear because they remind us about what is unpleasant in our polity. But the ability to hear these voices ensures the viability of a democratic political system. Rights are neither self-evident nor God-given; instead, they are "rules of the game" that guarantee the functioning of a particular type of political order. Just as the "right" to primogeniture was part of the infrastructure of an aristocratic polity, the right to free speech and assembly are critical to a democratic polity.

At first this link between speech and democracy might seem counterintuitive, given that it is often the majority that wants to silence the heretical views of the minority and does so in the name of democracy. In the early twentieth century, the good burghers of San Diego, for instance, were confident that in a referendum the majority of citizens would have chosen to silence the revolutionary Wobblies. But equating democracy with majoritarianism is an oversimplification. One important element of a democratic system is some mechanism for protecting the ability of minorities and especially poorly financed groups to convince the majority of their view. In a democracy it must be possible for the minority to become the majority. This is possible only insofar as the minority has the ability to articulate and publicize its issues and concerns. A permanent majority (or a permanent minority that governs in the name of an acquiescent populace) is not democratic if it insulates itself from challenge by making sure that alternative viewpoints are silenced.

The politics of public space is only one democratic process among many. Voting, opinion polling, and back-room bargaining among elites probably have more influence over policy. But many of the more profound challenges that have transformed politics have come from outside conventional channels. In Europe the social democratic movement emerged from socialist parties and trade unions that initially functioned under conditions of illegality. In the United States, the civil rights movement effectively employed demonstrations and protests when conventional political channels, including voting, were foreclosed. Today very few groups are disenfranchised but certain viewpoints are systematically disadvantaged and even excluded in a system that privileges the messages of corporations and established interest groups.[53] Under such conditions, mass demonstrations may still be the best way to inform leaders of the intensity of citizens' priorities. The government's response should not be to erect fences but rather to build bridges between citizens and policy makers.

ENDNOTES

1. This claim is made by David Rabban in his book *Free Speech in Its Forgotten Years* (New York: Cambridge University Press, 1997) and is true of the half-dozen constitutional law case books that I have studied. Some more historically oriented works, however, do emphasize the pivotal role of the IWW street-speaking fights. See, for example, Nat Hentoff's *The First Freedom: The Tumultuous History of Free Speech in America* (New York: Delacorte Press, 1980).
2. In *Emergence of a Free Press*, Leonard Levy shows that there were very few prosecutions for seditious libel in the period before and after the American Revolution (New York: Oxford University Press, 1985). For extensive examples of the courts' willingness to countenance restrictions on speech, see Michael Kent Curtis, *Free Speech, "The People's Darling Privilege": Struggles for Freedom of Expression in American History* (Durham, NC and London: Duke University Press, 2000).
3. Curtis, *Free Speech.*
4. Curtis, *Free Speech,* 216–240.
5. In 1940, Congress passed the Smith Act, which made it illegal to advocate refusal of military service and prohibited advocacy of the overthrow or destruction of the government by force. See Zechariah Chafee, Jr., *Free Speech in the United States* (New York: Antheum, 1969).
6. Rabban, *Free Speech.*
7. *The Industrial Worker*, August 17, 1911.
8. *The Industrial Worker*, November 17, 1909.
9. *The Industrial Worker*, April 1, 1909.
10. *The Industrial Worker*, January 1, 1910.
11. *The Industrial Worker*, January 1, 1910.
12. *The Industrial Worker*, August 12, 1909.
13. *The Industrial Worker*, December 12, 1909.
14. *The Industrial Worker*, November 2, 1909.
15. Melvyn Dubofsky, *We Shall Be All, A History of the Industrial Workers of the World* (Chicago: Quadrangle Books, 1969), 179.
16. Philip S. Foner, *History of the Labor Movement in the United States: volume IV: The Industrial Workers of the World, 1905-1917* (New York: International, 1965), 181.
17. *The Industrial Worker*, January 1, 1910.
18. Dubofsky, *We Shall Be All*, 191.
19. Rabban, *Free Speech*, 90.
20. *The Industrial Worker*, May 28, 1909.
21. Stanley Fish, for example, argues that abstract concepts such as free speech do not create a level playing field on which alternative political agendas compete; instead, rights themselves mask particular political projects. See Stanley Fish, *There's No Such Thing as Free Speech...and It's a Good Thing Too* (Oxford: Oxford University Press, 1994), 102. Wendy Brown worries about the disciplinary effect of rights and the way that rights talk translates political struggles into rigid moral absolutes. See Wendy Brown, "Revaluing Critique: A Response to Kenneth Baynes," *Political Theory* 28, no. 4 (August 2000), 469-479 and *States of Injury: Power and Freedom in Late Modernity* (Princeton, NJ: Princeton University Press, 1995).

22. Mary Ann Glendon, *Rights Talk: The Impoverishment of Political Discourse* (New York: Free Press, 1991).
23. Karl Marx, "On the Jewish Question," in *The Marx-Engels Reader,* ed. Robert C. Tucker (New York: Norton, 1978), 26–52.
24. *The Industrial Worker*, May 13, 1909.
25. Fish, *There's No Such Thing as Free Speech*, 102.
26. *The Industrial Worker*, April 1, 1909.
27. David Thelan, "Introduction," Leon Fink, "Labor, Liberty, and the Law: Trade Unionism and the Problem of the American Constitutional Order," and Joyce Appleby, "The American Heritage: The Heirs and the Disinherited," symposium on rights consciousness in *The Journal of American History* 74, no. 3 (1987), 795-925.
28. Cited in Rabban, *Free Speech*, 126.
29. Cited in Rabban, *Free Speech*, 126.
30. Claude Lefort, *The Political Forms of Modern Society* (Cambridge, MA: MIT Press, 1986).
31. John Dewey, "Freedom of Thought and Affection" and "Academic Freedom," *John Dewey: The Middle Works 1899-1924* (Carbondale: Southern Illinois University Press, 1976).
32. Zechariah Chafee, *Free Speech in the United States* (New York: Antheum, 1969), 411.
33. *Hague v. Committee for Industrial Organization* (1939) 307 U.S. 496. See also Chaffee, *Free Speech in the United States*, 409-438.
34. *Forsyth County v. Nationalist Movement* 505 U.S. 123.
35. "Fence Case Knocked Down: Supreme Court Won't Hear Challenge over Summit Perimeter," *The Gazette*, July 13, 2001, A4.
36. "Horror Stories from Protestors, Police," *Seattle Times*, December 7, 1999, A2.
37. "Court Vindicates City's WTO Riot Measures," *Seattle Times*, October 31, 2001.
38. "Judge Voids Convention Security Zone," *Los Angeles Times*, July 20, 2000, 1.
39. "Zoned Out," *The New Republic*, May 13, 2002, 14.
40. For an excellent overview of the politics around corporate branding in general and Nike's relationship with university athletics in particular, see Naomi Klein, *No Logo* (New York: Picador, 2000).
41. *Florida-Times Union*, April 13, 2002, A1.
42. Alisa Ulferts, "Protestors Who Put Up Tents in FSU Walkway Acquitted of Trespassing," *St. Petersburg Times*, September 26, 2002, 5B.
43. *St. Petersburg Times*, May 7, 2002.
44. Cited in *The Florida-Times Union Times*, April 13, 2002.
45. For example, the University of Maryland, College Park has a policy that "public speaking is limited to the Nyumburu Amphitheater. Public speaking elsewhere on campus is prohibited." The ACLU filed a suit challenging the policy on First Amendment grounds. See Peter Geier, "Students, ACLU Sue U of MD College Park Over Policy," *The Daily Record*, March 7, 2003.
46. "Zoned Out," *The New Republic*, 14.
47. Scott Street, "Promoting Order or Squelching Campus Dissent?" *The Chronicle of Higher Education*, January 12, 2001, A37.
48. John Dewey, *Democracy and Education: An Introduction to the Philosophy of Education* (New York: Macmillan, 1961).
49. Scott Street, "Promoting Order or Squelching Campus Dissent?"
50. Cited in "Zoned Out," 15.
51. Cited in Jamin B. Raskin and Clark L. LeBlanc, "Disfavored Speech About Favored Rights: *Hill v. Colorado*: The Vanishing Public Forum and the Need for an Objective Discrimination Test," *The American University Law Review* 51 (December 2001), 179-228.

52. See also Bonnie Honig, "Difference, Dilemmas, and the Politics of Home," in *Democracy and Difference: Contesting the Boundaries of the Political*, ed. Seyla Benhabib (Princeton, NJ: Princeton University Press, 1996), 257-277.

53. Steven Shiffrin, *Dissent, Injustice, and the Meanings of America* (Princeton, NJ: Princeton University Press, 1999).

3

THE PUBLIC FORUM DOCTRINE

Many things about the 1980 movie *Airplane* seem dated today: afros, feathered hair, leisure suits, parodies of jive talk, and jokes about pedophilia. There is one recurring scene, however, that captures the atmosphere of the 1970s particularly well. As each character enters the airport, a member of the Religious Consciousness Church gives him or her a flower and asks for a donation. The second time this happens to Ted Striker, the disillusioned former military pilot, he punches the cult member in the face. In the movie theater, audiences cheered.[1] Today, however, this scene elicits awkward silence; the joke does not resonate because the scenario that it mocks is so unfamiliar. Instead of religious groups in the airport there are cell phone kiosks, fast food outlets, duty-free shops, and designer boutiques.

In the 1980s airports began to clamp down on solicitation and political activity. Religious and political groups challenged the new restrictions excluding them from airport terminals and the resulting litigation made it to the United States Supreme Court. The petitioners, members of the Church of Krishna Consciousness, claimed that the prohibition on solicitation and leafletting violated their rights to free speech and inhibited their ability to exercise their religion. They argued that the airport is a public place that should be treated as a public forum. They emphasized that airports are owned and administered by government agencies and accessible to the general public. Furthermore, transportation hubs such as railways and ports have traditionally served as public gathering points, where everyone from peddlers to politicians have plied their wares. Airports are simply a modern-day variant of these traditional public forums and therefore should be treated in the same way. This litigation raises two issues that are central to this book. Is government-owned property always public? And how

47

do the laws governing public space enrich or inhibit a democratic culture of debate and dissent? This chapter explores the public forum doctrine, a set of rules that the American courts have developed in order to decide when political activity is permissible and when the government can prohibit unwanted speech on its property.

THE AIRPORT AS PUBLIC SPACE

In the summer of 1996 I was working for Jobs with Justice, a coalition of progressive labor and community organizations in Boston. One action that the coalition supported was a strike by the employees of a rental car company at Logan Airport. Only three picketers were allowed to stand at the entrance to the car lot and we were forbidden from distributing leaflets inside the airport itself. Every day we watched puzzled travelers whiz past the paltry picket line on the rental car company's courtesy vans. Without any chance to inform customers about their grievances, the discouraged union members caved in to management fairly quickly.

Almost five years later, after reading the Supreme Court decision in *Lee v. Krishna Consciousness,* I discovered that the union did theoretically have the right to distribute our leaflets within the airport terminal. In two related decisions handed down in 1992, the Court concluded that groups such as the Hare Krishnas were not allowed to solicit funds in the public areas of the airport, but they were permitted to pass out religious literature. Although the decision may seem like a reasonable compromise, the theoretical rationale had troubling long-term consequences. The majority of the justices agreed that the airport terminals operated by Port Authority of New York and New Jersey (a public agency) were not traditional public forums and therefore the higher standards of constitutional scrutiny adopted to protect First Amendment rights were not required. Once the Court concluded that the airport was not genuinely public space, the justices could use greater discretion in deciding whether charitable solicitation, leafletting, or any other kind of speech was appropriate.[2]

The designation "traditional public forum" is important because political activity is protected in such forums but not in other government-owned places. This principle was first articulated sixty years ago in a case called *Hague v. CIO* (cited in Chapter 1). In that decision Justice Roberts reversed existing precedent and held that "streets and parks may rest (in governments but) they have immemorially been held in trust for the use of the public and ...have been used for purposes of assembly, communicating thoughts between citizens, and discussing public questions. Such use of the streets and public places has, from ancient times, been a part of the privileges, immunities, rights, and liberties of citizens." This robust recognition of the importance of public space has been eviscerated in the past decade. The Supreme Court's application of the public forum doctrine has been confusing. It would be wrong, however, to place blame exclusively on the courts. They merely reflect a more broad-based consensus that public space has become an anachronism in a wired and wireless age of global telecommunications. Who needs the Hyde Park speakers' corner when there are countless Internet bulletin boards that are more accessible? Why worry about the right to distribute fliers when you can send email alerts? If political theorists were not able to address these questions, then there would be no reason to be troubled by the privatization of traditional public spaces. But the politics of public space does have distinctive benefits. Furthermore, studying the commodification of public space has lessons for those seeking to understand the recent transformation of the Internet.

THE SUPREME COURT AND THE PUBLIC SPHERE

The history of constitutional interpretation reflects two opposing theories of the public sphere. The first one assumes that the government in its role as property owner has all the same rights as any private individual. According to this "property rights" approach, public space is basically private space owned by the government. Once public space has been reimagined in this way, it can be regulated in whatever manner the responsible government agency sees fit. This approach was first articulated in a case called *Commonwealth v. Davis* (1897). Writing for the Massachusetts Supreme Court, Oliver Wendell Holmes concluded: "For the legislature absolutely or conditionally to forbid public speaking in a highway or public park is no more an infringement of rights of a member of the public than for the owner of a private house to forbid it in his house."

This analysis still holds considerable force today. In *Lee v. Krishna Consciousness* (1992) (hereafter *Krishna*), the Supreme Court followed a similar logic, holding that "where the government is acting as a proprietor managing its internal operations, rather than acting as lawmaker with the power to regulate or license, the government's action with respect to speech will not be subjected to…heightened review." In other words, the government plays two roles: legislator and shopkeeper. While wearing its shopkeeper hat, it may limit citizens' traditional liberties such as freedom of expression. If a bartender does not have to allow a political speech or preaching on his premises, why does the government?

At first this distinction seems to make sense. We would not expect community groups to hold their meetings in the Department of Motor Vehicles office, even though it is a public building. Nor would we want tax protesters to block up space in the post office when we are waiting to mail our Christmas packages. In order to avoid these scenarios, the court held that the government did not intend to create a public forum "in cases where the principal function of the property would be disrupted by expressive activity."[3] Although this seems reasonable, it actually gives an enormous amount of discretion to administrative agencies to prevent political activity that may be compatible with a site's other purposes. If the regulatory agency itself has the authority to exclude political speech, then truly public, multiple-use space could disappear altogether.[4]

The problem arises when we consider that all public places — even the archetypical examples such as parks and streets — have a "principal function." Parks are designed for recreation and streets are thoroughfares that are meant to facilitate the circulation of pedestrians and automobiles. Forbidding expressive conduct in all public places designed with something else in mind would be tantamount to forbidding it altogether. Although the government could create a place exclusively to serve as a public forum, it would probably be self-defeating. Its spatial segregation from other activities would guarantee its impotence. Political speech is often aimed at those citizens least likely to seek out such a place. Activists have many ways to reach people who are already interested in politics: phone trees, Internet bulletins, direct mailings, and lectures, to name just a few. The politics of the public sphere, however, is about the kinds of encounters that take place in the course of everyday life. It is a politics of the ordinary. The political encounters that take us by surprise in the streets have the distinctive capacity to interrupt our routines, our insularity, our solipsism. Unlike the information that we seek out in the controlled environment of our computer terminal, it is often the unexpected that can be transformative.[5] To say that our First Amendment rights can be expressed only in out-of-the-way places would be to vitiate the character of the public sphere.

The concept of a "designated public forum" is a product of the property rights approach. Only when the government decides to turn its property into a public forum does it truly become public, in the sense that it caters to rights-bearing citizens rather than consumers. In all other cases, it remains private. The alternative is the traditional public forum doctrine articulated in *Hague v. CIO*. This often-cited opinion established limitations on the government's ability to abdicate its political responsibility in the name of its administrative ones. I call this the participatory approach.[6] The rationale is that the impetus behind the First Amendment was to ensure an active citizenry capable of resisting tyranny and governing itself. It assumes that in order to avoid tyranny of the majority, we need to nurture a pluralistic, diverse society. The government therefore has the obligation to actively promote, or at least not to unduly hinder, the articulation and critique of political ideas. The image of ancient Athens, with Socrates, the notorious philosopher-critic engaging leading citizens in discussion about their most cherished values, inspires this approach.

Just as the majority of the jurors in democratic Athens decided that they could do without Socrates' provocations, the government of the United States is none too happy with its gadflies. The difficulty is that the First Amendment, with its blanket protections of speech, association, and religion, is a barrier to silencing cults, political protesters, anti-abortion activists, and homeless people. The current guideline is that government agencies must be particularly reluctant to limit speech if it takes place in a traditional public forum.[7] And in order to avoid this requirement, the solution is to narrow the definition of the traditional public forum. This is just what we see in the recent court decisions. In *Krishna*, the Supreme Court rejected the claim that an airport was a traditional public forum similar to the docks and wharves of an earlier epoch. Chief Justice Rehnquist wrote that "given the lateness with which the modern air terminal has made its appearance, it hardly qualifies as a property that has 'immemorially...time out of mind' been held in the public trust."

By interpreting the concept of a traditional public forum to mean the relic of a particular historical period rather than a general category, the justices managed to severely limit its scope. In his dissent, Justice Souter reached a similar conclusion, noting that Rehnquist's reading would effectively abandon the public forum doctrine altogether. He noted that in many places traditional public forums such as city streets are no longer the only focus of community life;[8] if new gathering places could not be recognized as public forums, then the entire concept would be meaningless. Airports have replaced train stations and wharves as the main transportation hubs. In the mid-1990s, even smaller airports such as Buffalo and Milwaukee already served four to six million travelers a year. Hubs such as Newark International Airport have over thirty million passengers and the number is growing. The kind of people who most often frequent airports are precisely those

Figure 3.1 Designated public forum in Muir Woods, California. (Mark Hsieh.)

who would seldom be found on the city streets. Businessmen and women who move from private homes to underground parking garages (or suburban corporate campuses) to shopping malls seldom enter public places unprotected by the modern shield—the automobile. Even in the airport, many passengers do not have to cross the public sidewalks because the underground parking garages are connected directly to the terminal buildings. This is relevant because free speech can only be limited if there are alternative forums for expression. The Supreme Court found that the restriction against solicitation in the airport was not too burdensome because the sidewalks outside the terminal presented a viable alternative. But exterior sidewalks and interior corridors are hardly equivalent, inasmuch as many passengers avoid the sidewalks altogether.

Even streets and sidewalks, however, are by no means secure in their status as traditional public forums. In a 1990 decision, *United States v. Kokinda*, the Supreme Court found that the sidewalk outside the post office was not a traditional public forum. In the plurality opinion, Justice O'Connor wrote that the post office was run "like a business" and therefore could forbid political activists from setting up an information table along its sidewalks. The decision has been particularly troubling to political groups in the twenty-four states and thousands of localities that use the initiative process to modify government policy. In order to get an initiative on the ballot, groups must gather a certain number of signatures in order to prove that the measure has significant citizen support. In most states, the number of signatures varies from five to ten percent of the total number of citizens who voted in the last election. Yet there are few places where groups can gather signatures. Private social spaces like shopping malls usually prohibit petitioners and many automobile-oriented suburbs have no alternative public gathering places (see Chapter 4). Businesses are not arranged on public streets but rather are located in privately owned strip malls surrounded by parking lots. The owners of businesses that attract a large cross-section of the population, for example, supermarkets can and often do forbid groups from soliciting in front of their property.[9] Although they may make exceptions for the Girl Scouts' cookie sale or the Salvation Army's Christmas bell ringing, they are much less likely to allow people to gather signatures for the controversial topics that come up on ballot initiatives, issues such as gay rights, single-payer health care, or banning affirmation action. The post office, a little oasis of public space in a sea of private ownership, is one of the few places on which signature gatherers have traditionally relied.

Emboldened by the *Kokinda* decision, in 1998 the Postal Service enacted a regulation that prohibits "soliciting signatures on petitions, polls, or surveys" in front of any post office. This restriction went far beyond existing rules that prevented solicitation that interfered with postal service activity. Arguing that the regulation "limits the ability of voters to reform their government," the Initiative and Referendum Institute (IRI), a nonprofit, nonpartisan group devoted to studying and strengthening direct democracy, filed suit.[10] The Initiative and Referendum Institute challenged the post office regulation, claiming that the prohibition on gathering signatures erected an important additional barrier that made it more unwieldy to use the initiative process. The IRI was joined by citizens' groups from across the political spectrum, including the ACLU, Citizens for Limited Taxation, and Nebraskans for Limited Terms. M. Dane Waters, President of the IRI, emphasized that the regulation clearly violated not only the First Amendment right to free speech but also the right to petition the government for the redress of grievances. Arthur Spitzer, Legal Director of the ACLU, argued that "sidewalks and similar outdoor areas open to the public, where people meet and greet each other, are also areas where people have a constitutional right to exchange political information and to seek signatures on petitions."[11] On December 31, 2003, U.S. District Court Judge Richard W. Roberts upheld the postal service regulation, explaining that the restriction on political activity was justified by a "significant governmental interest." What was this significant governmental interest? "(M)aking post offices and surrounding postal property attractive to customers whose payments fund USPS operations."[12] The property-rights approach to public space is victorious.

The Supreme Court has been closely divided on how to apply the public forum doctrine. In *Krishna*, five judges insisted that the airport did not constitute a traditional public forum. The other four reached the opposite conclusion. According to the dissent, a public space should serve as a public forum in all cases where its physical character is "suitable for discourse" and such use would not unduly disrupt its normal use. This proposed standard formalizes some of the characteristics that made public places like streets and parks favored sites of political activity in the first place. First, unlike public school classrooms or administrative offices, public forums are places where the general public has a right to be. Second, public forums function as informal meeting places for diverse people engaging in fairly varied activities. They are usually places such as transportation hubs and town squares that serve as social nodal points, the kind of places you might run into someone by accident or designate as a meeting point for a group. According to Justice Souter, the Port Authority airports are precisely these types of "multipurpose environments." Although post-September 11 security considerations may legitimately restrict access to terminals, there are still extensive public spaces located outside the security perimeter. Modern airports include extensive shopping facilities, exhibitions, and viewing decks; they function as a workplace for hundreds of thousands of employees. The public areas that are not leased to commercial vendors are physically suited to certain kinds of speech and solicitation. They tend to encompass spacious corridors and extensive waiting areas. These public areas are broken up by shops and other amusements meant to entice the enormous number of bored passengers waiting for their flights. If commerce were such a disruption to the normal function of air travel, it is hard to imagine why the airport of the twenty-first century looks so much like a shopping mall.[13]

The physical layout of the airport seems to contradict the rationale of the Supreme Court majority for banning the Krishnas. The majority of the justices found a legitimate state interest in controlling crowds and facilitating the free movement of people; however, this concern could be remedied with a more narrowly tailored restriction, for example, limiting the number of solicitors based on the space available or banning them from narrow corridors. Crowd control would be a reason to ban demonstrations or rallies but it is hard to

imagine how one or two leafletters could have such enormous consequences in a space designed to accommodate tens of thousands of
people a day. The real rationale behind the decision seemed to be the
fear that solicitation could involve fraud, harassment, and cause discomfort. This underlying motive was clear when Justice Rehnquist
worried that someone soliciting donations for groups such as the
Krishnas: "…can also commit fraud through concealment of his affil-
iation or through deliberate efforts to shortchange those who agree
to purchase."[14] Of course fraud is already illegal.[15] Furthermore, the
threat of fraud exists in all transactions and is not used to ban legitimate commercial activity.

Designating a place a "public forum" is crucial because it protects
legitimate speech from these types of prejudices. If the airport is not
considered a public forum, the Port Authority may enact any restriction that it finds reasonable. In a public forum, the Port Authority can
still take all precautions necessary to prevent fraud and harassment. It
can regulate solicitors' activities to prevent any additional congestion,
but it cannot enforce a blanket prohibition on speech in order to
achieve these goals when the same goals could be met by much more
narrow provisions. In the airport case, enforcement of existing prohibitions could achieve the legitimate state interest in preventing fraud
and harassment while not preventing religious activity and political
speech. A group should not be prevented from speaking based on an
unfounded suspicion that it might cause trouble.

As Justice Kennedy astutely pointed out, the idea of the First
Amendment is a *limitation on government*. Therefore, allowing government agencies to decide whether speech is permissible in a particular public place is problematic. Current public forum jurisprudence
"leaves the government almost unlimited authority to restrict speech
on its property by doing nothing more than articulating a non-speech-
related-purpose for the area, and it leaves almost no scope for the
development of new public forums absent the rare approval of the government."[16]

THE CANADIAN COURTS ON FREE SPEECH
ON PUBLIC PROPERTY

In 1991 the Canadian Supreme Court also considered whether airports
could outlaw expressive activity.[17] The petitioners, the Committee for
the Commonwealth of Canada, challenged Dorval Airport's (Montreal) rules against solicitation on airport property. Airport personnel
had forbidden them from displaying placards and handing out leaflets

outlining their political views. In a unanimous decision, the Canadian Supreme Court found that the airport rules violated Section 2b of the Canadian Charter of Rights and Freedoms, which guaranteed freedom of expression.

Several of the justices, however, noted that their reasoning departed from the American courts' public forum doctrine in significant ways. According to Justice Lamer, the public forum doctrine is a sleight-of-hand that the American courts have employed to justify balancing citizens' rights to free speech with the state's interest in efficiently managing government property.[18] This is unnecessary in the Canadian context because the Charter explicitly includes a "reasonable limits" clause which states that the Charter "guarantees the rights and freedoms set out in it subject only to reasonable limitation prescribed by law...."[19] This means that the Canadian courts can explicitly evaluate the importance of the government interest at stake to see if it should outweigh the presumption in favor of citizens' fundamental rights. United States courts, on the other hand, must interpret a categorical provision protecting free speech. The categorical approach would seem to provide a more robust protection of individual rights, however, the Canadian court's unanimous defense of political expression in airports suggests that this is not necessarily the case. Nor was this an isolated case. In *Churchill v. Greater Vancouver Transportation Authority* (2001), the Supreme Court of British Columbia decided that the Charter protected the free speech rights of citizens engaged in electioneering outside the restricted areas of train stations and bus stops. The petitioner, a member of the right-wing Canadian Alliance, was arrested after handing out leaflets in front of a Sky Train station. The court decided that as long as campaign workers did not block the entrance, they were free to hand out their leaflets and gather signatures.

In *Kokinda*, a case mentioned earlier, the United States Supreme Court took the opposite position and decided that nondisruptive political solicitation was not allowed on the sidewalk in front of U.S. Postal Service property. Having rejected the claim that the property was a public forum, the United States Supreme Court decided to leave discretion in the hands of the administrative authority that banned political activity. The Supreme Court of British Columbia, on the other hand, first acknowledged that campaign activity was a protected right under the Charter. Then it asked whether protecting that right would unduly undermine some state interest or interfere with the exercise of some important government function. The court felt that nondisruptive leafletting outside the fare-payers' area did not adversely affect transportation and therefore had to be considered protected speech.

With no provision for such transparent balancing, the American courts have had to develop legal doctrines such as "clear and present danger," "fighting words," and "public forum" in order to limit the right to free speech. Ostensibly, these rules are meant to identify apolitical criteria for distinguishing between different types of speech, but in fact they actually allow the courts to weigh First Amendment rights against other government interests, an undeniably political task. The public forum doctrine allows judges to believe that they are objectively *identifying* the places open to political activity in the past when they are actually *determining* the limits on political activity for the future.

The "traditional public forum" doctrine is supposed to distinguish places traditionally open to political speech from those devoted to other types of government and administrative activity. It provides a mechanism for balancing the interests of citizens and government, but it does so by placing too much weight on "tradition." It is unclear why tradition should necessarily be the key factor in deciding whether to allow political speech. The emphasis on "tradition" makes it difficult to decide how to deal with places such as airports and shopping malls that are distinctly modern variants of the ancient agora.

THE PUBLIC SPHERE

Why should we be concerned that the American courts and government bureaucracies are gradually restricting political and religious activity in public places? Such limitations accelerate the gradual disappearance of the public sphere that occurs through privatization. This in turn has consequences for democratic governance. It should be clear by now that I am using the term "public sphere" in a way that is quite different from the usual way it is invoked in political theory. The usage shares very little with the classical definition canonized by Juergen Habermas in his influential book, *The Structural Transformation of the Public Sphere.*[20] For Habermas the public sphere was an arena for rational debate about the common good.[21] In the public sphere that emerged in eighteenth-century Britain, rank and hierarchy were replaced by reason and judgment. According to Habermas, the public sphere was made up of an educated literary public that frequented the new coffee houses and private clubs. Due to the dubious legality of enlightenment associations in many parts of Europe, however, the public sphere existed "largely behind closed doors."[22] Thus, the term "public sphere" designated the norms and ideals of scholarly debate rather than a spatial location, let alone the disruptive, provocative politics of the streets. Although the classical public sphere has served as an important reference point in academic circles, it is less useful in understanding the role of the traditional public forum in contemporary politics. To shed light on our current legal dilemmas we need to look at the public sphere of the nineteenth and twentieth centuries, the period when working people claimed a right to the city by demonstrating on public squares and streets.[23]

Unlike the rarefied debates among friends in salons and cafés, the encounter between strangers on the street corner may look like fairly primitive politics. The beggar in the subway, the unwanted leaflet, the Hare Krishnas' solicitations do not have the sophistication of rational debate. Nor do they exhibit the criteria of what Habermas later called the ideal speech situation. There is no reciprocity when the beggar approaches the affluent. Given the fleeting opportunity for contact, the orientation is often less towards truth than towards provocation. The attempt to communicate is not framed in terms of mutual respect but confrontation, anxiety, and fear of otherness. This is illustrated beautifully in a "public service" advertisement produced by the New York City Transit Authority (NYCTA). Beneath a reminder that "Panhandling in the subway is illegal" was a cartoon in which a passenger was thinking the following:

> Uh, oh, come on, not me, not me. Oh pleeeeze don't come stand in front of me. Asking for money, great. Now the whole car's staring. What do I do? What do I do? I know. I'll pretend I'm reading my book. Look. I feel bad. I really do. But hey, it's my money. And how do I know what you are going to spend it on anyway? I don't. Sorry. No money from me.[24]

The same agency that sponsored that ad claimed that begging should not be protected by the First Amendment because it had no communicative content. Yet this claim is belied by the NYCTA's own propaganda. The agency's own ad campaign made it obvious that even before the panhandler said a word, his mere presence inspired an interior monologue in the passenger. The NYCTA argued that the beggar had no particularized message let alone one that would be understood by its audience, but the real problem is just the opposite. The subway patron understands the message only too well. The beggar draws attention to the vulnerability that we want to deny and reproaches us for our callousness. The suffering of the other is an indictment of our comfort and ease.[25]

This message can be conveyed in no other way because, as Marshall McLuhan put it, the medium is the message. The physical proximity of the homeless person reminds us that we cannot fully isolate ourselves from the casualties that our society produces. The effect of a disconcerting encounter cannot be approximated through an email. In the presence of another human being we cannot simply press delete and make her go away, as much as we may want to. Strikers on the picket line or beggars in the subway are part of the public sphere but not because they draw us into rational debate; instead, they draw our attention to the irrationalities produced by our society. Even if most of the time their message will not pierce the armor of our anxieties and prejudices, even experiencing those fears, defending those rationalizations, reminds us that we live in a shared world whose benefits are not distributed equally. Although the definitive characteristic of the Habermasian public sphere was the production of universal truth, the role of the public sphere today is to show that our truths are not universal.

CLINIC ACCESS

A critic might object that it is easy to romanticize the transgressive disturbing nature of the public sphere when one's own values are not being transgressed. As long as the picketers are strikers, most progressives are unlikely to be too troubled by confrontational tactics. Faced with unwanted solicitations for charity, even the feeling of guilt can serve as a kind of moral reminder. The defense of public protest, for progressives, has become more complex in the last decade as anti-abortion activists have become a visible presence in public space. Displaying shocking pictures of mutilated fetuses, blocking access to clinics, or providing sympathetic counseling, a new kind of protester has taken to the streets. If the public sphere is to be a site of political exchange, then it must also be open to those whose views are most disturbing to progressives. For those who identify with the left, the tactics of anti-abortion activists provide an important test of the general claim that confrontations between opposing political and ethical positions should not be outlawed in a vibrant democracy.

Two United States Supreme Court cases in the mid-1990s assessed the restrictions placed on pro-life activists demonstrating in front of abortion clinics.[26] In both cases, the court applied its higher standard of scrutiny since sidewalks were acknowledged as traditional public forums. The precise legal issue adjudicated in these cases, however, was different from the one in the airport cases discussed above. At stake was not a general regulation prohibiting protests but an injunction requiring that a specific group of pro-life protesters stop engaging in particular types of conduct (blocking traffic and harassing clients). In *Judy Madsen et al. v. Women's Health Center* (1994), the Supreme Court struck down a 300 foot protest-free zone around the clinic, but upheld a 36 foot buffer zone around the clinic entrance. This modified the decision of the Florida state court, which felt that based on the group's past tactics, such a buffer was necessary in order to ensure that they did not violate a statute preventing interference with public access to an abortion clinic. In essence, the Supreme Court majority found that content-neutral measures designed to prevent illegal conduct trumped the First Amendment guarantees.

The crucial question is whether such an injunction against harassment would be acceptable to people on the left if it were applied to Hare Krishnas or panhandlers. I think that the answer is yes. If a group of beggars harassed subway passengers, by following them, yelling at them, or encircling them, they should be stopped. If a large group of Hare Krishnas blocked the entrance to the airport terminals so that they could solicit the delayed passengers, they should also be banned from the airport. There are laws against fraud, harassment, public nuisance, noise limits, and so on, and these can and should be used against groups that turn a tacit provocation into an active threat. Anti-abortion activists, like strikers on the picket line, should be allowed to pass out leaflets but should not be permitted to block traffic or intimidate their targets.

The issue becomes more complex, however, when legislators attempt to protect clinic access by criminalizing leafletting and demonstrating as well as harassment. Courts in Canada have upheld the 1996 Abortion Services Act, which created a buffer zone around clinics and banned protest activities within the zone.[27] In 2000, the United States Supreme Court confronted a similar situation in *Hill v. Colorado*, which considered the constitutionality of a 1993 Colorado statute prohibiting "the willful obstruction of a person's access to medical counseling and treatment."[28] In order to achieve this objective, the statute prohibited obstructing access to a clinic or hindering entrance. This section of the legislation presents no problem inasmuch as it only prohibits conduct. Section 3, however, also makes it illegal to approach within eight feet of an individual in order to protest, leaflet, or communicate with her. A group of anti-abortion activists filed suit, claiming that the latter part of the statute violated their right to free speech. In their appeal to the United States Supreme Court, the activists argued that the statute discriminated against the pro-life viewpoint (e.g., the statute was not content neutral) and provided no alternative means of communication. In keeping with the trend towards restricting political speech in public places, the majority of the justices concluded that the statute was a permissible time, place, and manner restriction.

As noted in the previous chapter, a time, place, and manner restriction on speech is acceptable if it meets three criteria (the Ward test): it must be narrowly tailored to achieve a significant government interest, it must be content neutral, and it must leave open ample alternative channels of communication.[29] All three points were contested by the anti-abortion protesters, but they focused on the last two points. They noted that the statute only prohibited leafletting and communication at health care facilities, which they argued was clearly a euphemism for abortion clinics. This implied that the statute was not content neutral because its aim was to shield women seeking abortions from the pro-life message. In his dissent, Justice Kennedy agreed with the pro-life protesters, concluding that the statute was unconstitutional because it was clearly designed to criminalize the activities of anti-abortion activists and therefore discriminated against a certain viewpoint.

There was also disagreement about whether the restrictions left open alternative means of communication. The protesters felt that it would be impossible to engage pregnant women in conversation if they had to maintain an eight foot buffer zone. They would be forced to shout, which would engender an atmosphere of hostility when they wanted to offer nonthreatening pastoral counseling and education. Without being able to come within an arm's length of their target audience, pro-life "sidewalk counselors" could not even distribute a brochure with information on adoption agencies and support services for pregnant women. The majority of the justices, however, rejected this argument, emphasizing that closer contact was permissible if invited by the target audience.

The majority's position reflects an excessively rationalist understanding of political communication. The politics of the public sphere is not like a philosophy seminar. Each side does not systematically gather and assess the strongest arguments on each side of the issue. There is a high degree of chance, evasion, ideology, and circumstance in the development of our political views. The court's majority opinion does not acknowledge the reality of protest activity. Activists are trying to reach a specific target audience, usually one that would not otherwise seek out information about the particular cause. Even outside the highly charged atmosphere near an abortion clinic, most people are apathetic and unwilling to take the initiative to stop by an information table and ask for a brochure. Tactics such as leafletting are effective because they confront passersby with information that they would never seek. Receiving this information may be the beginning of a political conversation (perhaps a political argument) that otherwise would never take place. Although one-sided leaflets might not be the ideal form of political education, the alternative is simply to ignore opposing viewpoints altogether.

A critic might respond that abortion protest is a special case because of the history of violence associated with the fringes of the pro-life movement. According to this position, the violence of the pro-life movement makes it a legitimate target for government regulation. Abortion clinics have been bombed and doctors have been shot, therefore the very presence of anti-abortion protesters can create a climate of fear and intimidation. It is true that the line between provocation and intimidation is difficult to draw and fears and stereotypes will inevitably play a role in whose behavior is perceived as threatening. But the difficulty in finding some absolute criteria for distinguishing provocation from intimidation (and anyone who has walked a picket line must admit the line is blurry) is no reason to enact blanket prohibitions on the politics of protest. Protest activity is still the last resort for the powerless and must be protected. Intimidating or harassing behavior can be prohibited by enforcing existing laws or carefully tailoring new ones. By recognizing that a public place is a "traditional public forum," the court simply reminds itself to be extremely careful in evaluating restrictions on speech. The narrow legal standard adopted by the courts reflects today's widespread rejection of public life. This makes it all the more necessary to develop a politically relevant and ethically compelling approach to the public sphere.

RIGHTS AND POLITICAL PREFERENCES

The issue of clinic access poses an important challenge to those who defend a politics of confrontation in the name of democracy. At first pro-choice readers probably sympathize with the Canadian and United States courts' decisions that prevent protesters from gathering outside clinics. Having seen television images of groups of aggressive protesters blocking the way of vulnerable, isolated women, many will conclude that forceful government action is necessary. The crucial question for legislators and jurists, however, is when does a compelling government interest (such as protecting women's access to a legal medical procedure) outweigh protesters' right to free speech. Although it is clearly legitimate to prohibit harassment and intimidation, is it also acceptable to prevent all contact between members of groups with opposing viewpoints? The first step in answering this question involves considering whether alternative, less restrictive measures could meet the same objectives. In this case, it is relevant that the first part of the Colorado statute already banned protesters from blocking access to clinics. Furthermore, in 1994 Congress passed a federal statute, the Freedom of Access to Clinic Entrances Act (FACE) which explicitly prohibited the use or threat of force and physical obstruction to interfere with the provision of reproductive health services. The FACE statute is well designed to deal with the problem of violence and intimidation at abortion providers. The remaining question is whether less aggressive tactics such as leafletting and sidewalk counseling should be prohibited too.

Before answering this question it is important to acknowledge that encountering protesters at an abortion clinic undoubtedly causes discomfort at an already stressful time. Some protesters display enlarged models of a fetus in the first trimester and others call clinic staff baby killers. Is this discomfort a reason to prohibit them from trying to publicize their views? I do not think so. Protesters always cause discomfort in those whose views they seek to change. Union picketers hope to spark some sense of guilt in customers patronizing stores with unfair labor practices. Blacks sitting in at lunch counters wanted to make manifest the crisis and pain of racism by forcing whites to acknowledge it.[30] The point of protest is often to confront resistant or apathetic people with some alternative that would otherwise be ignored. Moreover, the spectacle of highly charged clashes between opposing viewpoints attracts the media attention that further diffuses a political message.[31] When the Court in *Hill* decided to protect citizens from "unwanted speech" it lost sight of the fact that the power of speech often lies in its capacity to disturb and agitate.

The *Hill* decision affects anti-abortion protesters in the short term but in the long term it could silence all forms of public protest. Some pro-choice activists might find the issue of clinic access so crucial that they are willing to sacrifice the principle of free speech, if a consistent application of the principle requires them to defend anti-abortion activists. This position has been developed at some length by literary-turned-legal theorist Stanley Fish. According to Fish, so-called principles are simply political preferences dressed up in universalistic language, which basically function as weapons of partisan struggle. Fish challenges the liberal orthodoxy on rights and insists that there is no good reason to subordinate one's substantive political goals in order to defend an abstract principle such as free speech. From Fish's point of view, it makes no sense for a Jewish lawyer to defend the Nazis at Skokie or a pro-choice leftist like me to express doubts about the *Hill* decision.[32] He is particularly contemptuous of well-meaning but befuddled liberals who lose sight of their political goals because of a slavish attempt to apply abstract principles consistently. According to Fish, speech is never *free* because most people believe that the principle of free speech should only extend to views they want to hear. Even the most ardent proponents of civil liberties believe that there is some form of expression that is outside the bounds of legitimate discourse.[33]

An initial reading of the public forum court cases provides support for Fish's view. The *Hill* decision, in particular, finds proponents of civil liberties like Justices Breyer and Ginsburg upholding prohibitions on speech and Justice Scalia, the most conservative member of the court and opponent of free speech in airports and post office sidewalks, sounding like an ACLU lawyer. This seems to confirm the thesis that principles such as free speech are employed instrumentally to further a particular political agenda. This may be true but that does not mean that it is something we should defend. We need to distinguish between the descriptive accuracy and normative legitimacy of this pattern. Even though both citizens and judges do interpret general principles through ideological lenses, this does not mean that they should jettison the general principles altogether. General principles such as free speech do not emerge from natural law or God or the original position. They are the sediments of previous struggles over power. As rules of the game, they are not politically neutral. They further a particular kind of political system. Rights to free speech, assembly, and petition are rules of the game that we call liberal-democracy and as long as we want to continue playing that game rather than, say, tyranny or aristocracy, there are good reasons for enforcing these rules. Speech is the primary mechanism that the minority can employ in order to convince adversaries and allies of its point of view and eventually become the majority. This claim does not mean that politics is basically rational and the best argument wins. Material interests pursued through webs of alliances and favors are far more important in understanding political outcomes. But activities such as protesting, campaigning, conversing, educating, dramatizing, and agitating that fall under the broader category of political speech are important tools for achieving political and social change.

What exactly would it mean to jettison "principle" (e.g., the principle of free speech) in the name of one's substantive political beliefs? From the pro-choice perspective it would involve arguing that abortion protesters should be muzzled because they want something bad (to intimidate a woman into carrying a fetus to term). This might be risky in the long term. If you think that you might someday strongly disagree with the majority about an important issue, then you might want to defend the principle of free speech inasmuch as it represents your best shot at preserving that same opportunity to try to become the majority yourself in the future. Is this tactic guided by an abstract principle, a substantive political agenda, or strategic thinking? It is governed by all three. Perhaps the most effective way to guarantee reproductive freedom in the long term is to protect the right to political dissent and to sustain pro-choice consciousness by engaging and refuting pro-life arguments. John Stuart Mill makes the same argument in *On Liberty*. He suggests that given human fallibility there is always a small possibility that one's own point is incorrect or partial and would therefore benefit from exposure to alternative views. But even if one's point of view is unassailable, defending it against alternatives will still strengthen and deepen it.[34]

Stanley Fish's critique of rights is based on a logical fallacy called "either-or." According to this fallacy, refuting possibility A is assumed to be a compelling argument for possibility B, when in fact there are multiple alternatives: C or D.[35] Fish suggests that if speech cannot be totally free then it is a ruse of power and a way of obscuring real interests. But there is a third alternative. "Free speech" may not be free because the government imposes limits, but it may still be worth supporting because of its systemic effects. Free speech may be a myth but one with salutary results. For example, the norm of frank speaking allows individuals to mock and demystify power. Furthermore, political speech often clarifies rather than obscures people's real interests by exposing them to critique and debate. These are democratic effects and it is not surprising that a democratic polity would protect them. In each court case, the judges must weigh the state's short-term interest (say, preventing traffic congestion or creating an attractive environment for postal service customers) against its long-term interest in sustaining a democratic system.

The traditional public forum doctrine is an example of such a balancing act. It is a compromise whereby the courts carefully review government regulations that restrict speech in places such as streets and parks that have historically served as sites of encounter and debate. The problem is that this doctrine does not do anything to protect nontraditional sites that have recently been created by new technologies and residential patterns, places such as Internet chat rooms, airports, and shopping malls (see Chapter 4). The compromise reached in the traditional public forum doctrine is no longer viable today. In order to come up with an alternative we need to spend less time identifying which spaces are traditional and devote more intellectual energy to reflecting on the meaning and value of the public realm.

ENDNOTES

1. Thanks are due to Ralph Shain for pointing out the way *Airplane* illustrates the disappearance of public forums.
2. In the public forums cases the standard is what Justice Scalia calls "intermediary scrutiny." A restriction must be "content neutral, narrowly tailored to serve significant government interest, and leave open ample alternative channels of communication." *Perry Ed. Assn. v. Perry Local Educators* 460 U.S. 37.
3. *Cornelius v. NAACP Legal Defense and Educational Fund* 473 U.S. 778. This case dealt with fundraising activities in a government office.
4. For a detailed analysis of the consequences of this restriction upon access to and use of public space, see Mike Davis, *City of Quartz: Excavating the Future in Los Angeles* (New York: Vintage, 1992).
5. As Robert Putnam points out in his book *Bowling Alone: The Collapse and Revival of American Community* (New York: Simon and Schuster, 2000), Internet communications lend themselves to hyperspecialization and thus segregation. Instead of talking to your neighbor about your interest (say, antique cars) and then his (gardens), you can communicate exclusively with owners of 1956 Edsels. For a fuller discussion of this issue, see Chapter 10.
6. In his article "Public Fora, Neutral Governments, and the Prism of Property," Calvin Massey calls this the affirmative approach. See *Hastings Law Journal* 50 (January 1999), 309–353.
7. The same applies to a designated public forum, but because a public forum is only so designated by the responsible agency, its decision really cannot be challenged in the courts. By definition, in the case of a designated public forum, there are no objective independent criteria for claiming public access.
8. Justice Souter, dissent to *Krishna v. Lee* 505 U.S. 672.
9. Some states, including California and Oregon, have interpreted their state constitutions to protect petitioning on publicly accessible private property. For a fuller discussion of this issue, see Chapter 4.
10. http://www.iandrinstitute.org.
11. http://www.iandrinstitute.org.
12. *Initiative and Referendum Institute v. United States Postal Service* (2003).
13. In Rehnquist's opinion there is a long paragraph describing "the disruptive effect" of solicitation, worrying that the decision about whether to donate money, to reach for a wallet, or to avoid the solicitor could delay travelers, causing them to miss a flight. If these were the actual concerns, it is hard to imagine that the numerous bars, luxury stores, duty-free shops, and kiosks wouldn't serve as similar distractions.

14. *International Society for Krishna Consciousness, Inc. v. Walter Lee* 505 U.S. 672 (1992).

15. There was no evidence presented that the Hare Krishnas engaged in illegal behavior, this was simply asserted by the court as a risk.

16. This comes from Justice Kennedy's decision concurring with the majority in *Krishna v. Lee*. He is referring to the standard established earlier that a traditional public forum must have the free exchange of ideas as its primary purpose. See *Perry Ed. Assn. v. Perry Local Educators' Assn.* (1983) and *Cornelius v. NAACP* (1985).

17. See note 9 in Chapter 1 for an explanation of the decision to analyze the Canadian court decisions as a point of comparison.

18. *Committee for the Commonwealth of Canada v. Canada* 4 C.C.R. (2d) 60 (1991). On this topic, see also Richard Moon, "Access to Public and Private Property Under Freedom of Expression," *Ottawa Law Review* 20 (1988), 339.

19. Section 1 of the Canadian Charter of Rights and Freedoms. For a brief discussion and sympathetic description of the reasonable limits clause, see Stanley Fish, *There Is No Such Thing as Free Speech…and It's a Good Thing Too* (Oxford: Oxford University Press, 1994), 104–105.

20. Jürgen Habermas, *The Structural Transformation of the Public Sphere: An Inquiry into a Category of Bourgeois Society* (Cambridge, MA: MIT Press, 1991)

21. Jürgen Habermas, "The Public Sphere: An Encyclopedia Article (1964)," *New German Critique* 3 (1974).

22. Habermas, *The Structural Transformation of the Public Sphere,* 35.

23. The phrase "right to the city" comes from Henri Lefebvre, the influential theorist of urbanism and social space. See his *Writings on Cities* (London: Blackwell, 1986).

24. Cited in Peter A. Barta, "Giuliani, Broken Windows, and the Right to Beg," *Georgetown Journal on Law and Poverty* (Summer 1999).

25. This case was handled by the United States Second Circuit Court of Appeals, *Young v. New York City Transit Authority* 903 F. 2d 146 (1990).

26. *Paul Schenck v. Pro-Choice Network* 34 F. 3rd 130 (1997); *Judy Madsen v. Women's Health Center* 512 U.S. 753 (1994).

27. The three cases decided by the Supreme Court of British Columbia, *Regina v. Watson* (2002), *R. v. Lewis* (1997), and *Demers v. R* (2003), all upheld the constitutionality of the Abortion Services Act of 1996. At the time of this writing, the Supreme Court of Canada had not ruled on this issue.

28. Jamin B. Raskin and Clark LeBlanc, "Disfavored Speech About Favored Rights: *Hill v. Colorado*, the Vanishing Public Forum, and the Need for an Objective Speech Discrimination Test," *The American University Law Review* (December 2001), 190.

29. *Ward v. Rock Against Racism* 492 U.S. 937 (1989).

30. See Martin Luther King, "Letter from a Birmingham Jail."

31. Raskin and LeBlanc, "Disfavored Speech About Favored Rights," 185.

32. Stanley Fish, *The Trouble with Principle* (Cambridge, MA: Harvard University Press, 1999). Fish, *There Is No Such Thing as Free Speech.*

33. Fish, *There Is No Such Thing as Free Speech,* 102–119. Fish notes that after celebrating the virtues of toleration and unregulated publication, Milton emphasizes that toleration should not extend to "popery, and open superstition." John Locke makes a similar caveat in his "Letter Concerning Toleration."

34. John Stuart Mill, *On Liberty* (Indianapolis: Hackett, 1978).

35. For example, it would be a logical fallacy to claim that the failure of a command economy (A) legitimizes a free market (B), when there might be a system of regulation (C) that is superior to them both.

4

THE MAULING OF PUBLIC SPACE

Bridgewater Township is a community of 40,000 located in New Jersey. Like earlier cities that were traditionally situated at the intersection of transportation routes, it owes its location to the confluence of Routes 287 and 78, two superhighways. Although Bridgewater was originally a bedroom community serving professionals who worked in New York, it gradually developed its own local economy with offices, businesses, and services. What it lacked was a sense of place. Local residents dreamed of a town center, some ideal composite of a New England village green and a Tuscan piazza, a place where old people could gossip, young people could *farsi vedere* (make themselves seen), mothers could bring young children while getting a latté, a sandwich, or some postage stamps. After over a decade of discussion, in 1988 they inaugurated Bridgewater Commons—a mall.[1]

The Bridgewater Commons Mall was not originally the initiative of commercial real estate developers. After years of research and debate, local government planners and community groups decided that a carefully designed shopping mall was the form of development best suited to maintaining the small town's quality of life and avoiding the strip mall aesthetic. Individual retailers could not provide the capital necessary to implement a comprehensive plan that included environmentally sensitive landscaping and rational traffic management. More importantly, a traditional downtown could not guarantee the most highly prized amenities: safety, cleanliness, and order.

The Bridgewater Commons and hundreds of supermalls like it have long troubled architects and critics who bemoan the homogeneity, sterility, and banality of the suburbs.[2] Approaching the mall primarily as an aesthetic or even a sociological issue, however, overlooks the enormous political consequences of the privatization of public space. Public sidewalks and streets are practically the only remaining available sites for unscripted political activity. They are the places where insurgent political candidates gather signatures, striking workers publicize their cause, and church groups pass out leaflets. It is true that television, newspapers, and direct mail constantly deliver a barrage of information, including political leaflets. But unlike the face-to-face politics that takes place in the public sphere, these forms for communication do not allow the citizen to talk back, to ask a question, to tell a story, to question a premise. The politics of the public sphere requires no resources—except time and perseverance. Public spaces are the last domains where the opportunity to communicate is not something bought and sold.

And they are rapidly disappearing. Such places are not banned by authoritarian legislatures. The public is not dispersed by the police. Their disappearance is more benign but no less troubling. The technology of the automobile, the expansion of the federal highway system, and the growth of residential suburbs has changed the way Americans live. Today the only place that many Americans encounter strangers is in the shopping mall. The most important public place is now private. And that is probably not an accident.

The privatization of public space poses a number of conceptual challenges for public policy makers. Does the ownership or use determine whether a particular place is truly private? How should the right to private property be weighed against the legitimate state interest in sustaining a public sphere? Does it violate the First Amendment right to free speech if a shopping mall prohibits orderly political speech? Are suburban malls meaningfully different from downtown developments?

The United States Supreme Court has tried to answer these questions in a series of decisions that have determined government policy defining the public sphere. The Supreme Court's doctrine in "the shopping mall cases" reflects a growing unwillingness to engage the broader political issues emerging from rapid social change. By insisting that the First Amendment only limits what government agencies can do, the Court has effectively closed its eyes to the privatization of public space.

THE SHOPPING MALL CASES

The Supreme Court addressed the implications of private ownership of quasi-public spaces in a series of cases decided between 1946 and 1980. The Court first considered the issue in 1946 in *Marsh v. Alabama*, which dealt with a Jehovah's Witness who was arrested for distributing religious pamphlets in the business district of a company-owned town. The majority decided that the arrest violated the freedom of the press and freedom of religion guaranteed by the First Amendment and applied to the states under the Fourteenth Amendment. The opinion written by Justice Black emphasized that all citizens must have the same rights, regardless of whether they live in a traditional municipality or a company-owned town. He noted that a typical community of privately owned residences would not have had the power to pass a municipal ordinance forbidding the distribution of religious literature on street corners. Why then, should a corporation be allowed to do so?

The company, Gulf Shipbuilding Corporation, based its argument on the common law and constitutional right to private property. If an individual does not have to allow Jehovah's Witnesses into her home, why should the company have to allow them on its property? The court, however, rejected this logic. It cited a long list of precedents—cases involving bridges, roads, and ferries—to establish that the right to private property is not absolute. Especially when a private company performs public functions, it opens itself up to greater government scrutiny and regulation. Given that the town was freely accessible to outsiders, it implicitly invited in the general public, thereby voluntarily incurring quasi-public obligations. The concept of "invitee" went on to play an important role in desegregation cases. According to the Court, "The more an owner, for his advantage, opens up his property for use by the public in general, the more do his rights become circumscribed by the statutory and constitutional rights of those who use it."

The opinion concluded that property rights must be weighed against other state interests. Justice Black emphasized that a democracy had a compelling state interest in maintaining free and open channels of communication so that all of its residents could fulfill their duties as citizens: "To act as good citizens they must be informed. In order to enable them to be properly informed their information must be uncensored." A concurring opinion by Justice Frankfurter stated that fundamental civil liberties guaranteed by the Constitution must have precedence over property rights.

Based on the reasoning in *Marsh v. Alabama*, it would seem likely that the right to free speech would apply to other private arenas that are similarly open to a broad public. In a 1972 decision, *Lloyd Corp. v. Tanner*, the Court considered whether First Amendment guarantees extended to the shopping mall.[3] This time, however, the majority upheld the mall's policy forbidding the distribution of handbills on its premises. The owners could exclude expressive conduct, even when it did not disrupt the commercial functions of the mall. Writing for the majority, Justice Powell argued that a shopping mall was not the functional equivalent of a company town, because it was not a space where individuals performed multiple activities. It was simply devoted to shopping. Although it was true that the shopping mall implicitly invited the general public onto its premises, this did not transform it into a public space. According to Powell, political activists misunderstood the invitation if they turned the mall into a public forum; the invitation to the public was only to shop. Moreover, because the First Amendment only limited "state action" there was no constitutional basis to apply it to private entities.

In *Lloyd v. Tanner* the Court did not overrule *Marsh v. Alabama*; instead it emphasized how the two cases differed. The mall was no company town. Basically, the Court concluded that activists had other opportunities to engage in political activity. They could make use of the public roads and sidewalks on the perimeter of the shopping mall. The assumption was that citizens had other chances to be exposed to diverse ideas and viewpoints. Because they presumably spent at most part of their day at the shopping mall, they could become informed citizens elsewhere.

Although the Court tried to emphasize the differences of fact between the two cases, it actually modified its view of the relevant doctrine. In the *Lloyd* decision there was no idealistic discussion of the free exchange of ideas necessary to maintain an informed citizenry. Rather than considering the goal of the First Amendment—presumably to foster the free expression characteristic of a democracy—the Court focused narrowly on the supposed absence of state action. It decided that private property does not "lose its private character merely because the public is generally invited to use it for designated purposes."

It is puzzling that the justices in *Lloyd* did not really analyze the logic of *Marsh v. Alabama* on the critical issue of state action. In *Marsh*, Justice Black suggested that the enforcement of state criminal trespass laws constituted state action. If the state may make no law abridging freedom of speech, then it cannot pass a criminal trespass statue penalizing a citizen simply for engaging in nondisruptive expressive conduct in a place where he or she would be legitimately allowed to enter. This same logic was used in a much more famous case, *Shelley v. Kraemer,* which was decided by the same court in 1948. In that case, the Supreme Court struck down a restrictive covenant preventing residents from selling their homes to blacks. The contract was undeniably private, however, it could not be enforced without "the active intervention of the state courts, supported by the full panoply of state power." According to this decision, private actors could not use the police and the courts to enforce practices that violate constitutional rights. In *Lloyd v. Tanner* (1972) the Supreme Court decided to overlook these precedents, assuming a much narrower definition of what constitutes state action.

The last shopping mall case, *Pruneyard Shopping Center v. Robins* (1980) dealt with a group of high school students who attempted to gather signatures for a petition protesting a U.N. resolution condemning Zionism. The California State Supreme Court originally found in favor of the students, ruling that the state's criminal trespass law would constitute state action for the purposes of the First Amendment. The shopping mall owners appealed to the United States Supreme Court, claiming that their Fifth Amendment right not to be deprived of "private property, without due process of law" was violated by the California decision. They argued that the mall was no public forum. To require that the mall allow political solicitation was tantamount to "taking without just compensation." The owners also claimed that the right to exclude others is an essential component of the definition of private property.

The *Pruneyard* decision, which governs to this day, articulated a mediating position. The Supreme Court rejected the mall owner's claim to absolute dominion over its property. Drawing upon a long history of precedents regarding public regulation of private property, the court concluded that the due process clause only required that the laws "not be unreasonable, arbitrary, or capricious and that the means selected shall have a real and substantial relation to the objective sought." The right to exclude others would only be decisive if the mall owners could prove that allowing orderly political speech would substantially decrease the economic value of their property.[4]

The Court, however, also rejected the students' claims to protection under the free speech clause of the First Amendment. Because the facts of the case were substantially the same as those in *Lloyd v. Tanner*, the Court saw no reason to reconsider the issue. They still insisted that the mall was private and therefore beyond the reach of the Bill of Rights. But there was a second issue at stake. The students had challenged the shopping center's policy under both the U.S. and the California State Constitution. The language of the California free speech clause was more expansive. Article 1, § 2, of the California Constitution provides:

> Every person may freely speak, write and publish his or her sentiments on all subjects, being responsible for the abuse of this

right. A law may not restrain or abridge liberty of speech or press.

The U.S. Supreme Court found that there was no reason why a state or federal statute could not guarantee access to the public areas of private malls. In other words, the court did not find any constitutional prohibition against legislation protecting political speech in places where citizens were normally allowed to be. This finding was consistent with an earlier decision, *Hudgens v. NLRB* (1976), which held that striking workers had no First Amendment right to picket in a mall, but they could assert such a right under federal labor laws protecting the processes associated with collective bargaining.[5] Since the decision fourteen states have considered whether their own state constitutions protect expressive conduct in shopping malls. Only five—California, Oregon, New Jersey, Colorado, and Massachusetts—recognized broader protections for speech.[6]

PRIVATIZATION AND PUBLIC POLICY

Over twenty years have passed since the Supreme Court's decision. Although the law has not changed in that period, society has. There is something quaint and anachronistic about reading the old shopping mall cases. They describe the world we take for granted as something new and marvelous and they could not even imagine the world in which we would soon live. Writing in 1972, Justice Powell described the Lloyd Center in Portland Oregon like this:

> The Center embodies a relatively new concept in shopping center design. The stores are all located within a single large, multi-level building complex sometimes referred to as the "Mall." Within this complex, in addition to the stores, there are parking facilities, malls, private sidewalks, stairways, escalators, gardens, an auditorium, and a skating rink. Some of the stores open directly on the outside public sidewalks, but most open on the interior privately owned malls. Some stores open on both. There are no public streets or public sidewalks within the building complex, which is enclosed and entirely covered except for the landscaped portions of some of the interior malls.[7]

This futuristic mall had 60 shops and 1000 parking spaces. Compared to today's supermalls, the Lloyd Center is a neighborhood corner store. By 1990 there were over 300 mega-supermalls with at least five department stores and three hundred shops. The West Edmonton Mall has over 800 shops, 11 department stores, 110 restaurants, 20 movie theaters, 13 night clubs, a chapel, a large hotel, and a lake.[8] In the United States there are twenty-three square feet of shopping mall space for every person.[9]

In 1972, the Court concluded that this new concept in shopping, "sometimes referred to as the 'Mall,'" in no way resembled a company town. It seemed obvious that a mall was simply devoted to a single activity, shopping, whereas a town was defined by the physical proximity of diverse spaces and activities, housing and services, leisure and work, consumption, education, and production. A mall is a place you visit; a town is a place you live. But this has been slowly changing.[10] Industry watchers report that the average visit to a "leisure time destination" (a mall with sophisticated design elements, restaurants, and movie theaters) lasted four hours as compared to just one hour at a conventional mall.[11]

The mall has become an entertainment mecca, a major employer, and a premier vacation destination. The Travel Industry Association of America (TIA) reported that shopping is the number one vacation activity in America. The Mall of America in Bloomington, Minnesota attracts 42.5 million visitors annually.[12] Its hundreds of retail establishments are not the only attraction: it has a wedding chapel, the nation's largest indoor amusement park, a post office, a police station, and a school.

The mall is also a workplace. The West Edmonton Mall has over 15,000 employees. Although they do not manufacture automobiles or aircraft carriers, they do produce the spiral of fantasy, desire, and consumption that is the basis of the North American service economy.

The mall is becoming not only a genuine multi-use facility, but a completely self-contained homotopia of suburban life. In the morning the doors open to waiting seniors, the famous mall-walkers who appreciate the controlled climate, cleanliness, and safety. At night the security guards have to herd out the lingering teenagers, who are in no rush to go home to their monotonous housing developments.[13] The mall is clearly the nodal point of social life, but is it the equivalent of a downtown business district?

Not exactly. The shopping mall is so attractive because it combines the pleasures of public life with the safety and familiarity of the private realm. Ironically, the suburban megamall was intended to be an oasis of urbanity and civilization. Victor Gruen, the Viennese architect who designed the prototype of the modern mall, was motivated by a progressive vision. He wanted to recreate a vibrant, pedestrian-oriented, multi-use area that captured the excitement of urban space. An immigrant from Vienna, he was inspired by the glass-enclosed atriums of Europe, particularly the gallerias of Milan and arcades of Paris. In 1956 he built Southdale in Edina, Minnesota, the first multi-level, enclosed, climate-controlled mall. He thought that the mall could serve as a community center and nodal point for civic identity in the suburbs.[14] He realized that many people long for the vitality, diversity, beauty, and stimulation of public space. Gruen astutely predicted that when public space is not available, people would flock to private simulacra. But the private provision of public places is a Faustian bargain. Once developers possess the power of property rights, they usually exercise them to create the highly orchestrated and controlled environments that eviscerate the diversity that animates public space.

Following in Gruen's footsteps, contemporary mall designers have used their formidable skills to simulate the old-fashioned downtown of our imaginations. Faux antiquarian signs suggest that shopping corridors are actually city streets and the central atrium is the town square.[15] Some malls, such as Faneuil Hall Marketplace in Boston, incorporate restored historical buildings in order to create the atmosphere of reassuring urbanity that many Americans identify with the past. Other malls play freely with period and place in order to incorporate images widely associated with a sophisticated and alluring public life. The Borgota, a mall in Scottsdale, Arizona, for example, was built to resemble a walled village in thirteenth- century Italy. Replete with an imitation church bell tower, bricks imported from Rome, and signs in Italian, it appeals to affluent consumers' fantasies about public space.[16] These design elements reflect the developers' claim that the mall is a "city within a city" (The Mall of America) or "an urban village" (Universal City Walk).[17]

When animal rights protesters went to court to gain access to the "public" areas of the Mall of America, they tried to make use of the mall's semiotic system for their own ends. They claimed that the mall presented itself as a multi-use downtown business district and therefore should be governed by the principles set out in Marsh v. Alabama. Faced with petitioners trying to engage in protest activity, the Mall of America, however, quickly retreated from the semiotics of "Main Street USA" and embraced a more conventional defense of private property.

In some cases, the claim that malls are contemporary community centers is based on more than imagineering.[18] Increasingly the mall is a civic center as well as a shopping destination. The local and county government in Knoxville, Tennessee, for example, has located essential government services in a shopping mall on the periphery of town, the Knoxville Center. In an effort to "take the services to the people," the city encourages Knoxville citizens to visit "City Hall at the Mall," where they can pay their property taxes, renew their drivers' licenses, mail letters, and apply for marriage licenses. There is also a police station and a community room.[19] The consequence of this convenience is that the shopping center effectively serves as a moat of private space that insulates public functionaries from protest activity. The leasing arrangement opens up a potentially Kafkaesque scenario in which the aggrieved citizens try vainly to gain access to the city hall only to be turned away at the gates of the mall by unaccountable private security forces. Lest this scenario seem fantastic, imagine a group of antiwar activists who want to deliver a petition to the city government, but they are turned away at the entrance to the mall because they are wearing T-shirts that say "Give Peace a Chance."

The "City Hall at the Mall" may be an extreme example, but it is emblematic of a trend toward multi-use malls. An April 1999 survey by the journal *Shopping Center World* found that half of the 150 new projects under construction are multi-use malls. Some of these are the New Urbanist-inspired developments that try to mimic the appeal of old-fashioned downtowns (see Chapter 6). They link higher density housing with office and retail space, all unified by architectural cues evoking the turn of the century. Fifty of the new multi-use malls include office space, libraries, housing, or hotels.

One such project is the new Towers at Zona Rosa, a shopping mall situated ten minutes from downtown Kansas City. Although the plan relies on 30,000 foot department stores to anchor the retail plaza, it also includes loft-style apartments situated above boutiques and cafés. Underground parking, decorative street lamps, indigenous plants, and outdoor tables are among the lifestyle-enhancing amenities. As theme parks, megamalls, and gated communities merge, nostalgic recreations of the village green replace actual public space.[20]

Living at the mall might still seem unusual, but it is a culmination of a dynamic that has been accelerating throughout the 1990s—the emergence of what Joel Garreau has called Edge Cities. The growth of Edge Cities reflects a complete transformation of the spatial structure of postwar American life. The typical pattern of bedroom communities situated along the outskirts of urban cores is disappearing. He reports that Americans no longer sleep in the suburbs and work in the city. In dozens of cities including Houston, Boston, Tampa, and Denver, there is more office space outside the central business district than within it.

This new office space is built in ~~Edge Cities~~, suburbs that now incorporate millions of square feet of commercial development.[21]

There are undoubtedly positive sides of this development. As more companies relocate to the suburbs, the average American's commute time decreases. But as workplaces become more and more decentralized, the density needed to support public transportation such as commuter railroads also disappears. Your suburban office park may be closer to your home, but it is probably not served by the subway, which leads to greater automobile dependence, traffic congestion, pollution, and the blight of endless parking lots. It becomes increasingly commonplace to move from home to office to shopping mall in the automobile. The Edge City citizen need never traverse public space. It becomes possible to spend an entire day or lifetime without encountering street corners, bus stops, or park benches.

The new Edge City geography poses a challenge to the doctrine established by the Supreme Court. If private space takes on a public character in cases like the company town when it colonizes every aspect of life, then it is time to reconsider the character of the mall. But this is unlikely to happen. As recently as 1992, the Supreme Court held that labor organizers had no right to try to contact potential members by passing out leaflets in the parking lot of a Lechmere's store, this despite the fact that the only alternative space was a 46 foot wide grassy strip separating the lot from the highway.[22] In 1999 the Minnesota State Supreme Court heard a challenge from an animal rights group that was prevented from peacefully protesting in the common area of the 4.2 million square foot Mall of America. The protesters argued that the mall was a public space because it had been heavily subsidized by the state, which provided $186 million in public financing.[23] The Justices found that "neither the invitation to the public to shop and be entertained...nor the public financing used to develop the property are state action for the purposes of free speech" under the Minnesota Constitution.[24]

POLITICS AND THE PUBLIC SPACE

This string of defeats is a setback for political activists and proponents of an active public life. But it could have the unintended consequence of channeling debate over privatization into the political arena and out of the closed chambers of the court. If judicial intervention will not protect the public sphere, then political action still presents an alternative. Congress or state legislatures could pass statutes mandating that malls of a certain size must provide access to community groups. They could also establish guidelines to extend broader protections for political activity. One way to do this would be to pass legislation applying speech and petition guarantees to the functional equivalents of traditional public forums. As indicated in the *Pruneyard* decision, there is no constitutional provision that would invalidate these kinds of laws. Because labor unions are dependent on tactics such as the picket line, they would be powerful proponents of such a law and useful allies for other activist groups fighting to maintain access to public space. As the Seattle-inspired euphoria wanes, the struggle for such legislation could unify labor and other social movements.

Even in areas where such tactics were unsuccessful at the state level, it would still be possible to adopt similar strategies at the local level. The obvious place is to start is to support downtown business districts and other public places that still encourage diversity and invite political activity. But this individualist solution, by itself, is naïve. Collective action is also necessary. When new large-scale mall developments are proposed, citizens have the most leverage to demand some form of continued public access. The support of local government agencies, town councils, and planning boards is crucial for a project on the scale of the modern mall. By building and upgrading roads, modifying zoning, and approving permits, localities still have bargaining power over some aspects of development. They could negotiate a policy guaranteeing free access to a community booth or public courtyard in the mall.[25] For example, in 1991 the Hahn Company, which owns thirty malls in California, signed an agreement with the American Civil Liberties Union that allows leafletting and petitioning in most of its malls. In New York, Democratic state legislators have introduced a bill mandating that privately owned complexes with at least 20 stores and 250,000 square feet of commercial space designate an area where citizens can congregate to engage in non-disruptive political activity.[26] In 1988 a similar bill was defeated in the state legislature.[27]

Why are these tactics seldom even employed let alone successful? Although malls like the one in Bridgewater manage to preserve natural oases such as "Mac's Brook," they fail to protect oases of publicness in a privatizing world. And this is not only the fault of greedy developers. Most people do not value the disruption and unease caused by other peoples' political speech. One of the appeals of the mall is precisely that it provides an environment carefully designed to exclude any source of discomfort. As Benjamin Barber put it, shopping malls and theme parks sell a sanitized substitute for public life "where people can experience the thrill of the different without taking any risks."[28] The soothing lighting, polished surfaces, pleasant temperature, and enticing displays are not the only allure; part of the fantasy involves entering a world where no homeless person, panhandler, or zealot can disturb the illusion of a harmonious world. We appreciate free speech in the abstract but often avoid it in reality.

In this mauling of public space, democratic theorists have confronted extremely sophisticated marketing experts, and the democratic theorists have been the losers. The political theorists who are most concerned with democracy have failed to offer a compelling rationale to challenge the privatization of public space. By concentrating on the value of speech rather than the importance of space, they turn the public sphere into an abstraction. We need to engage in more careful reflection on the reasons why we should protect free speech *and* public space.

In academic circles, theorists argue that deliberation between citizens is the most promising way to reach rational political decisions. Moreover, they stress that rational, public-spirited discussions are necessary to legitimate democratic procedures and make sure that politics does not degenerate into mere struggles over power. These theories of deliberative democracy are indebted to Jürgen Habermas's influential work on the ideal speech situation. The basic idea of the ideal speech situation is something like this: when we engage in conversation we assume that other participants are telling the truth, speaking sincerely, and oriented toward mutual understanding. When these conditions are realized, then a rational consensus can emerge.[29]

I believe that one reason for the popularity of deliberative democracy is that it is based on a certain optimism about the efficacy of ideas. Although our convictions may also be resistant to change, they are much more malleable than the built environment. Confronted with a landscape filled with strip malls, decaying supermalls, forbidding seas of concrete parking lots, and urban high-rises isolated in unkempt wastelands, it is tempting to focus on democratic theories rather than the more intractable problem of democratic practices.

At first it seems as if this emphasis on "deliberative democracy" is precisely what is needed to reinvigorate our commitment to the public sphere, whether it is comprised of street corners with soap boxes and speakers or their modern equivalents. Deliberative democracy reinforces traditional justifications of the speech clause of the First Amendment. But the concept of deliberation will not be useful if it emphasizes the rationality that emerges from the ideal speech situation. Let's face it. Nothing approaching the ideal speech situation ever happens in the mall. The ideal speech situation is basically an extremely idealized depiction of the norms of scholarly journals or conferences. We need free speech and public places not because they help us, as a society, reach a rational consensus but because they disrupt the consensus that we have already reached too easily. Reasonable arguments often just reinforce distance, whereas public space establishes proximity. This proximity has distinctive properties that democratic theorists often overlook. We can learn something from facing our fears and evasions that we cannot learn from debating principles. The panhandler and the homeless person—they do not convince us by their arguments. Rather, their *presence* conveys a powerful message. They reveal the rough edges of our shiny surfaces. The union picketer and right-to-lifer confront us with meaningful and enduring conflict. Provocative speech cannot be something that happens elsewhere—in academic journals, conferences, mass mailings, and highly scripted town meetings. It must sometimes be literally in your face for it to have any impact. For a robust democracy we need more than rational deliberation. We need public places that remind us that politics matter.

In New Jersey, at least, malls will be part of this public. That is the implication of a decision reached by the New Jersey State Supreme Court on June 13, 2000. In a unanimous vote, the Court held that Mill Creek, another New Jersey mall, could not restrict free speech by forbidding political groups from leafletting. Although the owners could place reasonable restrictions on expressive conduct to make sure that politics did not disrupt the commercial activities of the mall, they could not deny access to the only place left in New Jersey where there is an opportunity for face-to-face contact with large groups of people. By a circuitous route, the dream of Bridgewater comes true and the residents will get a commons.[30]

THE MALL GOES DOWNTOWN: BUSINESS IMPROVEMENT DISTRICTS

Among sophisticated city dwellers, it has become commonplace to criticize the vulgarity, homogeneity, and sheer ugliness of the suburban shopping mall.[31] Strip mall-style development with its garish signs, immense parking lots, and brutal architecture draws the bargain hunter not the connoisseur. Even the more upscale suburban shopping malls, with their faux marble surfaces, skylit atriums, and classical music can barely disguise the standardized, middle-brow goods they sell. So downtown business districts, with their historical buildings, unique shops, and slightly transgressive mix of seediness and sophistication continue to have some appeal. But do these areas foster a different kind of public life? I pose this question because academics writing about the mall often give in to the temptation to dress up unreflective elitism as cultural criticism. As Pierre Bourdieu's *Distinction* and David Brooks's *Bobos in Paradise* have shown us, "alternative" forms of consumption—items such as Turkish kilims, espresso drinks, high-end outdoor gear, or ultra-modern furniture—function to distinguish the educated, upper-middle classes from their petit-bourgeois parents, business elites, and the Budweiser-drinking masses.[32] In order to avoid facile criticism of the suburban mall, the final section of this chapter focuses on the way that the malling of America has transformed the core downtown neighborhoods of urban centers such as New York City.

Business Improvement Districts (BIDs) have been at the forefront of the attempt to apply the logic of the shopping mall to downtown centers. There are over 1000 BIDs in the United States and more than forty in New York City alone.[33] BIDs are geographically contiguous areas that vote to assess property owners a special fee in order to provide additional services. These services include sanitation, security, and landscaping. Some BIDs employ uniformed personnel to provide tourists with directions and discourage criminal activity. Others install benches, enforce uniform exterior décor standards, and distribute maps featuring local businesses. They have been widely credited in the press for improving the quality of life in downtown commercial districts.

BIDs have been popular with both city officials and business owners. For government officials, they provide additional tax revenue to fund needed services in the most visible areas of the city. Business interests support BIDs because the structure allows them greater control over their own tax payments. Revenue collected through the BID is spent exclusively in the district and reflects the priorities of business owners. Because assessments are mandatory, setting up a BID overcomes the free-rider problem that plagues voluntary associations such as the Chamber of Commerce. At the same time, business interests maintain complete fiscal control, thereby avoiding the interference of government bureaucrats, local residents, and other citizens. With budgets in the tens of millions of dollars, these publicly regulated, private governments are reshaping the political landscape of downtown.

The proliferation of Business Improvement Districts (a phenomenon that goes by many names including special assessment district or business improvement zone) is a response to competition from the suburban shopping mall. The BID is, in effect, a centralized management structure that allows dispersed downtown retailers to imitate and incorporate successful elements of the mall. For a shopping mall it is fairly easy to provide common spaces, maintain cleanliness, and orchestrate a high degree of visual and spatial coherence. Because the entire mall is owned by a single developer who leases space to individual stores, centralized control is guaranteed through property rights, rules, and detailed lease restrictions.[34] In most downtown business districts, streets and plazas are public; small businesses coexist alongside large chains in buildings that they may either rent or own. The BID, unlike the mall, has to rely on governmental powers such as eminent domain, taxation, fines, and zoning in order to mimic the effects of centralized control. The enabling legislation in Arkansas gives some idea of just how wide-ranging the power of business improvement districts can be. They are allowed:

(1) To acquire, construct, install, operate, maintain, and contract regarding pedestrian or shopping malls, plazas, sidewalks or moving sidewalks, parks, parking lots, parking garages, offices, urban residential facilities including, without limitation, apartments, condominiums, hotels, motels, convention halls, rooms, and related facilities, and buildings and structures to contain any of these facilities, bus stop shelters, decorative lighting, benches or other seating furniture, sculptures, telephone booths, traffic signs, fire hydrants, kiosks, trash receptacles, marquees, awnings or canopies, walls and barriers, paintings or murals, alleys, shelters, display cases, fountains, child-care facilities, restrooms, information booths, aquariums or aviaries, tunnels and ramps, pedestrian and vehicular overpasses and underpasses; (2) To landscape and plant trees, bushes and shrubbery, grass, flowers, and each and every other kind of decorative planting; (3) To install and operate, or to lease, public music and news facilities; (4) To construct and operate childcare facilities; (5) To construct lakes, dams, and waterways of whatever size; (6) To employ and provide special police facilities and personnel for the protection and enjoyment of the property owners and the general public using the facilities of the district; (7) To prohibit or restrict vehicular traffic on the streets within the district as the governing body may deem necessary and to provide the means for access by emergency vehicles to or in

these areas; (8) To remove, by agreement or by the power of eminent domain, any existing structures or signs of any description in the district not conforming to the plan of improvement; and (9) To do everything necessary or desirable to effectuate the plan of improvement for the district.[35]

In other words, BIDs can exercise far-reaching governmental powers against individual property owners in order to transform an existing neighborhood into a "managed environment" with quaint matching signs and manicured plazas. In some cases they can even eliminate seedy businesses that might scare off the target consumer demographic. All this is done with minimal input from neighborhood residents, citizen groups, or even commercial tenants.[36]

Business Improvement Districts have imitated the environment of the suburban shopping mall as well as its management structure. The shopping mall, like the theme park, tries to create an atmosphere "in which the emphasis on safety and tidiness is supposed to make visitors feel secure and happy so they'll spend money and come back."[37] To this end, BIDs devote, on average, twenty percent of their budget to sanitation and twenty-five percent to security.[38]

These downtown shopping districts try to achieve a mix of urban and suburban values. Their appeal is due to the energy, variety, visual stimulation, architectural distinctiveness, and cultural opportunities distinctive of urban centers.[39] At the same time they mimic the safety, cleanliness, order, and familiarity that has proven such an effective formula in suburban malls. This allows consumers to enjoy the traditionally urban pleasures of proximity to diverse strangers in a setting where any risk of threat, disruption, disorientation, or discomfort has been removed.[40] This is a formula that was perfected in "festival marketplaces" such as Faneuil Hall in Boston, Riverwalk in New Orleans, the Cannery in San Francisco, and South Street Seaport in New York. Each project transformed a historic district into a zone of leisure and consumption, filled with restaurants, chain boutiques, and kiosks specializing in local color. Wildly successful from a commercial point of view, these projects have been criticized for transforming distinctive, mixed-use districts into formulaic, sanitized tourist traps.[41] Festival marketplaces sell a simulacra of the city as tableau or spectacle, something to be enjoyed visually but not experienced kinesthetically: the city without its smells, sensations, or dangers. They cleverly integrate design cues that evoke nostalgia for an imagined urban past with the safety, cleanliness, and familiarity of the suburban mall.

SOCIAL AND POLITICAL CONSEQUENCES OF BUSINESS IMPROVEMENT DISTRICTS

Whereas most commentators have focused on an aesthetic critique of festival marketplaces and the Disneyfication of downtown, they over-look the political and social consequences of this transformation, par-ticularly the impact of Business Improvement Districts on democratic governance. BIDs pose several challenges to a democratic polity. First, political influence in a Business Improvement District is usually directly proportional to the value of one's property, thereby violating the basic democratic principle of one-person, one-vote. Second, BIDs increase the impact of the already powerful business community on local government. Finally, BIDs, as private, nonprofit organizations, may be able to circumvent the constitutional provisions that require local governments to protect the civil liberties of their citizens.

In San Francisco, like most municipalities, the creation of a BID and its priorities depend on the support of the majority of property owners in the district. But all property owners do not have equal votes. Votes are apportioned in relation to the value of commercial property, there-fore a very small cadre could effectively control the decisions of the BID. Although oligarchical control is acceptable, a monarchy is ruled out, at least in San Francisco, where the weighted vote of one individ-ual cannot surpass forty percent.[42]

There have been several court cases challenging the anti-democratic decision-making structure of Business Improvement Districts. The most notable decision involves New York's Grand Central BID, which encompasses 71 million square feet of commercial space (nineteen per-cent of Manhattan's total office space) and has a budget of over $10 million. Robert Kessler, a shareholder in a co-op apartment building in the district, argued that the governance structure, which guaranteed thirty-one seats to property owners, seventeen seats to tenants, and four seats to government appointees, violated the constitutional princi-ple of one-person, one-vote. In 1997 the United States District Court found in favor of the BID and the decision was upheld a year later by the Second Circuit Court of Appeals.

From a legal perspective, the issue was how to interpret the prece-dent established in *Avery v. Midland County*, the case in which the Supreme Court applied the doctrine of one-person, one-vote to local government. Although the court clearly stated that cities and counties must guarantee personhood suffrage, it left open the question as to whether this doctrine applied to the myriad diverse and overlapping sub- and supra-local institutions. The Supreme Court noted that "a

special-purpose unit of government assigned the performance of functions affecting definable groups of constituents more than other constituents" might be exempt from the principle of one-person, one-
vote.[43] In subsequent litigation, the court recognized at least one such
exception. It held that the governing board of a local watershed management district designed to provide irrigation could be elected exclusively by agricultural interests.[44] In *Kessler*, United States Circuit Court
Judge Kearse concluded that the Grand Central Business Improvement
District (BID) was similar to the water management district: it existed
for the purpose of promoting business. Due to its limited scope and
disproportionate impact on property owners, one-person, one-vote
did not apply.[45]

Although it is certainly true that Business Improvement Districts
exist in order to promote business interests, they still have a significant
impact on local residents. The range of services provided by well-
funded BIDs—security, sanitation, social services, and capital
improvements—is similar to that of local government. Furthermore,
the Grand Central BID's foray into social services illustrates some of
the dangers that arise when a business lobby takes on quasi-govern-
mental power. The controversy involved a program designed by the
Grand Central Partnership (a Business Improvement District) to tackle
the problem of homelessness by providing shelter and job training.
There were two accusations levied against the program, which resulted
in litigation.[46] Over forty participants in the job-training program
claimed that the Partnership violated state and federal minimum wage
laws. Under the auspices of "job training," homeless people were paid
$1.16 per hour to serve as outreach workers.[47] The second accusation
dealt with the nature of the work that fell under the category of "outreach." Four former outreach workers claimed that they were told by
supervisors to use all means necessary in order to remove homeless
people from the district. They admitted to beating homeless people
and destroying their belongings. These statements corroborated the
stories of homeless people who claimed they had been beaten and
threatened by Partnership employees.[48] After an investigation, the
Department of Housing and Urban Development (HUD) requested
that the BID return the unused portion of a $547,000 grant that had
been awarded to subsidize its work with the homeless. Andrew Cuomo,
assistant secretary of HUD, explained, "We are not in the business of
subsidizing thuggery."[49]

The example of the HUD grant also illustrates another under-appre-
ciated political consequence of the proliferation of BIDs. Although

BIDs are widely lauded for raising additional tax revenue from businesses, they also are more effective at competing for scarce resources from city coffers. This is another lesson that BIDs have learned from shopping mall developers, who have been very successful at getting a variety of government subsidies in order to lure commercial development to a particular locality. In the suburbs, these subsidies usually include tax abatements and public funds for site development and roads. BIDs have made downtown more effective at lobbying for the enactment and enforcement of pro-business laws and gaining resources such as extra police protection or direct subsidies.[50] To take one example, the Wall Street BID offered to offset some of the costs (towards space and equipment) if New York City located a police substation in the district. Even though it was not an under-served area, the police department complied.[51] Decisions such as that one further exacerbate inequalities between neighborhoods in the distribution of essential services. Not only do Business Improvement Districts benefit from their ability to pay for higher levels of service, they may also receive a greater proportion of city resources, as cost-sharing rather than need becomes a criterion for distributing scarce resources. Although it is true that a voluntary Chamber of Commerce, large corporation, or interest group will also be effective at influencing local government, the BID formalizes this influence by creating a strong institutional mechanism.

BIDs aspire to imitate the controlled environment and unified management of the shopping mall but public ownership of the streets and common spaces imposes a serious limitation on their ability to do so. Unlike mall owners, local police officers are limited in their ability to eject homeless people, preachers, street performers, and leafletters from common spaces downtown. But what happens if private security forces do so? Take, for example, the homeless people who were intimidated and forced to leave the Grand Central District. Had the police tried to evict them, they could have complained to the city review board in charge of police misconduct. The homeless victims also could have brought a lawsuit under a federal statute that provides redress to any citizen deprived of any right secured by the Constitution and laws. But because this statute only applies to rights violations undertaken by a person "acting under color of law,"[52] neither of these remedies is available to someone intimidated or threatened by a private security force.[53]

This raises the possibility that local governments may rely on private proxies to employ tactics that are forbidden to government actors.

Although the Bill of Rights prevents the government from limiting individuals' right to free speech, movement, and assembly, it is unclear what would happen if a private government such as a BID tried to do so. Imagine a scenario in which a Business Improvement District adopted a code of conduct that banned skateboarding, lying on benches, loitering, and leafletting. A BID could claim that it was not a state actor, and therefore the Constitution did not apply. If this failed, the city could lease or give the streets, sidewalks, and plazas to the BID, which had already assumed the cost of policing and maintaining them (see Chapter 5). Armed with this designation as private property, the BID would be a step closer to its goal of transforming downtown into a specialty mall.

CONCLUSION

The malling of America is not limited to the suburbs. The shopping mall is an icon of fantasy, leisure, and consumption at the same time as it is a symbol of homogeneity, sterility, market stratification, and social control. If Rem Koolhaas is right and shopping provides the only public space that still exists, then the difference between the city street and the suburban mall may be diminishing.[54] According to *The Harvard Design School Guide to Shopping*, urbanism itself has become a specialized form of shopping that exploits icons such as Madison Avenue or Times Square by turning them into "Brand Zones." In order to understand this process we need to pay attention to both commodification and privatization. Studies of *commodification* tend to focus on the cultural dimension of this negative dialectic between city and mall. We also need an analysis of *privatization* that uncovers the political and legal mechanisms allowing the public areas of the city core to look and act like suburban malls.

The growing influence of Business Improvement Districts is problematic for two reasons. The governance structure of most BIDs violates norms of democratic accountability by giving a disproportionate voice to property owners over other community interests and possibly by circumventing statutes and principles ensuring the protection of civil liberties. BIDs also exacerbate existing inequalities in the provision of government services in order to create marketable "Brand Zones" within the city. It is not surprising that the wealthy and powerful would prefer to govern themselves without interference from everyone else. What is surprising is that a democracy is willing to let them.

ENDNOTES

1. The story of Bridgewater is recounted in Joel Garreau's *Edge City: Life on the New Frontier* (New York: Doubleday, 1991), 42–45.
2. John Hannigan, "The Saturday Essay: Who Wants to Spend Their Life in a Theme Park?" *The Independent*, Nov. 28, 1998, T1.
3. In an earlier case, *Food Employees v. Logan Valley Plaza* 391 U.S. 308 (1968) the court ruled that a labor union could picket a supermarket located in a shopping mall, despite the objections of the mall manager. For a full discussion of the shopping mall cases, see Brady C. Williamson and James A. Friedman, "State Constitutions: The Shopping Mall Cases," *University of Wisconsin Law Review* (1998), 883–903; Curtis J. Berger, "Pruneyard Revisited: Political Activity on Private Lands," *N.Y.U. Law Review* 66 (1991), 663–691.
4. For a critical view of this argument, see Richard Epstein, "Takings, Exclusivity and Speech: The Legacy of *Pruneyard v. Robins*," *The University of Chicago Law Review* 64 (Winter 1997), 21–56.
5. *Hudgens v. NLRB* 424 U.S. 507 (1976) was an important decision because it over-turned *Food Employees v. Logan Valley Plaza* 391 U.S. 308 (1968), the first shopping mall case. The decision held that striking workers did have a First Amendment right to protest unfair labor practices in front of their employer's store, even though it was located in a mall. In weighing the issues, the court concluded that the employees had no alternative place to protest, inasmuch as their message was directly linked to the commercial activity of a store located in the mall. In contrast, *Hudgens* stated that "property does not lose its private character merely because the public is generally invited to use it for designated purposes."
6. Mark Alexander, "Attention, Shoppers: The First Amendment in the Modern Shopping Mall," *Arizona Law Review* 41 (Spring 1999), 1–47. Alexander notes that many of the nine states which have rejected petitioners' free speech claims rely on the Supreme Court doctrine of "state action" even though their own constitutional provisions provide a broader guarantee similar to the language in the California constitution.
7. *Lloyd Corp. v. Tanner* 407 U.S. 551 (1972).
8. Margaret Crawford, "The World in a Shopping Mall," in *Variations on a Theme Park: The New American City and the End of Public Space*, ed. Michael Sorkin (New York: Hill and Wang, 1992), 3.
9. Eds. Chuihua Judy Chung, Jeffrey Inaba, Rem Koolhaas, and Sze Tsung Leong, *Harvard Design School Guide to Shopping* (Cologne: Taschen, 2001).
10. For a detailed account of the transformation of the shopping mall, see William Severini Kowinski, *The Malling of America: An Inside Look at the Great Consumer Paradise* (New York: Morrow, 1985).
11. Jim Walker, "Visionary's Quest: Columbus-Based Developer Yaromir Steiner Determined to Build Better Shopping Center," *The Columbus Dispatch*, June 9, 2002, 1E.
12. Melissa Levy, "On the Road Again," *Minneapolis Star Tribune*, July 16, 2001, 1D.
13. Kowinski, *The Malling of America*, 26–52.
14. See Victor Gruen and Larry Smith, *Shopping Towns USA: The Planning of Shopping Centers* (New York: Reinhold, 1960). See also Witold Rybczynski, *City Life* (New York: Touchstone, 1995), 206–207.
15. Some of the Mall of America's promotional literature reads: "[The] Mall of America will be a city within a city, unlike other malls....It will be divided into four distinctive city streets providing four unique shopping and visual environments." Brief of Amicus Curiae from the Minnesota Civil Liberties Union, presented in the case *State v. Wicklund*.

16. Kowinski, *The Malling of America*, 233.

17. "Universal City Walk: An Architect's Dream: A Conversation with Jon Jerde," Universal City Press Release, 1993. Cited in Aida Hozic, *Hollyworld: Space, Power and Fantasy in the American Economy* (Ithaca, NY: Cornell University Press, 2001), 6.

18. The term "imagineering" suggests "engineering and image" à la Disney. The term comes from Keally McBride, *Social Imagineering*, unpublished manuscript, 2002.

19. Jennifer Niles Coffin, "The United Mall of America: Free Speech, State Constitutions, and the Growing Fortress of Private Property," *University of Michigan Journal of Law Reform* 33 Summer 2000), 615–649.

20. Craig Kellog, "Shopping and Housing Mix in New Kansas City Mall," *Architectural Record* 187, no. 2 (1999), 56.

21. Garreau, *Edge City*.

22. *Lechmere, Inc. v. NLRB* 502 U.S. 527 (1992).

23. The mall is also protected by City of Bloomington police and the only police substation is located on mall property. For a more thorough discussion of this case see Coffin, "The United Mall of America."

24. Mike Kaszuba, "Megamall Not Public Space, Court Rules," *Minneapolis Star Tribune*, March 12, 1999, 1A.

25. Many other malls, including those operated by the Rouse Company (the developer of many visible projects such as Faneuil Hall in Boston), routinely provide a booth for community groups. See Witold Rybczynski, *City Life* (New York: Simon and Schuster, 1995), 209.

26. Anne Miller, "Mall Drops T-Shirt Charges," *The Times Union*, March 6, 2003, B1.

27. Anne Miller, "Malls, Main Street Intersect in Debate; As Anti-War Voices Seek a Public Outlet, Private Property Issues Arise," *The Times Union*, March 7, 2003, A1.

28. Benjamin Barber, "Malled, Mauled and Overhauled: Arresting Suburban Sprawl by Transforming the Mall into Usable Civic Space," in *Public Space and Democracy*, ed. Marcel Hénaff and Tracy B. Strong (Minneapolis: University of Minnesota Press, 2001), 206.

29. See Jürgen Habermas, *Theory of Communicative Action, Vol. 1*, tr. Thomas McCarthy (Boston: Beacon, 1984); Jürgen Habermas, "What is Universal Pragmatics," *Communication and the Evolution of Society*, tr. Thomas McCarthy (Boston: Beacon, 1979). For an excellent secondary source, see Simone Chambers, *Reasonable Democracy: Jürgen Habermas and the Politics of Discourse* (Ithaca, NY: Cornell University Press, 1996).

30. Molly J. Liskow, "Leafletting Rules to Balance Mall's and Speakers' Rights," *New Jersey Lawyer*, August 28, 2000, B8. For the full text of the decision, see *Green Party of New Jersey v. Hartz Mountain Industries, Inc.*, New Jersey Supreme Court, A-59, June 13, 2000.

31. For an example of the best cultural criticism of the mall, see Crawford, "The World in a Shopping Mall," 3–30.

32. Pierre Bourdieu, *Distinction: A Social Critique of the Judgement of Taste* (London: Routledge and Kegan Paul, 1986); David Brooks, *Bobos in Paradise: The New Upper Class and How They Got There* (New York: Simon and Schuster, 2000).

33. Richard Briffault, "A Government for Our Time? Business Improvement Districts and Urban Governance," *Columbia Law Review* 99 (March 1999), 365–477.

34. Kowinski, *The Malling of America*, 53–63.

35. See Arkansas Statute 14-184-115 (1995). Cited in Clayton P. Gillette and Paul B. Stephan III, "Constitutional Limits on Privatization," *American Journal of Comparative Law* 46 (1998).

36. Some BIDs, for example, those in New York, guarantee representation to non-property owners, but even there business people, especially landlords, dominate the membership of the governing boards. One study of eight BIDs in New York City found that 67% of members were business people; in the five remaining BIDs 75% of the board members were either business people or legal professionals. (Briffault, "A Government for Our Time?" 412.)

37. Stephen C. Fehr, "Property Owners Commit to Revive D.C.: In Heart of District a $38.5 Million Push for Safety, Cleanliness," *The Washington Post*, July 27, 1997, A20 (citing views of downtown business owners).

38. Briffault, "A Government for Our Time?" 396.

39. Paul Goldberger, "The Rise of the Private City," in *Breaking Away: The Future of Cities: Essays in Memory of Robert F. Wagner*, ed. Julia Vitullo-Martin (New York: Twentieth Century Fund Press, 1996), 136–137.

40. On festival marketplaces, see M. Christine Boyer, "Cities for Sale: Merchandising History at South Street Seaport," in ed. Michael Sorkin, *Variations on a Theme Park: The New American City and the End of Public Space* (New York: Hill and Wang, 1992), 181–204.

41. Bernard Frieden and Lynne Sagalyn, *Downtown, Inc.: How America Rebuilds Cities* (Cambridge, MA: MIT Press, 1990).

42. Tom Gallagher, "Trespasser on Main St.: (You!)," *The Nation*, December 18, 1995.

43. *Avery v. Midland County et al.* 390 U.S. 474 (1968).

44. The courts decided that local school board elections were not exempt from one-person, one-vote. In *Salyer Land Co. v. Tulare Lake Basin Water Storage District,* the Court determined that the water storage district, by virtue of its limited purpose and financing structure, could be governed by affected property owners exclusively.

45. "Voting Scheme for Board Okayed," *City Law*, November/December, 1998.

46. A similar lawsuit was brought by homeless plaintiffs against the Fashion District BID in Los Angeles. The suit was settled out of court. Although the BID denied wrongdoing, it also promised that its security contractor, Burns International Security, would not search, harass, or order homeless people to "move along." See Marla Dickerson, "Fashion District Group Agrees to Settle Homeless Lawsuit," *Los Angeles Times*, August 14, 2001.

47. "Homeless Workers: BIDs Failed to Pay Minimum Wage," *City Law*, March/April 1998. The article reported that U.S. District Court Judge Sonia Sotomayor ruled that the program participants were entitled to the minimum wage.

48. Heather Barr, "More Like Disneyland: State Action, 42 U.S.C. 1 1983, and Business Improvement Districts in New York," *Columbia Human Rights Law Review* (Winter 1997), 399–404. The accuracy of these later accusations is a matter of controversy. At least one of the four workers retracted the accusations and another claimed that he was pressured to retract. The BID did settle at least two lawsuits by homeless people injured by outreach workers.

49. Thomas Lueck, "Grand Central Partnership Is Subject of U.S. Inquiry," *New York Times*, May 26, 1995, A7.

50. Briffault, "A Government for Our Time?" 427–428. To cite one specific example, the Riverhead Business Improvement District successfully lobbied the town board to enact legislation requiring that any social service agency wanting to relocate in the district must get a special permit. See Mitchell Freedman, "Riverhead to Govern Downtown Tenants," *Newsday*, May 9, 2002, A30.

51. Briffault, "A Government for Our Time?" 462–463.

52. Barr, "More Like Disneyland," 404, 408–411. The statute quoted is 42 U.S.C. 1 1983.

53. Of course, a homeless person who was physically injured or whose property was destroyed could bring a criminal complaint or a civil suit for damages. The former is difficult, given how closely private security forces work with police (sometimes sharing a substation). The latter has been pursued successfully by homeless individuals. One plaintiff won a $27,500 judgment against the Grand Central Partnership. See David Stout, "For a Troubled Partnership: A History of Problems," *New York Times*, November 8, 1995, B6.
54. Eds. Chuihua Judy Chung, Jeffrey Inaba, Rem Koolhaas, and Sze Tsung Leong, *Harvard Design School Guide to Shopping* (Cologne: Taschen, 2001).

5

GOD, CAESAR, AND THE CONSTITUTION

In December 1998 the municipality of Salt Lake City and the Church of Jesus Christ of Latter-Day Saints (the Mormons)[1] held a joint press conference announcing plans to develop a pedestrian plaza by closing a block of Main Street to vehicular traffic. Located in the heart of downtown Salt Lake City, the proposed plaza connected residential neighborhoods to the north with the central shopping areas to the south. On the east and west, the block was flanked by property owned by the Latter-Day Saints (LDS) Church, including the Mormon Tabernacle and Temple. The LDS Church had long coveted this block of public property, which is located in the heart of Temple Square, the Vatican of the Latter-Day Saints. The LDS Church sought to create a unified campus in the heart of the city that "celebrated and retold the story of the Mormon Church's founding and beliefs."[2] On April 13, 1999, the City Council voted to approve the sale of the property to the church.[3]

During the negotiations preceding the sale, the Salt Lake City Planning Commission had suggested that the city attach certain conditions to the sale in order to make sure that the public purpose of the project was not jeopardized. According to the city, the church-owned plaza would enhance the vitality of downtown by funneling residents and visitors towards the two shopping centers. It would create an aesthetically pleasing focal point linking residential neighborhoods, church property, and downtown commerce. In order to achieve this, the Planning Commission mandated that the new plaza had to be maintained in a manner that encouraged and invited public use. Furthermore, it specified that "there be no restrictions on the use of this space that are more restrictive than is currently permitted at public parks."[4] The ordinance adopted by the City Council did not include this later provision.[5]

Public access to the plaza was guaranteed by an easement attached to the deed of sale. An easement is a "non-possessory property right." In other words, the city does not own the property but has a contractual right to use it for certain purposes. According to the language of the easement, the public had the right to pass through the plaza but not to engage in a whole range of conduct such as "loitering, assembling, partying, demonstrating, picketing, distributing literature, begging...." The easement specified that the deal should "not be deemed to create or constitute a public forum, limited or otherwise...."[6]

The First Unitarian Church of Salt Lake City, however, objected to the deal on First Amendment grounds. They did not like the idea that the Mormons could buy a core block of downtown and then restrict residents' right to criticize the Mormon Church, proselytize for other faiths, or petition the local government on the main plaza. In court they argued that the new plaza (which the LDS Church called an ecclesiastical park) was a traditional public forum and therefore expressive conduct could be regulated but not forbidden. They claimed that the First Amendment applied to the plaza because the easement was a property right held by the city. Because the municipal government retained a property right, its acquiescence to the LDS Church's restrictive rules constituted state action for the purpose of the First Amendment.

Initially, the District Court held in favor of the Mormons who argued that their newly created "ecclesiastical park" did not constitute a public forum. As the language of the easement made clear, neither the city nor the church intended to create any sort of public forum.[7] The Tenth Circuit Court of Appeals, however, reversed the decision of the lower court. According to Justice Seymour, Salt Lake City's attempt to create a "First Amendment free zone" was unconstitutional. The right to free speech on public property was not something the city could sign away. The rationale for this decision drew upon the Supreme Court's public forum doctrine. It cited previous cases in which the Supreme Court had distinguished among traditional public forums, designated public forums, and nonpublic forums. Salt Lake City clearly did not intend to create a public forum, therefore the question was whether the plaza was a traditional public forum. The court concluded that the plaza was similar to streets and thoroughfares (the archetypical examples of traditional public forums) because it played a key role in the circulation of pedestrian traffic. Furthermore, the court held that the city could not simply decide to waive the First Amendment rights of its citizens by decreeing that the plaza was not available for speech and assembly. Instead, the physical characteristics and traditional uses of the space had to be assessed. Given its features and location, it is not surprising that the area had often served as a forum for dissenting speech, especially speech critical of the Mormon Church. The court concluded that the plaza was a traditional public forum and therefore the rules forbidding speech and assembly by non-Mormons were unconstitutional.[8]

The second issue that the court had to consider was whether the easement was enough government involvement to trigger the application of the Bill of Rights. On this issue the court was somewhat inconsistent. Initially, it suggested that government ownership was not essential for deciding whether a place was considered public. It noted that privately owned spaces such as sidewalks and mailboxes have been considered public due to government regulation. In the end, however, the court stressed the pivotal role of the easement. The prohibitions against speech and assembly would stand if the land were entirely private. Although the city could not forfeit citizens' rights to exercise civil liberties on quasi-public property, it could forfeit the easement. And that is precisely what Salt Lake City did.

With the legal issue decided, the political controversy emerged with renewed vehemence. Emboldened by the court decision, critics of the LDS Church took the opportunity to pass out leaflets and hold mini-demonstrations on the plaza adjacent to its Tabernacle. The powerful LDS Church, which paid over eight million dollars for a block of Main Street, tried to exercise its clout in city hall. Initially Mayor Rocky Anderson said the city would not give up the easement. But the LDS Church has considerable influence in Salt Lake City. Two months later, the mayor reversed himself and expressed support for a proposal giving up the easement in exchange for a parcel of church-owned land in the western part of the city.

CIVIL LIBERTIES IN INTENTIONAL COMMUNITIES

This case raises a number of issues that complicate our attempt to theorize the relationship between public space, civil liberties, and democracy. Most notably it introduces two new dimensions of the First Amendment into the analysis: the Free Exercise clause and the Establishment clause. In addition to protecting speech, the First Amendment states that Congress shall make no law respecting an establishment of religion or prohibiting the free exercise thereof. Both parties to the debate over the plaza raised the issue of religious freedom. The Mormons argued that the restrictions on behavior in the plaza (which included rules against profanity, drinking, and inappropriate dress) were part of their religious practice. They claimed that by disallowing such behavior codes on church property, the government was prohibiting the free exercise of the Mormon religion.

The ACLU (American Civil Liberties Union), on the other hand, suggested that allowing the Mormons to purchase a traditional public forum was a violation of the Establishment clause. According to the ACLU, "the purpose and effect of the City's conduct in this case is to advance the Mormon religion by protecting the Church's speech while preventing unwanted speech."[9] By selling a block of Main Street, the city was endorsing one religion by treating it more favorably than others.[10] If taken to an extreme, such sales could have serious repercussions for religious pluralism in the United States. Municipalities could sell public places (perhaps at a nominal price) to favored religious denominations, which could then enforce rules prohibiting leafletting critical of the favored church or local government.

The controversy over the plaza also raises the broader issue of how to handle constitutional challenges to the practices of intentional communities. By intentional communities I mean groups of individuals, both religious and secular, that live together in order to share ritual life and pursue collective political or moral goals.[11] In *Marsh v. Alabama*, the courts found that a company town should be treated like other municipalities. But what about towns or neighborhoods that are founded by religious denominations or political groups? If individuals voluntarily choose to live in a place such as a commune, monastery, or phalanstery in order to live according to distinctive religious or political beliefs, should the courts intervene to enforce liberal norms? Few people would argue that monks in a monastery who voluntarily made a vow of silence have the right to free speech. But what about a situation in which a town has been built around a mission on church lands? Do the lay residents still have the right to free speech, assembly, due process, and religious freedom? Does the outcome change if residents live in privately owned homesteads in a town planned, built, and governed by an intentional community?

Intentional communities founded by religious sects have traditionally had more autonomy from the state than ones sponsored by political groups. The reason is that religious activity is protected by the First Amendment but there is no equivalent constitutional right to association. When disputes between co-religionists have arisen, the courts have generally deferred to the internal decision-making process of the denomination, even when this has violated due process.[12] The Supreme Court felt that if it began to scrutinize the principles of ecclesiastical law, it would be interfering in the internal governance of a religious order, which would be a violation of the "free exercise" clause of the First Amendment.[13] As long as members could simply leave the religious community, their membership implied consent to have disputes resolved by the church's procedures.

The insulation of associations from judicial oversight is not necessarily an anomaly within the American system of government. For most of American history, the Bill of Rights has been applied only to the federal government. Over the course of the twentieth century, the Supreme Court developed the doctrine of incorporation, which applies the Bill of Rights to the actions of states and municipalities, thereby transforming American federalism and the rights consciousness of American citizens. This chapter considers whether judicial oversight should also extend to intentional communities that exercise political power and territorial control.

In the nineteenth century, self-governing communities had a great deal of autonomy from both federal and state governments. There were hundreds of micro-theocracies and utopian communes flourishing in the United States. Groups such as the Shakers, Oneida Perfectionists, Amish, Mennonites, Zoar, Owenites, and Fourierists among others controlled small territories where they could live according to their beliefs.[14] These intentional communities ranged in size, composition, and governing structure. The Oneida Perfectionists' community consisted of about two hundred people living in a complex composed of two sprawling mansions.[15] The Harmony Society built a town inhabited by nine hundred members living on small homesteads.[16] The Mormon city of Nauvoo had 15,000 inhabitants at its zenith.[17] The question for political theory is whether civil liberties (like those encoded in the Bill of Rights) should restrict the actions of these micro-polities just as they restrict the actions of Congress, the states, and local governments. Are these micro-polities similar to other municipalities that must respect diversity and allow dissent, or are they more like voluntary associations that can demand orthodoxy and allegiance? This question was widely debated in the late nineteenth century, a time when micro-theocracies and utopian societies were proliferating in the United States.

The best-known and most controversial intentional community in American history was founded in 1830 by Joseph Smith, leader of the Church of Latter-Day Saints (the Mormons). After being forced to leave New York and Missouri, the Mormons founded a new settlement in Nauvoo, Illinois. They sought a high degree of political autonomy in order to govern their community according to theocratic principles. This autonomy was reflected in the Nauvoo Charter, which established an independent militia and a City Council made up of a mayor, four aldermen, and nine councilors. The Latter-Day Saints also had ecclesiastical courts that adjudicated disputes between members. The Nauvoo Charter, however, was short-lived. In 1845 the Charter was revoked and Joseph Smith was murdered in jail. Under the leadership of Brigham Young, the Mormons went West and settled in the barren desert of Utah, a sparsely populated and unincorporated territory where they could develop their distinctive political institutions.

Mormon political autonomy was controversial in the late nineteenth century. Clergyman Josiah Strong suggested that the hierarchical structure of Mormonism threatened republican institutions because Mormons tended to follow the dictates of their Church elders and vote as a block.[18] J. H. Beadle, the editor of the only non-Mormon paper in Utah, argued that the problem with Mormonism was not polygamy (an issue of intense national concern in the 1880s) but theocracy. He claimed that in Utah the rule of law was subordinate to ecclesiastical policy and Gentiles (non-Mormons) were "subjected to all the annoyances of petty tyranny" and surveillance.[19] The United States Supreme Court was also concerned with the political autonomy exercised by the Mormons. In *Mormon Church v. the United States* (1889), Justice Bradley noted that the Mormons exercised "immense power in the Territory of Utah," which it employed "in constantly attempting to oppose, thwart, and subvert the legislation of Congress and the will of the government of the United States."[20] According to these critics, the threat posed by Mormonism lay in its challenge to the sovereignty of the United States.

The tension between communal autonomy and national unity has a long and controversial history in the United States. Although the Mormons were treated with particular suspicion and hostility, they were only one of a large number of religious and political groups that sought to control territories where they could live according to their beliefs. In 1874 the Mennonites petitioned Congress for land on which they could build an exclusive religious community. They sought guarantees including religious freedom, exemption from military service, and the "right to live in closed communities, with their own form of local government."[21] This desire for sovereignty, however, was particularly contentious. According to Senator George Edwards, a leading opponent of the bill, "Fundamental to successful republicanism (is) homogeneous unity of the whole body of citizens of a State" with everyone "in the body of the community living as friends and neighbors." The country could not survive "if distinctions prevailed…locating men of special religious or special political or social ideas exclusively in one place."[22] Although the bill failed, the proliferation of utopian residential communities continued unabated. Numerous religious and political groups established model villages in which their distinctive ideologies were reflected in the built environment as well as the laws.

Charles Fourier's phalanstery, or "unitary dwelling" was particularly influential and inspired dozens of groups to try to build physical environments that overcame the conflict between city and country, rich and poor, men and women by an enlightened arrangement of space and resources.[23] Utopian socialism is something of a historical relic today, but religious groups such as the Mennonites and the Amish continue to argue that legal control over their territorially bounded communities is essential for maintaining the viability of their religion and culture.[24]

Should these religious and political communities be treated as municipal governments or voluntary associations? The answer depends, in part, on diversity, scale, and property ownership. The more that an intentional community resembles a family—an exclusive association based on intense intimate bonds—the less it should be treated like a polity. On one end of the continuum would be small homogeneous enclaves made up of group members living on collectively owned property. The numerous communitarian socialist experiments of the late 1800s and communes of the 1960s would fall into this category. On the other end of the continuum would be large diverse cities inhabited by both members and nonmembers who own individual private property. An example would be a place like Salt Lake City that functions as does any other municipality in the United States.[25] The difficulty lies in deciding how to treat the numerous configurations that lie in between these two extremes, such as the larger utopian communities built in the late 1800s, places such as Harmony, Pennsylvania that had nine hundred residents and Amana, Iowa, a "communistic" village with about two thousand residents.

One argument made for exempting intentional communities from constitutional protections is that members give up certain rights when they freely choose to live in one. This argument, however, is only valid insofar as all members choose to affiliate as adults and none are born into the community as children. Although this was true of many short-lived communal experiments, others, such as the Amana, flourished over several generations. Because most members were born in Amana,

Iowa, the issue of choice becomes more complicated.[26] Should towns like Harmony and Amana be treated the same as other municipalities that are required to respect free speech and religious freedom, even though this would weaken their unity and undermine their distinctiveness? Should they be forced to adopt the principle of one-person, one-vote rather than be governed by Church elders?

A critic might respond that posing these questions is anachronistic, given that free speech jurisprudence was not applied to the states until the 1920s and the principle of one-person, one-vote was not applied to municipalities until 1968.[27] Even if the issue is anachronistic from a legal perspective, it is still highly relevant from a theoretical perspective. Furthermore, even though I am not familiar with any nineteenth-century court case dealing with free speech in religious communities, at least one dissenter did consider challenging the use of excommunication to silence internal critics. An incident that took place at Zoar, a separatist religious community located in Ohio, confirms that there were dissenters who argued that the protection of free speech should not stop at the gates of intentional communities. In 1896, Levi Bimeler, a descendant of the community founder, came to criticize the Zoar practice of refusing to provide any financial settlement to members who withdrew or were expelled. Because individuals had no right to wages or property, they were totally dependent on the society. According to Bimeler, this caused excessive conformity. Bimeler published a newspaper expounding his views and the Zoarites threatened him with expulsion. He wrote, "The U.S. Constitution guarantees freedom of speech and press. We avail ourselves of this guarantee for a good purpose." But Bimeler's legal counsel warned him that he had little chance of prevailing in court. The threat of expulsion worked. Shortly thereafter the newspaper ceased publication.[28]

Although this incident was somewhat unusual, the nineteenth-century courts did often have to decide whether to intervene in the affairs of intentional communities. The issue was usually property rights rather than civil liberties. On numerous occasions, the courts considered whether the contracts binding individuals to intentional communities should be enforced. This litigation usually arose out of complaints brought by disaffected apostates who sought compensation for their contributions to the collective property of the society. The court had to decide whether to invalidate what Carol Weisbrod has called the utopian contract, an agreement whereby individuals pledged their property and labor in return for support as long as they remained members of the community. In one case, the plaintiff argued that such contracts should be voided because they deprived the individual of "the constitutional power of acquiring, possessing, and protecting property." Others noted that the structure of utopian societies facilitated the abuse of power and diminished the possibility of individual choice. According to Samuel Tilden:

> If its [the intentional community's] internal police extends to the supervision and control of the minutest personal concerns; if its fundamental law is an unqualified submission of its members to their irresponsible rulers, and if the penalty with which those rulers are armed is a forfeiture of all he possesses by any member who shall be ejected from or shall leave the association,—can it be that a society so constructed and possessing such powers shall not frequently work great individual wrong and oppression?[29]

Tilden argued that the hierarchical governance structure, indoctrination, and collective property characteristic of utopian communities render the possibility of individual choice illusory. The courts, however, usually rejected this argument.[30] Chief Justice Mellen explained that "one of the blessings of a free government is, that under its mild influences, the citizens are at liberty to pursue that mode of life…best suited to their inclination and habits."[31]

Tilden and Mellen drew their conclusions based on two different understandings of liberalism. One emphasized that a liberal society cannot tolerate illiberal practices within its borders. The other suggested that a free government must allow individuals and groups considerable latitude in how they pursue their distinctive concept of the good life. The following section analyzes these two alternate interpretations and considers whether liberal theory requires that intentional communities be granted considerable latitude to regulate their territory as they see fit, even if this means that they do not protect the civil liberties of their members.

LIBERALISM, PERFECTIONISM, AND SUBFEDERAL SOVEREIGNTY

The governing norm today is that micropolities—including those founded by intentional communities—should be subject to judicial oversight and treated as state actors.[32] Dissenting political and legal theorists, however, have argued in favor of granting intentional communities sovereign immunity. These arguments include the benefits of federalism, the sanctity of private property, and the right to free association. In "The Outer Limits of Community Self-Governance in Residential Associations, Municipalities, and Indian Country: A Liberal Theory" Mark Rosen provides a particularly thorough defense of what he calls "sub-federal sovereignty."[33] He claims that liberalism requires that subfederal units have significant discretion in their ability to make laws or rules that reflect their values, even if these practices violate existing criminal and constitutional law.[34] In this section, I summarize Rosen's defense of community self-governance and expose some problems with his view. By critically engaging his argument, we can attain insight into the relationship between liberal constitutionalism and illiberal micro-polities.

According to Rosen, liberalism requires that communities, under certain circumstances, be able to opt out of the practices, rules, and laws that govern the dominant society. He notes that the history of the United States is animated by religious and political groups such as the Mormons, Mennonites, Icarian Socialists, Shakers, Harmonists, and Oneida Perfectionists that sought autonomy from the corruption of mainstream society in order to create a more perfect community. Similarly, Native Americans on reservations have adopted their own laws and practices in order to protect their cultural distinctiveness.[35] Native Americans in the United States and Canada benefit from special legislation guaranteeing limited autonomy and territorial sovereignty. Other groups have tried to use generally available legal tools such as restrictive covenants on property or incorporation as a municipality in order to promote communal self-governance. The courts have generally been unsympathetic to these attempts. For example, a California court invalidated the theosophists' attempt to form an exclusive residential community association, and a federal court rejected the Satmar Hassidim's effort to form a special school district that would allow gender-segregated education for their children.[36]

Rosen argues that liberal theory requires that liberal governments grant autonomy to such "perfectionist zones," which he defines as geographically bounded areas in which distinctive groups can govern themselves according to their cultural, political, or religious values. According to Rosen, the core doctrine of political liberalism is that the state should maintain neutrality towards competing understandings of the good. Among these understandings of the good is "political perfectionism," a doctrine that is composed of two elements: a belief in Government Socialization and Interconnected Welfare.[37] *Government*

Socialization is a theory, dating back at least as far as Plato and Aristotle, that emphasizes that individuals' identity, moral judgment, and rational capacities are largely a product of the laws and social institutions of their community. Because people are profoundly shaped by their environment, the laws governing the community have a significant impact on individual virtue. The related concept of *Interconnected Welfare* refers to the belief that an individual's potential for self-actualization (salvation, rational development, virtue, etc.) is influenced by the conduct of the community as a whole. For some sects this implies the conviction that God holds the entire community of believers responsible for the behavior of its members. More generally, the standpoint of political perfectionism implies that it is difficult if not impossible to live a righteous or virtuous life when governed by sinners. Rosen argues that the principle of subfederal sovereignty requires that residential communities, Indian reservations, and municipalities be exempted from federal laws and constitutional oversight.

At first it would appear that political perfectionism cannot be reconciled with political liberalism and, in fact, John Rawls reaches this conclusion. Rawls insists that "There is no reason, then, why any citizen, or association of citizens, should have the right to use the state's police power to decide constitutional essentials or basic questions of justice as that person's, or that association's, comprehensive doctrine, directs."[38] Rawls argues that in the original position (where individuals choose principles of justice without knowing their personal characteristics, capacities, or concept of the good) rational individuals would never consent to give this authority to a person or group. The implication is clear: any conception of the good that "can only survive if it controls the machinery of state…will cease to exist in the well-ordered society of political liberalism."[39]

From Rosen's perspective, however, Rawls deduces the wrong conclusion from his own initial premises. In the original position, individuals do not know whether they are political perfectionists. Given that uncertainty, they might choose a system of "sub-federal sovereigns," which would allow political perfectionists to live in communities controlled by their own rules while the rest of the population would be governed by the individualistic principles of the United States Constitution. In other words, political liberalism requires a system of subfederal territories (Indian reservations, residential communities, municipalities) in order to accommodate the worldviews of perfectionists and nonperfectionists alike.

Of course, there would be some limitations on these self-governing territories. Given that the core liberal value is the individual right to choose his or her conception of the good, perfectionist communities could not unduly coerce their neighbors or their own members. Perfectionist groups believe that salvation (or virtue) depends on the behavior of society at large. As long as these groups seek to influence others by example or persuasion they present no problem for a liberal society, but once they advocate forcible or violent conversion, then they cannot be accommodated in a liberal polity. This means that subfederal sovereigns might legitimately be prevented from organizing a militia, stockpiling weapons, or engaging in aggressive conduct toward outsiders.

The second limitation is more complex inasmuch as it addresses the ways in which perfectionist groups may influence members. According to Rosen, members of perfectionist communities must have the ability to "opt out." Again, this reflects the basic liberal stance that individuals must be able to choose among competing conceptions of the good. In order to have a meaningful possibility of exit, the community cannot be excessively punitive towards defectors. For example, it cannot threaten to harm remaining family members. Also it must provide a basic education that would ensure a viable existence in the outside world. Rosen calls this the "compatibility requirement," because it ensures that group members have the ability to survive in the broader society. This does not mean that everyone must be trained to take advantage of all the opportunities of modern life. Socialist communities would not have to train investment bankers and Luddites would not have to prepare computer programmers, but they would have to provide the skills that ensure basic compatibility with the outside world.[40]

Scholars of liberalism and multiculturalism have debated whether an exit option sufficiently protects individuals from antiliberal practices. In *Multicultural Jurisdictions*, Ayelet Shachar challenges the argument that vulnerable group members are adequately protected by the right of exit.[41] First, she argues that the right of exit solution is problematic because it imposes the entire burden of resolving conflict on the individual, absolving both the state and the community of responsibility for finding a solution. She also points out that those who take advantage of the exit option and flee their home and community are usually the most vulnerable members. They are the individuals with the least power to influence internal change or protect themselves within the community's legal system. In other words, the exit option is unfair because it places all of the costs on the injured insider, who is usually one of the most powerless members of the group. Finally, this "solution" to the problem of internal oppression does not take seriously enough the difficulty involved in leaving behind one's family, friends, economic support, religious community, and way of life.[42]

This provision that members of perfectionist residential communities must be able to opt out opens up a Pandora's Box of problems that starkly reveal the limitations of Rosen's liberal defense of subfederal sovereigns. Many of the conflicts between the federal government (or judiciary) and perfectionist groups emerge from the way rules and practices limit members' capacity to make meaningful choices. Take, for example, the ongoing conflict between the government and the Fundamentalist Church of Jesus Christ of Latter-Day Saints, a religious sect that practices polygamy and child marriage.[43] The government believes that a child under a certain age has not developed the capacity for judgment and the sense of self that is necessary to choose a life-long partnership. Moreover, a young girl married to a much older man, especially as a second or third wife in a household, will not be able to develop a capacity for critical thinking or self-actualization distinct from that of the family unit. Yet nontraditional family arrangements are precisely the practices that subfederal sovereignty seeks to accommodate. This example suggests that it is difficult to decide whether a certain practice poses a threat to the community member's capacity for choice or whether it simply violates dominant group morality.

There are plenty of communal norms that do not impinge on individuals' ability to revise their concept of the good. One controversial issue—veiling—would seem unproblematic from this perspective. Requiring that all women and girls wear the *chador* would not inhibit their ability to reject Islam. Although such a dress code might be inconsistent with liberalism as a theory of the good, because it regulates an area outside the domain of limited government, it would not violate a version of political liberalism that accommodated subfederal sovereignty. But there are many other examples that expose the tension between political liberalism and political perfectionism. Imagine that there is a group that believes women's domestic role precludes paid work outside the home. To this end girls are educated in basic literacy and home economics but receive no additional academic or pre-professional training. Rosen states that "a community's decision not to educate their girls would violate the compatibility requirement" because it would make women defectors unable to function in the broader society. But this extreme example (providing *no* education to girls) is less revealing than the much more likely scenario in which a community educates women for a very particular, narrow role. Basic literacy and domestic training would not violate the compatibility requirement.[44] Because women educated in this way could get employment and carry out basic bureaucratic tasks, such an educational program would be acceptable under the proposed doctrine of communal autonomy, even though it violates statutory and constitutional principles of equal treatment. The problem is that such an education would hardly seem to foster the political judgment that we expect of citizens, let alone the ability to reflect upon the norms governing one's community.

The right of exit is meaningless in a society that is organized to preclude exposure to other ways of thinking. If political liberalism requires that individuals have a meaningful possibility of rejecting their community, then severe restrictions on heterodox sources of information are unacceptable. In order to evaluate critically a particular worldview, adherents must have some access to alternative viewpoints. The United States Supreme Court addressed this issue in *Yoder v. Wisconsin*, a case in which the Amish challenged a state law requiring compulsory attendance at secondary schools. In his dissent, Justice Douglas argued that "If his parent keeps his child out of school beyond the grade school, then the child will be forever barred from entry into the new and amazing world of diversity that we have today....If he is harnessed to the Amish way of life by those in authority over him and if his education is truncated, his entire life may be stunted and deformed."[45] The Amish themselves acknowledged this point. They wanted to exempt their children from compulsory secondary education precisely because it posed a threat to their way of life by exposing adolescents to a seductive and threatening alternative lifestyle.

The circulation of alternative religious and political views also poses a problem. Many perfectionist groups are also deeply committed to proselytizing as a means of propagating their faith. Mormons, Hare Krishnas, evangelicals of all sorts, and especially Jehovah's Witnesses have received considerable protection from the United States Constitution in their mission to spread their faith by distributing religious literature from door to door. What if these sects wanted to exclude other religious or political groups from canvassing in their neighborhoods? This would prevent community residents from obtaining exposure to other views and it would also provide the group with an unfair advantage by exempting their own members from the challenging alternatives with which they confront outsiders. Of course, one solution would be for all communities to close their territories to outside viewpoints, but this would achieve the balkanization that would make any conception of a national polity meaningless.

A proponent of subfederal sovereignty might respond that child marriage, girls' education, and free speech are some of the difficult issues that could be resolved in different ways in different institutional contexts. To me they reveal a fundamental problem that either undermines political liberalism or reveals that Rosen (and other liberal defenders of subfederal sovereignty) reaches the wrong conclusion about what liberalism requires. Each of these three examples illustrates the way a community's practices may conflict with the liberal belief that the individual should be capable of revising his or her conception of the good based on rational grounds. This principle of the "revisability of ends" is a core liberal doctrine.[46] From this principle liberals deduce the necessity of things such as public education and free speech. In *Multicultural Citizenship: A Liberal Theory of Minority Rights*, Will Kymlicka argues in favor of supporting "societal cultures" because he believes that they provide a structure that facilitates the development of individual autonomy and choice.[47] But how should a liberal state treat groups or localities that try to inhibit rather than foster these capacities in some if not all of their members? And how should it deal with specific practices, such as restrictions on speech and press that undermine rather than encourage the ability to reflect upon one's way of life?

I am not convinced that liberal theory, at least in its Rawlsian variant, can answer these questions in a satisfying fashion. How could individuals in the original position, ignorant about whether they will be liberals or perfectionists, secular humanists or religious fundamentalists, decide how much control communities should have over their members? If salvation is the reward for faith and obedience, then too much critical thinking and individual freedom might well lead to damnation. Moreover, why should those who have the benefit of guidance from the law (or faith) even try to imagine how they would order society if they were ignorant of it? *A Theory of Justice* implicitly relies on a liberal conception of the person and without these presuppositions, trying to reflect behind a veil of ignorance would simply yield indeterminacy.

In *Political Liberalism*, a set of essays responding to twenty-five years of criticism of *Theory of Justice*, John Rawls acknowledges that the mechanism of the original position only yields his two principles of justice if one assumes certain things about the individuals reflecting behind the veil of ignorance. According to his "political conception of the person," "citizens...view their persons as independent from and not identified with any particular such conception with its scheme of final ends."[48] Citizens "are seen as capable of revising and changing [their conception of the good] on reasonable and rational grounds, and they may do so if they desire."[49] This view is at odds with the principle of "Government Socialization" which emphasizes that only individuals trained in virtue are capable of exercising choice. Those that lack a certain kind of moral upbringing may well be led astray by individual reflection. Rawls's political conception of the person is also clearly at odds with the conception of personhood in cultural traditions that assume that rational and reasonable grounds are those legitimated by authority, not those chosen by the individual.[50] Rawls recognizes this tension between political liberalism and metaphysical or authoritative belief. He insists that "in [citizens'] political thought, and in the discussion of political questions, [they] do not view the social order as a fixed, natural order, or an institutional hierarchy justified by religious or aristocratic values."[51] He concludes that the process of public reason at the heart of political liberalism cannot accommodate the arguments that are distinctive of religious and moral principles.[52]

In *Political Liberalism*, Rawls essentially acknowledges that his theory is not a universally valid theory of justice but rather an account of why liberal individuals in a liberal polity should choose certain principles. This does not mean that the thought experiment of the original position has no value as a heuristic device. To the contrary, it is extremely effective at encouraging citizens of a liberal polity to more fully understand why it is legitimate and necessary to protect individual freedom and expand equality. It does little, however, to resolve conflicts between different approaches to the good, which are based on fundamentally opposed understandings of the relationship between the individual, the community, and the source of ultimate meaning.

The upshot of this discussion is that liberalism does not provide a compelling rationale for "sub-federal sovereignty." If individuals in the original position do not know whether they are liberals or perfectionists, then there is no way of determining which principles they will choose. If the individuals deliberating all reflect the political (e.g., liberal) conception of the person, then Rawls is probably right in concluding that they will not allow autonomy for communities that restrict individual freedom and inhibit members' choice of ends.

This reading of liberal theory shows the weaknesses of the argument that the micro-polities set up by intentional communities should be exempt from constitutional protections because they are voluntarily chosen by residents. It demonstrates why territorial micro-polities within a liberal-democratic state should not be able to opt out of protecting the civil liberties of their residents. Even when individuals choose to live in an intentional community with restrictive rules, they must have the opportunity to stay informed of alternatives, to encourage internal change, and to seek external redress. Although intentional communities should have some autonomy in establishing rules and practices that reflect their vision of the good life, when they govern territories they must still be subject to government oversight and limited by constitutional protections. Senator George Edwards misidentified the problem when he insisted that "homogeneous unity" throughout the nation was essential for republican government. Diversity and conflict are endemic (and, I would suggest, positive forces) in modern society, therefore territorially distinct pockets of "homogeneous unity" are particularly dangerous for a democracy. They create individuals who are incapable of recognizing others as equal citizens and communities that have so few cross-cutting ties that they may become incapable of communicating let alone acting together.

PERFECTIONIST ZONES TODAY

A critic might object that the legal and theoretical dilemmas raised by religious and political utopias are a nineteenth-century concern. Many communities such as the Owenites and Oneida Perfectionists have disappeared and a once powerful sect like the Shakers now has less than five hundred members. Flourishing groups such as the Latter-Day Saints have jettisoned their theocratic aspirations, giving both God and Caesar their due. In Salt Lake City, as in other municipalities, governing territory is the responsibility of the secular administration, which is distinct from the church's authority over spiritual matters. During the plaza controversy, Salt Lake City never claimed to be exempt from the free speech provisions of the Bill of Rights.

Although the spatial practices of late nineteenth-century communitarians might be anachronistic, the theoretical questions raised by these micro-polities are not. Furthermore, new intentional communities are emerging to replace the ones that have disappeared. In California the Theosophical Society tried to found an exclusive residential community by writing restrictive covenants limiting the sale of property to society members.[53] In New York the Satmar Hassidim successfully petitioned the state legislature to create a specially drawn school district in order make it possible to educate their children in gender-segregated public schools. The control of territory continues to be an important mechanism for creating highly unified and distinctive communities.

Although the courts struck down both attempts to increase the secular power of religious communities, Congress has moved in the opposite direction. It has tried to increase the autonomy and secular authority of religious groups. In 1993, Congress passed the Religious Freedom Restoration Act, which prohibited the government from substantially burdening religious exercise. After this statute was struck down by the Supreme Court in 1997, Congress drafted a controversial new law called the Religious Liberty Protection Act. This was later modified and in July 2000 Congress unanimously passed the Religious Land Use and Institutionalized Persons Act. This bill stated that "no government shall...impose or implement a land use regulation...that imposes a substantial burden on...religious exercise...unless [it] is in furtherance of a compelling government interest...."[54] It means that religious institutions can petition the federal courts claiming exemption from municipal zoning regulations. These initiatives demonstrate that there is considerable political support for positions like the one that Rosen defends, for example, the idea that perfectionist communities (at least religious ones) should be exempt from generally applicable laws.

These new perfectionist zones are not isolated farming communes but suburban megachurches that combine worship with recreation, education, consumption, and even housing. Megachurches are congregations with over 2000 members that provide a variety of nontraditional services. For example, the 12,000 member Community Church of Joy in Glendale, Arizona has a 187 acre campus with a school, conference center, bookstore, and mortuary. It is also raising funds to expand by building a housing development, a hotel, and water-slide park.[55] Among the amenities provided by the 22,000 member Southeast Christian Church in Louisville, Kentucky are a 50,000 square foot activities center, a bank, a school, restaurants, and shops. One megachurch even has a McDonald's. The churches are designed like shopping malls with the sanctuary taking the place of the anchor store.

These megachurches raise important issues about how to treat a religious entity when it also incorporates many aspects of secular life. According to the *New York Times*, "These churches are becoming civic in a way unimaginable since the 13th century and its cathedral towns. No longer simply places to worship, they have become part resort, part mall, part extended family and part town square."[56] We do not have to look back to thirteenth- century Europe to find religious sects that governed micro-polities. Nineteenth-century America provided plenty of examples.

ENDNOTES

1. In this chapter I use the Mormons and the LDS Church interchangeably to refer to the Church of Jesus Christ of Latter-Day Saints.
2. L. Martin Nussbaum, "ACLU Invades Mormon Church Grounds," www.rothberger.com/newslettersarticles. This article was published in the newsletter of the law firm Rothberger, Johnson, & Lyons, which submitted an amicus brief on behalf of the LDS Church.
3. The general background information comes from T. R. Reid, "Salt Lake City Street Fight: Mormons and 'Gentiles' Duel Over Speech Rights," *Washington Post*, December 23, 2002, A01.
4. *First Unitarian Church of Salt Lake City v. Salt Lake City Corporation* 308 F. 3d 1118 (decided October 9, 2002).
5. Craig Axfo, one of the plaintiffs in the lawsuit, claimed that there was no public input between the Planning Commission meeting in March 1999 (which specified that rules could not be more restrictive than those currently permitted at public parks) and the City Council meeting in April 1999 (which forbade expressive conduct). See "Two Views on Ending Controversy on Main Street Plaza, A Plaza Not as Described," *Salt Lake Tribune*, November 24, 2002.
6. *First Unitarian Church of Salt Lake City v. Salt Lake City Corporation* (2002).
7. Bradley Snyder, "LDS Leaders Defend Stand on Main Plaza," *Desert News*, November 17, 2002.
8. *First Unitarian Church of Salt Lake City v. Salt Lake City Corporation* (2002).
9. American Civil Liberties Union, Appellants' Reply Brief; www.acluutah.org/msreply.htm.
10. American Civil Liberties Union, Complaint filed by plaintiffs in the United States District Court of Utah, Central Division; www.acluutah.org/mscomplaint.htm.
11. For an excellent discussion of the tradition of judicial deference to religious authority, see Nancy Rosenblum, *Membership and Morals: The Personal Uses of Pluralism in America* (Princeton, NJ: Princeton University Press, 1998), 73–111.
12. The Supreme Court held, "whenever the question of discipline, or of faith, or ecclesiastical rule, custom, or law have been decided by the highest of these church judicatories to which the matter has been carried, the legal tribunals must accept such decisions as final." *Kedroff v. Saint Nicholas Cathedral* 344 U.S. 94 (1952), at 195.
13. See *Serbian Eastern Orthodox Diocese of America and Canada v. Milivojevich* 426 U.S. 696 (1976). For a more complete discussion of these issues, see Rosenblum, *Membership and Morals*, 73–111.
14. Carol Weisbrod, *The Boundaries of Utopia* (New York: Pantheon, 1980).
15. Dolores Hayden, *Seven American Utopias: The Architecture of Communitarian Socialism, 1790–1975* (Cambridge, MA: MIT Press, 1976), 199.
16. Hayden, *Seven American Utopias*, 111.
17. In 1845 the population of Nauvoo, Illinois, was estimated to be between twelve and twenty thousand. Hayden, *Seven American Utopias*, 113.
18. Weisbrod, *The Boundaries of Utopia*, 24.

19. J. H. Beadle, *Life in Utah; Or the Mysteries and Crimes of Mormonism. Being an Exposé of the Secret Rites and Ceremonies of the Latter-Day Saints, with a Full and Authentic History of Polygamy and the Mormon Sect from its Origin to the Present Time* (Philadelphia and Chicago: National Publishing, 1870), 212–213.

20. *Mormon Church v. United States* 136 U.S. 1 (1889).

21. Weisbrod, *The Boundaries of Utopia*, 42.

22. See *Congressional Record* 43 (1874), 3054–3058, cited in Mark Rosen, "The Outer Limits of Community Self-Governance in Residential Associations, Municipalities, and Indian Country: A Liberal Theory" *Virginia Law Review* 84 (September 1998), 1055.

23. Robert Owen inspired about fifteen communities and Charles Fourier's work provided the model for about thirty Phalanxes. See Dolores Hayden, *The Grand Domestic Revolution* (Cambridge, MA: MIT Press, 1982), 35.

24. The most important Supreme Court case in which this argument was made is *Wisconsin v. Yoder* (406 U.S. 205 {1972}). The Old Order of Amish challenged a state mandatory education law on the grounds that the socialization into mainstream society involved in public schooling would threaten the viability of their way of life. Other examples of recent litigation over communal autonomy include the Rajneeshpurams' unsuccessful attempt to incorporate as a municipality in Oregon and the Satmar Hassidim's ongoing attempt to set up a special school district in Kiryas Joel, New York.

25. Sixty-nine percent of Utah's residents are Mormons; www.saltlakechamber.org.

26. The True Inspiration Congregation was founded in Germany in the 1700s and migrated to the United States in 1842. A group of around 2000 eventually settled in Amana, Iowa, where they maintained collective property until 1932. See Hayden, *Seven American Utopias*, 225–243.

27. See *Avery v. Midland County* 390 U.S. 474 (1968). This case applied the principle of one-person, one-vote to elections for County Commission.

28. Weisbrod, *The Boundaries of Utopia*, 99. According to Weisbrod, three issues of the paper were published. Acting on the advice of counsel, Bimeler ceased publishing after the expulsion threat. Levi Bimeler's newspaper was reprinted in E. O. Randalls, "The Separatist Society of Zoar: An Experiment in Communism—From Its Commencement to Its Conclusion," *Ohio History* 8 (1899), 1–105.

29. Samuel Tilden, "Considerations in Regard to the Application of the Shakers for Certain Special Privileges," in *The Writings and Speeches of Samuel J. Tilden*, ed. John Bigelow (New York: Harper & Brothers, 1885), I:95; cited in Weisbrod, *The Boundaries of Utopia*, 44.

30. There are records from nine nineteenth-century court cases dealing with utopian contracts and each one was decided in favor of the defendant society. See Weisbrod, *The Boundaries of Utopia*.

31. *Waite v. Merrilli* (1826), cited in Weisbrod, *The Boundaries of Utopia*, 130.

32. See *State v. Celmer* (404 A 2d 1, N.J.), which adjudicated the constitutionality of a New Jersey statute that gave certain municipal powers to a religious organization. The court found that the statute violated the Establishment Clause.

33. Mark Rosen, "The Outer Limits of Community Self-Governance in Residential Associations, Municipalities, and Indian Country: A Liberal Theory" *Virginia Law Review* 84 (September 1998).

34. Chandran Kukathas makes a similar argument that minority groups should have a wide latitude to practice their own traditions, even if those traditions violate the liberal rights of certain members. He bases this argument on the freedom of association. See "Are There Any Cultural Rights," *Political Theory* 20 (1992), 105–139 and "Liberalism and Multiculturalism," *Political Theory* 26 (1998), 686–699.

35. In this section I argue that residential community associations and municipalities should not be exempted from scrutiny under federal laws, including the Constitution. There may be distinctive reasons for making an exception in the case of Indian reservations, that are governed by treaties and akin, in certain ways, to separate nations. See Will Kymlicka, *Multicultural Citizenship: A Liberal Theory of Minority Rights* (Oxford: Clarendon, 1995), 27–30.

36. *Taormina Theosophical Community v. Silver*, 190 Cal. Rptr. 38, 44–45 (1983) held that the proposed residential community violated the California Civil Code. *Board of Education of Kiryas Joel Village School District v. Grumet* 512 U.S. 687 (1994).

37. Rosen takes for granted that liberalism and political perfectionism are opposed to each other. Many liberal theorists, including William Galston, Joseph Raz, and Jeremy Waldron suggest that liberal perfectionism is a coherent position. According to Waldron, "Perfectionism is simply the view that legislators and officials may consider what is good and valuable in life and what is ignoble and depraved when drafting the laws...." [See "Autonomy and Perfectionism in Raz's *Morality of Freedom*," *Southern California Law Review* 62, no. 4 (1989), 1102]. The elements of a liberal perfectionist view usually include a commitment to personal autonomy, equal respect and toleration. For the purposes of this argument, however, I am adopting Rosen's definition that highlights the cases in which liberalism and perfectionism come into conflict.

38. Rawls, *Political Liberalism*, 62; cited in Rosen, "The Outer Limits of Community Self-Governance."

39. Rawls, *Political Liberalism*, 196–197.

40. Rosen argues that reflection in the original position does not yield a single necessary solution to the problem of education. The level of education that the federal government would require depends on whether people are more or less risk averse, in other words whether they think it is more or less likely that they will want to leave the community. He proposes an "Immigrant" and a "Median Model," calibrated to different levels of risk aversion. See Rosen, "The Outer Limits of Community Self-Governance," 1098–1106.

41. Ayelet Shachar, *Multicultural Jurisdictions: Cultural Differences and Women's Rights* (Cambridge: Cambridge University Press, 2001). Although Shachar focuses on personal rights systems (which are not territorial but based on nomoi group membership), her argument applies even more forcefully to situations in which nomoi groups control territories. Following Robert Cover, she defines nomoi groups as groups that maintain a normative universe in which law and cultural narrative are inseparably related. (2).

42. Shachar, *Multicultural Jurisdictions*, 41.

43. This sect splintered off from the Mormon Church. The mainline Church of Jesus Christ of Latter-Day Saints outlawed polygamy over a century ago.

44. Recently a New York court held that the State Constitution only required that the state provide basic literacy and mathematical skills necessary to work in service sector jobs. (See "New York Civil Liberties Union v. State of New York," *New York Law Journal*, July 11, 2002, 24.)

45. *Yoder v. Wisconsin* 406 U.S. 205 (1972).

46. See, for example, Joseph Raz, *The Morality of Freedom* (Oxford: Clarendon, 1986) and *Ethics in the Public Domain* (Oxford: Clarendon, 1994). Raz defends an approach to liberalism that he calls perfectionist (as opposed to neutral). He argues that the way to foster human flourishing is to secure the conditions for personal autonomy. This, in turn, requires cultural diversity so that there is "an adequate range of options" from which to choose (1986, 372).

47. Kymlicka, *Multicultural Citizenship*, 82–93.

48. Rawls, *Political Liberalism*, 30.

49. Ibid.

50. In *Political Liberalism*, Rawls distinguishes between rational (e.g., self-interested and taking efficient means to their own ends) and reasonable. Reasonable citizens refrain from making truth claims about their own private views and beliefs. Unreasonable citizens assert that "their beliefs alone are true." (61) This is unreasonable because it provides no compelling way to convince other citizens of the veracity of their claims. For a critique of Rawls' privileging of the political point of view over comprehensive doctrine, see Monique Deveaux, *Cultural Pluralism and Dilemmas of Justice* (Ithaca, NY: Cornell University Press, 2000), 91–92.

51. Rawls, *Political Liberalism*, 15. Rawls continues, "These other points of view (e.g., religious or philosophical doctrine) are not, in general, to be introduced into political discussion of constitutional essentials and basic questions of justice." (15–16)

52. Rawls acknowledges that individuals have "comprehensive philosophical and moral doctrines" that motivate their preferences for public policy and hopes for an "overlapping consensus of reasonable religious, philosophical, and moral doctrines...." This consensus is achieved through public reason, the domain in which citizens only evoke principles that "all citizens, whatever their religious view, can endorse." (10)

53. In *Taormina Theosophical Society v. Silver* (1983) this attempt was struck down by a California appeals court, which found that it violated several provisions of the California Civil Code. For a brief discussion of this case, see Rosen, "The Outer Limits of Community Self-Governance," 1086.

54. Cited in Jonathan Weiss and Randy Lowell, "Supersizing Religion: Megachurches, Sprawl, and Smart Growth," *Saint Louis University Public Law Review 21* (2002), 313–329.

55. Patricia Leigh Brown, "Megachurches as Minitowns," *New York Times,* May 9, 2002, F1.

56. Brown, "Megachurches as Minitowns."

6

BRAVE NEW NEIGHBORHOODS

The Golden Gateway Center is a retail and residential complex made up of 1254 apartments. The development, which is protected by doormen and roving security patrols, includes four high-rise buildings and a group of townhouses located in downtown San Francisco. Since 1982, the Golden Gateway Tenants Association has distributed a newsletter to all residents. In the early 1990s, however, the building management challenged this practice. Under threat of litigation, it backed down and accepted the newsletter, stipulating that it be distributed in "a reasonable manner." The conflict re-emerged in 1996 when the Tenants Association stepped up its activities in response to the policies of a new building manager. Management retaliated, revising the building standards to prohibit all leafletting (except information placed on laundry room bulletin boards) and sought the help of the court to enforce this ban. On August 30, 2001, after over five years of litigation, the California State Supreme Court decided that the management's action did not violate the tenants' right to free speech.

For those unfamiliar with First Amendment jurisprudence, this decision must seem somewhat puzzling. Although a member of the Tenants Association can mail a letter or make a phone call to her neighbor, she cannot slip a leaflet under her neighbors' doors. As Kathryn Mickle Werdegar, one of the dissenting justices, put it, the Court's decision implies that it would be legal for an apartment complex to forbid tenants to speak with each other on the premises altogether. The United States Constitution provides no protection against this Huxleyan scenario. The reason is straightforward. The First Amendment to the Constitution of the United States begins "Congress shall make no law…"; it only places limitations on state actors. Because the Golden

Gateway Center and not the government was responsible for banning the leaflets, the First Amendment is irrelevant.

What made this case particularly important was the fact that it significantly tightened California's expansive protections of free speech. Unlike the United States Constitution, California's founding document (like that of many states) specifies, "Every person may freely speak, write and publish his or her sentiments on all subjects..." (Art. I, 2:a). In *Pruneyard*, a groundbreaking decision twenty years earlier, the California State Supreme Court decided that the free speech clause extended to privately owned shopping centers, which could restrict but not prohibit political activity in their public areas. The *Golden Gateway* decision implies a repudiation of *Pruneyard* and its robust defense of free speech.

This *Golden Gateway Center* decision is also significant because it is one of the first cases to deal with the right to political speech in private residential communities. By private communities I mean large developments such as condos, gated communities, co-ops, and apartment complexes where residents' units are not accessible to public streets but linked together by private hallways or roads. Most private communities are governed by residential community associations. Tenants in apartment complexes are only a small part of a large and growing category of people who live in private communities. Almost ten percent of Americans reported that they live in communities that are surrounded by walls or fences or where entrance is controlled by entry codes or security guard approval.[1] An estimated 47 million Americans lived in 231,000 neighborhoods governed by Residential Community Associations (RCAs) and the number is growing.[2] In Los Angeles and San Diego counties, seventy percent of new housing developments are governed by RCAs.[3] The trend, however, is not restricted to Southern California. Approximately fifty percent of all new homes built in major metropolitan areas nationwide fall under the jurisdiction of RCAs.[4]

Although these developments satisfy dreams of safety, privacy, and community, the people who live in them risk becoming cut off from public life. If tenants cannot put fliers under their neighbors' doors, then there is no reason why homeowners in private communities should be able to distribute information on political candidates or local churches, let alone challenge the policies of their homeowners' association. Political life and community are correspondingly diminished.

In this chapter I argue that private residential communities restrict political activity and explore the negative consequences for a democratic polity. At first this claim might sound counterintuitive, given that residential community associations provide an opportunity for political participation through neighborhood governance. In many communities, however, flourishing civic life is more image than reality. Drawing upon the theories of Thomas Jefferson and Alexis de Tocqueville, I show that the modern phenomenon of neighborhood government differs from its precursors: the ward system and town meeting.

RESIDENTIAL COMMUNITY ASSOCIATIONS

Residential Community Associations (RCAs) are nonprofit corporations created by real estate developers and regulated by the state. They function as a kind of neighborhood government. Their authority over residents is established through legally binding restrictive covenants attached to property deeds. These covenants provide mechanisms for maintaining common facilities such as roads and recreational facilities and govern the use of individual units. There are at least four types of RCAs that are distinguished by different forms of ownership: cooperatives, condominiums, common interest developments (CIDs), and homeowners' associations. In a cooperative, the corporation owns the common spaces and all units and the individual member has a lease guaranteeing exclusive rights to occupancy of a unit. In condominiums and common interest developments, an individual holds title to a unit and the association holds title to the common elements. A homeowners' association is somewhat different insofar as the association itself does not own any property but it can still charge mandatory fees and enforce stringent rules in order to maintain the appearance and character of the neighborhood.

Although residential community associations are often categorized as voluntary associations, their form and function more closely resemble that of local governments. Membership is not voluntary. All property owners in a given development are members and must pay mandatory assessments that fund services such as maintenance of common areas and security. The majority of property owners cannot dissolve the association because it usually exists in perpetuity; the deed to the land mandates membership in the residential community association, which enforces rules designed to protect property values and sustain the particular character of the community.[5] Even changing the rules is often difficult because of provisions that require super-majoritarian voting or mandate the approval of all residents, even when only a small minority attend meetings.[6] These rules range from the famous restrictions on class cues such as laundry lines and cars on blocks to more overtly political restrictions prohibiting campaign signs and American flags.[7] Failure to pay assessments or infractions can result in heavy fines and RCAs can put a lien on a homeowner's property to ensure payment.

For political theorists, the conflicts surrounding RCAs pose some important conceptual issues.[8] RCAs offer an opportunity for community building and local political activity. They encourage neighbors to come together in order to pursue shared goals, organize social activities, and develop community resources. Although participation in RCAs may be low,[9] they provide an institutional structure for dealing with dissent or crisis when it emerges and administering consensus as long as it lasts. RCAs make it possible for residents to exercise control over the character of their community by raising or lowering mandatory assessments in order to provide collective services and enforce standards. Given that local government often seems remote and rigid, disaggregating decisions to the neighborhood level is one way to deepen democracy.

On the other hand, RCAs can also be exclusionary.[10] They represent economically and often ethnically homogeneous neighborhoods that pursue private goods and undermine shared public values.[11] In Houston, Kansas City, New Jersey, and Montgomery County, Maryland the government refunds property taxes to homeowners in areas where RCAs provide services such as trash and snow removal.[12] Critics claim this allows the wealthy to opt out of their obligations to the broader community. This is particularly apparent in debates about the provision of public recreational facilities. Wealthy neighborhoods can afford facilities such as swimming pools that poor neighborhoods cannot afford.[13] And why would voters approve taxes to build public facilities when elite and middle-class neighborhoods provide their own? More generally, RCAs reinforce homogeneity and encourage the "not-in-my-backyard" (NIMBY) politics that shifts burdens such as garbage dumps and highway interchanges to less well-organized poor neighborhoods. In other words, RCAs encourage the bonding of similarly situated people but do nothing to bridge the enormous gulfs that separate black and white, rich and poor.[14]

In a purely procedural sense, residential community associations look democratic. They provide the opportunity for homeowners (but usually not tenants) to vote for representatives to manage their affairs. Decisions are reached by procedures clearly outlined in the property deed, which functions as a kind of constitution. But, as Michael Walzer points out, associations that are internally democratic may nevertheless weaken democracy in the larger polity by loosening the bonds of citizenship that link us to diverse others.[15] When residents participate in neighborhood governance, they gain political skills and information. Insofar as such associations are homogeneous and focus on parochial concerns, however, they are not effective at serving as forums for public deliberation, building solidarity, or representing difference.[16] How can we decide whether the positive aspects of participation outweigh the balkanizing effects? To answer this question we must have a theory of democracy and civil society. Thomas Jefferson and Alexis de Tocqueville, two of the most important theorists of local democracy, can help.

TOCQUEVILLE AND JEFFERSON ON LOCAL GOVERNANCE

Proponents argue that residential community associations are part of a long, vibrant tradition of local self-government in the United States.[17] Initially, the writings of Jefferson and Tocqueville seem to reinforce the claim that residential community associations facilitate the participation in local governance that is essential to both liberty and democracy. In *Democracy in America*, Tocqueville argued that local self-government protected the spirit of liberty from the encroachment of despotism. Similarly, Jefferson thought that participation in small, self-governing units was the only way for Americans to sustain a meaningful sense of citizenship.

A closer look at Jefferson's description of the local, self-governing units that he called wards, however, reveals how they were supposed to differ from contemporary residential community associations.[18] Jefferson proposed subdividing counties into wards of about six square miles. These micro-polities would be responsible for an elementary school, a company of militia, a justice of the peace, police and constable, road maintenance, and poor relief. Furthermore, they would select jurors and assemble "at their Folk-house" to vote in elections. "Every man in the State would thus become an acting member of the common government, transacting in person a great portion of its rights and duties."[19] The wards would also be forums for deliberation about issues of national concern. Jefferson proposed that citizens of each ward would assemble in order to reach decisions about fundamental constitutional issues.[20]

There are several features of the ward system that differentiate it from the form of neighborhood governance that is predominant today. First, the ward was supposed to be responsible for services that directly benefited individual property owners (roads, policing) as well as more solidaristic initiatives such as education and poor relief. Residential community associations (RCAs), on the other hand, are concerned exclusively with property interests and have no redistributive role. The fact that Jefferson even mentions poor relief suggests that wards were to be diverse areas inhabited by rich and poor alike, not economically homogeneous enclaves. In the early 1800s it was logistically difficult to create wards exclusively of rich or poor. Given the constraints of primitive transportation, the rich had to live close to the working and middle classes who served as domestic workers, agricultural laborers, tradespeople, and shopkeepers. The wards were political units that brought members of different classes together and therefore differed from contemporary residential community associations, which tend to aggregate the interests of similar individuals. Wards were supposed to be microcosms of the broader polity, whereas RCAs are more like interest groups that represent a particular strata.

Jefferson also envisioned the wards as forums for the direct participation of citizens in self-government. In contrast, modern RCAs are usually governed by professional management companies rather than resident-volunteers let alone by the membership itself. According to one 1990 survey, twenty-seven percent of community associations were self-managed (by elected representatives or volunteers); the other seventy-three percent were run by management companies or professional on-site staff.[21] Finally, Jefferson's emphasis on selecting jurors, voting, and deliberating about national issues suggests an "outward" orientation towards politics rather than an "inward" orientation towards narrowly local concerns. The ward system reflected Jefferson's conviction that citizens needed "more public space than the ballot box" and "more opportunity to make their voice heard in public than election day."[22] It was a mechanism for encouraging citizenship rather than protecting property values.

According to Hannah Arendt, Jefferson was concerned that the United States Constitution gave citizens power in their capacity as private persons rather than citizens. He worried that if each individual strictly pursued his own private interest, then the future of the republic would be in jeopardy. The goal of the ward system was to fight this tendency and reinforce Americans' identity as citizens. By providing a meaningful opportunity for political discussion and action, the micropolity was supposed to cultivate a sense of public responsibility. Jefferson succinctly summed up the purpose with the maxim, "Love your neighbor as yourself, and your country more than yourself."[23] The wards were supposed to be a way to connect love of one's neighbor and love of country. Residential community associations, on the other hand, do not foster the same outward orientation. They encourage citizens to behave as private property owners and to privilege neighborhood interests over those of the polity.[24]

Even more than Jefferson, however, Alexis de Tocqueville is usually credited with a sympathetic view of the relationship between civic associations, local self-government, and democracy.[25] Like Jefferson, Tocqueville was also concerned with the excessive privatism that he observed in the United States. For Tocqueville, the greatest threat to liberty was the tendency of democratic peoples to turn away from public concerns, to live side by side, unconnected by interpersonal ties, uniform in their isolation. He also noted that the mediocrity of American culture seemed to foster conformism and stifle individual thought. Tocqueville felt that mass society (which he called "democracy" in a sociological sense) was dangerous. Despite the ostensible freedom of speech, American society inhibited the cultivation and expression of diverse opinions that are necessary for freedom and meaningful self-government.[26] He suggested that one way to counterbalance this tendency was to encourage the circulation and defend the legitimacy of dissenting views.

Tocqueville's most famous solution to the problem of conformist mass society was to strengthen the local institutions and voluntary associations that trained men in their roles as citizens and checked the expansion of the central state. Local autonomy was part of his recipe for ensuring pluralism in an era of increasing sameness. But the small municipalities that he admired in the 1830s were very different from the private governments that proliferate today. Like Jefferson, Tocqueville appreciated the link that local government created among people of different social classes, which he felt provided guidance for the lower orders and inspired magnanimity in their superiors. Regardless of what one thinks of these "benefits" today, it is clear that they are not achieved in exclusive buildings and homogeneous neighborhoods.

Proponents of RCAs often invoke Tocqueville as their champion because of his insight into the democratic effects of local self-government. Taking this one point out of context, however, gives a misleading understanding of Tocqueville's analysis. The governance typical of RCAs actually provides an uncanny illustration of Tocqueville's greatest fear: democratic despotism. His main worry was that America would become so concerned with private gain and commercial endeavors that it would lose both the capacity for individual liberty and public spirit. In Volume II of *Democracy in America* Tocqueville used the term "democratic despotism" to describe the voluntary embrace of paternalistic government. Tocqueville believed that popular sovereignty was likely to yield a benign form of despotism because people were more likely to give up their freedom to the demos, a sovereign with whom they identify. According to Tocqueville, democratic citizens accept this despotism "because every man, when he is oppressed and disarmed, may still imagine, that whilst he yields obedience it is to himself he yields it, and that it is to one of his own inclinations that all the rest give way."[27] In other words, individuals voluntarily abdicate their own political agency and trust in a paternalistic state that reflects the values they share with others. Although the "citizens" may ritualistically participate in periodic elections, administrators make the real decisions and individuals concentrate on their private affairs. The result is that "this rare and brief exercise of their free choice (e.g., voting in elections), however important it may be, will not prevent them (citizens) from gradually losing the faculties of thinking, feeling, and acting for themselves, and thus gradually falling below the level of humanity."[28] For Tocqueville the consequences of this insidious privatism are serious; the man who is unconcerned with public affairs loses his humanity.

A critic might respond that it is unfair to take Tocqueville's concern with centralized administration and apply it to the despotic effects of small-scale phenomena such as RCAs.[29] A close reading of the text, however, shows that it was not primarily the level of government but the degree of conformism that worried Tocqueville. In fact, Tocqueville felt that despotism in small matters was the most threatening. He explained:

> It must not be forgotten that it is especially dangerous to enslave men in the minor details of life. For my own part, I should be inclined to think freedom less necessary in great things than in little ones, if it were possible to be secure of the one without possessing the other. Subjection in minor affairs breaks out every day, and is felt by the whole community indiscriminately. It does not drive men to resistance, but it crosses them at every turn, till they are led to surrender the exercise of their will. Thus their spirit is gradually broken and their character enervated.[30]

According to Tocqueville, the habit of obedience and conformism in "minor affairs" enervates the spirit of liberty necessary to prevent democratic despotism.

The habits of freedom, self-government, and public interest may be fostered or stifled in local and sublocal governments. In practice, however, residential community associations have tended to undermine democratic practices and strengthen despotic ones. This is a consequence of their history and structure. CC&Rs (conditions, covenants, and restrictions) are the constitutions of residential community associations. They are legally enforceable contracts that are drawn up by real estate developers in order to protect property values. CC&Rs routinely outlaw all visible signs of difference, from nonconforming paint colors to political signs to garage sales. Many restrict the circulation of leaflets, unsolicited newspapers, or canvassers in the name of privacy and safety. CC&Rs are designed to make change or modification impossible and to discourage any type of collective action, instead resolving conflict through bureaucratic procedures.[31]

Tocqueville outlined several remedies that may prevent the growth of democratic despotism: voluntary associations, a free press, and the courts. Voluntary associations overcome the individual's isolation and make it easier to resist the conformism demanded by mass society. An independent judiciary provides even the weakest individual with some redress against oppression and the arbitrary actions of government. A free press is another critical way of overcoming isolation and sustaining democracy because local newspapers and pamphlets inform individuals and link them together. It is this latter function that is most in jeopardy in neighborhoods and buildings that want to be politics-free zones. Although residents may still subscribe to home delivery newspapers, they may not have access to the small-scale, issue-driven pamphlets that are usually used to inform neighbors about local politics. Also, in some residential communities, the connections forged by ringing doorbells for a candidate or cause are foreclosed. Without communication there is no community.

IMAGINARY COMMUNITIES AND MUNICIPALISM

Many residents would reject the suggestion that their neighborhoods foster atomization; they choose "common interest developments" precisely because such developments provide opportunities to build community and overcome the isolation of traditional suburbs.[32] But the community of many of these new developments might be described as "imaginary community." An imaginary community is a group that is sustained by perceived similarities in lifestyle and absence of conflict. It is a community that is reinforced by similar patterns of consumption and cultural cues rather than shared activities and practices.[33] In an imaginary community, collective identity results from individuals identifying with a particular location. Strict rules ensure a high degree of homogeneity so that the illusion of shared values won't be shattered.

It would be an error to associate imaginary community exclusively with suburban gated communities. Gated communities may highlight this exclusiveness, but both urban and suburban neighborhoods are usually racially and economically homogeneous. Levels of participation in politics and neighborhood governance are approximately the same in gated versus non-gated communities; nor does participation differ significantly between RCAs and informal neighborhoods.[34] Nevertheless, the proliferation of private communities reflects the desire for imaginary community and the fear of crime and difference that is widespread in contemporary America.[35]

Imaginary communities exhibit characteristics that urbanist Richard Sennett identified over thirty years ago in his book *The Uses of Disorder*.[36] He argued that individuals choose to live in homogeneous neighborhoods for much the same reason that adolescents cling to rigidly defined cliques. The alienation of adolescence comes from the fact that teenagers' physical maturity is seldom accompanied by the set of experiences necessary to adapt to new situations. They often seek a purified identity and environment in order to ensure that the range of unknown experiences is limited and controlled. Yet these unsettling encounters are the ones that force us to become flexible and capable people. Adults choose homogeneous neighborhoods for the same reasons. It allows them to avoid the kind of encounters that might force them to question their values and identity. Although everyone would probably choose to avoid unfamiliar and unsettling encounters, the affluent are particularly able to isolate themselves.[37] They are the ones with the resources to live in gated communities or doorman buildings. They go to work in private cars rather than crowded buses where one might chat with a friend or try to avoid unwanted attention. Unlike the poor who need to rely on neighbors to borrow a lawnmower or an extra chair for a dinner party, the affluent are able to use wealth to achieve a kind of personal autarky. They have the tools to realize the fantasy of community solidarity by avoiding the social interactions that sometimes cause conflict.

These brave new neighborhoods of nearly identical luxury dwellings are marketed to appeal to a certain fantasy. They provide a way of evading the irreconcilable social antagonisms that pervade modern life. They make it possible to avoid the potentially unbearable encounter with the stranger (the homeless person, ghetto youth, poor white trash redneck) who forecloses the possibility of pure community.[38] Moreover, they disguise the fact that this pure community is itself impossible to achieve.

When Benedict Anderson characterized the nation as an imagined community, he emphasized the way that the narrative of the nation creates "a deep, horizontal comradeship" through (invented) shared histories and symbols rather than face-to-face interactions.[39] The term "imaginary community" should also evoke a sense of comradeship that is fostered by shared symbols rather than common experiences. For example, in suburban neighborhoods similar standards of lawn maintenance and Christmas décor become symbols of shared values and concerns. But the term "imaginary" has a pejorative connotation that "imagined" does not. An imaginary community suggests a simulacra, a copy with no original. Richard Sennett made the same point when he juxtaposed "the projection of community solidarity" with the absence of "community experience."[40] He argued that "the images of communal solidarity are forged in order that men can avoid dealing with each other."[41] White picket fences and porch swings function metonymically, evoking a feeling of community without the discomfort of actual community-building, things like time-consuming meetings, social obligations, or nasty gossip.[42] The part stands for, and in fact substitutes for, the whole.

But perhaps this is painting an excessively bleak vision. After all, people seek and often find opportunities for social interaction and friendship in these new residential communities. There may be an element of urban snobbery in the assumption that suburbanites suffer from isolation and anomie. In his influential study *The Levittowners*, Herbert Gans found that contrary to expectations, the postwar Long Island suburbs provided an active social and political life. The physical environment of Common Interest Development, in particular, would seem to foster community interaction and identity. By providing shared recreational amenities and meeting spaces, such developments facilitate social interaction between neighbors. Studies on this issue are inconclusive. There is little consistent evidence that social activity is either higher or lower in gated communities and common interest developments. It seems plausible that the community building features might be counterbalanced by the physical (large lots, few sidewalks) and cultural features of suburbia. Recently, the New Urbanism has tried to remedy this by transforming the physical features of suburbia. The intentions and many of the strategies of the New Urbanism are laudable but it is difficult to achieve the goal of revitalizing public life without addressing the underlying economic structures and cultural dispositions that caused the retreat into privatism in the first place.

NEW URBANISM: THE ARCHITECTURE OF
IMAGINARY COMMUNITY

Critics have suggested that the New Urbanism is the architectural embodiment of imaginary community.[43] Perhaps this is Disney's fault. For many people, the concept of New Urbanism is linked to the town of Celebration, Florida. Due to the involvement of the Walt Disney Corporation, the town has received considerable attention from the press and the scholarly community. Some of this attention has been critical, emphasizing the strict rules or kitschiness of the neo-traditionalist style, which evokes Disneyland's Main Street.[44] Much of it, however, has been nuanced analysis of the contradictions between the theoretical aspirations of the New Urbanism and the reality of the fairly conventional, upscale suburb that its proponents build.[45]

The New Urbanism, the architecture and planning movement pioneered by Andres Duany and Elizabeth Plater-Zyberk, illustrates the way that private simulacra come to substitute for public spaces. In New Urbanist communities, "public" space becomes an amenity to be purchased by affluent consumers on the real estate market. And I suspect that people like me are precisely the demographic to whom these savvy marketers want to sell it. This target group is made up of people who love old houses, who appreciate the ability to walk to a café, movie theater, or restaurant and desire easy access to a swimming pool, playground, and garden (but do not have the space or time to provide them for their families). And, even though we hate sprawl, strip malls, and traffic we occasionally (and guiltily) shop at Target. The New Urbanism fulfills all these desires, combining an urban life that is sanitized and nonthreatening with a suburban environment that features community and charm. Replete with sidewalks, porches, parks, and turn-of-the-century-style signs and lampposts, New Urbanist communities are carefully designed to reproduce the atmospherics of small town life.

In theory, one of the central goals of the New Urbanism is to provide an alternative to the intense privatism of the suburbs. In order to achieve this, Duany and Plater-Zyberk have proposed compact walkable neighborhoods: mixed-use and mixed-income development, plenty of parks and playgrounds, and neo-traditional architectural styles.[46] The New Urbanism artfully deploys the semiotics of community. The wraparound porch set back just a few feet from the street is the physical embodiment of the spirit of the New Urbanism. The porch, an icon of the neo-traditionalist style, is supposed to facilitate informal contact with neighbors, thereby building a sense of community. In New Urbanist developments the houses are set on small lots but residents can take advantage of generous collective amenities:

parks, playgrounds, open space, and community centers. But the "public" spaces are, in fact, privately owned. The charm of these neighborhoods deflects the question of why these features are available at premium prices to privileged consumers but not to those outside their borders.

Figure 6.1 Haile Plantation, a New Urbanist community in Gainesville, Florida. (Duane Bernstein.)

While researching this issue, I began to reflect about the difference between the New Urbanism and the old urbanism, a label that might apply to Leslieville, my neighborhood in Toronto. Leslieville could have served as an inspiration for New Urbanist principles. It is a mixed-income, mixed-use area. The range of socioeconomic classes represented, however, is much wider than the mix of middle-class and extremely affluent that inhabits New Urbanist developments. There are several public housing projects, including one for the disabled, two nursing homes, small apartments above rundown stores, and many Victorian-era brick row houses. The retail area of Queen Street East is fairly eclectic; trendy modern design stores are located next to seedy bars where grizzled men start drinking before noon; antique stores are adjacent to fish 'n chips places and pawnshops. Large row houses have been converted into duplexes, accommodating a wide variety of family types. There are plenty of professionals with children, gay couples, immigrants, and old-timers. A few blocks away there are old ware-

Figure 6.2   A house on Bertmount Avenue, Toronto. (Margaret Kohn.)

houses and factories. A few are still functioning, others are leased to artists and nonprofits, and a handful are being converted into luxury condominiums.

The three New Urbanist neighborhoods that I am most familiar with—Haile Plantation, Town of Tioga, and Celebration (all in Florida)—look very different from my neighborhood in Toronto. Part of the difference is inevitable due to the newness of the New Urbanist developments. Leslieville shows the signs of gradual transformation over time. Modernist apartment buildings coexist and often clash with the dominant Victorian style and are interspersed with small in-fill townhouse projects built in neo-traditionalist style. The built environment is a rough record of changing aesthetics, priorities, and needs. Although it would be unfair to criticize places like Celebration for their newness, it is legitimate to note that they are planned to resist change. Restrictive covenants and detailed design guidelines guarantee a high degree of homogeneity in building styles. Because the homeowner's association and its lawyers are able to enforce rules restricting architectural innovation, such towns will consistently project the image of turn-of-the-century small-town America. This has certain advantages; it protects property values and prevents architectural fads from marring the image. But it also means that New Urbanist developments will never reflect the sense of history that planners and residents so admire. Rather than conveying a specific history and geography, the neo-traditionalist building style seems to remove the developments from time and space and situates them in a dream-like alternative dimension. By means of extraction, reduction, and recombination, the architecture creates a new, anti-geographical space.[47]

I do not object to the architecture of the New Urbanism as much as the gap between the theory and the practice of the movement. Or to be more precise, the difficulties of realizing the laudable goals of the New Urbanism reveal some fundamental problems with the theory. One goal is to decrease the dependence on the automobile by creating walkable towns and integrating commerce into residential neighborhoods. Most New Urbanist neighborhoods, however, are located in remote suburbs where large swaths of land make it possible for developers to engage in ambitious, large-scale planning and recoup their heavy investments in infrastructure. Given the remote location, public transportation is seldom available and bicycling or walking to work is impossible. The Town of Tioga, a 500-acre New Urbanist development located nine miles west of downtown Gainesville, for example, is not served by public transportation. And no buses enter Haile Plantation, a more established New Urbanist community of over 4000 residents, located eight miles from the town center. Rather than decreasing reliance on the automobile, these projects increase the need for two cars. Although the virtues of walkability are touted in theory, the built environment contradicts this claim. Even modest townhomes in the Town of Tioga feature two-car garages.

Proponents would respond that even though public transportation connections between New Urbanist developments and the downtown core may be lacking, sidewalks and biking trails facilitate auto-free living within. It is true that Haile Plantation features extensive sidewalks and jogging trails. But my informal conversations with residents gave me the impression that most rely on their cars, even for a trip to the Haile Village Center. A real estate agent told me that many neighborhoods are a mile or two (a twenty minute walk) away from the Haile Village Center. Given that the houses are situated on cul-de-sac roads designed for privacy not efficiency, it is often necessary to drive even when the destination is within the development.[48] And no one relies on the Village Center for basic necessities. Groceries, hardware, computer supplies, and pharmaceuticals all require a trip to the ubiquitous big box retailers outside.[49] Although a handful of real estate agents, doctors, and lawyers may be able to bike to their offices in the Village Center, most retail employees cannot afford the high rents in Haile Plantation and most residents work at high-paying jobs miles away at the University of Florida or Shands Hospital. At first glance these quaint, neo-traditionalist neighborhoods look like an attempt to resist the sterility of big-box retailers and strip malls that have marked the landscape of Florida. But the two actually exist in an almost symbiotic relationship. The intimate alluring space of the "Olde Towne Center" is not a challenge to the strip mall but an oasis meant to shield residents from its ugliness while still allowing them to take advantage of its conveniences.

Most New Urbanist towns also fail to realize the ideal of creating a mixed-income environment. Typically, they contain a range of housing styles and prices but even entry-level homes are priced well above the median for the region. In the Town of Tioga, for example, the lowest-priced "Cottage Homes" start at $197,000, compared to the median housing price in Gainesville of $125,800.[50] There is a similar disparity in the case of Celebration, Florida, the famous Disney-built town. Celebration advertises itself as an inclusive, mixed-income community, yet in 2003 the least expensive units—two bedroom condos—started at $175,000, well above the median sales price for larger homes in Orlando, $132,600.[51] Haile Plantation does feature some small units that cost around $140,000 (about the same cost as other new construction in area) but these are not integrated with more expensive properties. Instead, the development is segregated into about 45 different neighborhoods, guaranteeing that modest two-bedroom bungalows are far removed from villas and mansions.

In the sales brochures for Celebration, the Town of Tioga, and Haile Plantation, there is much emphasis on public space. Many homesites in New Urbanist neighborhoods are smaller than sites in other suburban neighborhoods (in order to facilitate walkability) but community amenities are more extensive. In theory, everyone benefits when dozens of lawns are replaced by well-equipped playgrounds, running trails, and parks. Of course, these amenities are not really public spaces. They are owned by the community association and accessible to residents. In Haile Plantation prominent signs emphasize that the trails are open only to residents and their guests. But a closer look suggests that the recreational amenities are not even open to all community members. In Haile Plantation, the recreational facilities—a golf course, swimming pool, and tennis courts—are not the collective property of residents. They are owned by a private club. Both residents and nonresidents alike may choose to pay a hefty initiation fee ($3000 for access to all facilities) and monthly dues of up to $210 in order to make use of them.[52] Instead of providing public space, Haile Plantation encourages residents to become members of a conveniently located but high-priced Golf and Country Club. The Village Meeting Hall functions on similar commercial principles. Advertised as a civic center, it is actually a catering hall which charges $500 to $750 for wedding receptions and conferences.[53] When asked whether local nonprofits, civic groups, or residents could use the Village Meeting Hall, I was informed that they could as long as they paid the $750 fee *per use*. This was not exactly what Thomas Jefferson had in mind when he wrote that ward residents would gather "at their Folk House" for public deliberation.[54]

Places like Haile Plantation, Celebration, Town of Tioga, and countless other new developments sell consumers the dream of a place linked together by more than proximity and property values. The icons of the village center, town hall, and neighborhood pool are powerful marketing tools that trade upon a longing for public places. This longing is fueled by the sterile, ugly commercial spaces outside the boundaries. But in the hands of private developers public places such as community centers are transformed into commodities, Through the process of commodification they are changed from places that integrate people across class and racial lines into ones that separate them according to different levels of consumption. A village meeting hall that charges groups $750 for a single evening is prohibitively expensive and serves no civic purpose. Similarly, a recreation center with an initiation fee of up to $3000 stratifies the community rather than bringing it together.

New Urbanism has received widespread attention because of its distinctive architectural style and ideology. But other high-end residential developments also feature traditional Southern architecture and extensive communal amenities. What distinguishes the New Urbanism is the integration of retail and residential units within a single planned development. A bustling commercial center is a key component of the small-town ambience and community identity that developers seek to create. But unlike traditional downtowns that have publicly owned streets and plazas, the town center of a New Urbanist community is often private property. In Celebration, the streets and parks are owned by a property management company controlled by Disney.[55] The streets of the Haile Village Center are owned by the homeowners association. Bob Kramer, the developer and president of the homeowner's association, explained that the decision to retain ownership of the streets in the Haile Village Center was not motivated by the desire to maintain proprietary control.[56] The aesthetic vision for downtown was inconsistent with county standards. Brick sidewalks and nonstandard street lighting would not have been allowed on county-maintained streets. Ironically, in order to recreate the atmosphere of a traditional public place, the village center had to be privately owned. In its attempt to create an aesthetically coherent environment with old-fashioned lanterns and cobblestone streets, the Haile Plantation Corporation may have unwittingly created a mechanism for increasing control over activity on the street.

Does it matter that the streets in the Haile Village Center are owned by the homeowners' association rather than the county? The answer to this question depends on whether the courts decide to treat residential community associations as the equivalent of governments. If RCAs are treated as municipalities, then it does not matter which entity owns the streets. If, on the other hand, streets owned collectively by homeowners are treated as private property, then it may be possible to enforce rules against free speech, religious expression, or equal protection, that violate constitutional protections. The lower courts have handed down inconsistent rulings and the Supreme Court has not yet heard a case dealing with this issue.

According to Bob Kramer, Haile Village Center does not have rules against passing out leaflets, picketing, or demonstrations, but he emphasized that such rules could be enacted if the need arose, inasmuch as it was private property. It seems unlikely that such restrictions would withstand judicial scrutiny, given the logic of existing legal precedents. The Haile Village Center is open to residents and outsiders alike and includes a full range of houses, businesses, stores, and commercial property. This makes it very similar to the company town in *Marsh v. Alabama* (see Chapter 4). According to *Marsh,* all citizens must have the same rights, regardless of whether they live in a traditional municipality or a company-owned town. This implies that citizens should also have the same rights, regardless of whether they live in a town owned by a development company or a residential community association. Over the past two decades, however, the Supreme Court has become less willing to give priority to civil liberties over private property rights. Given the increasingly conservative composition of the court, it is possible that the Supreme Court could overrule *Marsh* and reassert a more absolutist understanding of private property.

The New Urbanism's impact on civil liberties is still unresolved. The residential–retail mix makes New Urbanist developments more like traditional towns and therefore more likely to be treated as municipalities. On the other hand, if the courts overturn *Marsh* and treat private towns as private property, then individuals living in these enclaves will be even more cut off from civic life. If people live, work, work out, and shop entirely on private property, then they may never have to be exposed to the variety of ideas and people that inhabit the larger polity.

The structure of private residential communities (in New Urbanist communities and old suburbs) potentially constrains the opportunities for political activity, especially dissent. The United States Constitution has traditionally provided limitations on the level of conformity that democratic majorities—acting through their state institutions—can exact. A new problem emerges, however, when democratic majorities (and nondemocratic property managers) exercise substantial control over residents' lives but do so through private institutions. In order to understand this threat, the next section analyzes the relevant legal doctrine that emerged from litigation challenging restrictions on free speech in two private residential communities: a condominium and a gated community.

TWO COURT CASES:
THE GALAXY TOWERS AND LEISURE WORLD

The privatization of neighborhoods has direct political consequences when it affects our capacity to reach informed decisions as voters. When private residential communities such as high-rise apartment buildings ban leaflets and signs, they undermine citizens' capacity to recognize and adjudicate competing views. The Galaxy Towers case, decided by the New Jersey Appellate Court in 1994, dramatically illustrates the way that control of space can lead to a monopoly on political information. The Galaxy Towers is a luxury condominium consisting of three high-rise buildings, an underground parking garage, and an attached mall. Ninety percent of the voters in Electoral District Six lived in the Galaxy Towers and the Condominium Association was involved in local politics. It distributed materials and actively canvassed in support of candidates for the town council and school board. The opposing organization, the Guttenberg Taxpayers Association, was not allowed on the premises. Although the Guttenberg Taxpayers Association carried the rest of the town by two to one, Galaxy residents supported the condo association slate almost unanimously. Without access to Galaxy voters, the Taxpayers Association had no chance to present its case to the majority of the districts' voters; it filed suit and the New

Jersey Appellate Court ultimately ruled for the plaintiffs, finding that there was no possibility for meaningful electoral competition under the existing rules.[57]

This decision was possible in New Jersey, one of the few states to interpret its state constitution broadly enough to apply to social places that are not owned by the state. Had Galaxy Towers been located in virtually any other state, the condo associations' monopoly on political activity would probably have remained intact. Yet such a monopoly seems patently to violate the most fundamental principles of a democratic political system. It is impossible to make an informed judgment between rival options without exposure to arguments from both sides. Like citizens in an authoritarian regime, residents of Galaxy Towers were a captive audience for the condo associations' message.

One objection might be that the informal monopoly allegedly exercised by the condo association was not really a monopoly because Galaxy residents could get political information at their workplace or on the street as well as through the news media or by mail. Today email would be cited as an ideal alternative. Although other modes of communication do exist, the enormous disparity in voting patterns between the condo and the town suggests the power of the face-to-face canvassing that took place in the buildings. The many companies who invest millions of dollars in expenses and commissions for their salespeople recognize that face-to-face contact has a distinctive power. Just as in the case involving the Golden Gateway Center in San Francisco, the architectural form of the building cut off individual units from public space, thereby curtailing residents' access to dissenting views. There simply was no alternative way to engage in "direct" democracy. Although a leafletter could stand on the street outside the Galaxy mall (also a private space), the condo residents would probably not pass him by because they had their own, internal entrance. The residents who drove directly from high-rise office buildings to the condo's private underground parking lot could go days without ever entering public space. Although the mail or news media were still accessible, these expensive forms of communication were hardly viable alternatives for modestly financed candidates for the local school board or town council.

It is especially troubling when apartment complexes or gated communities try to limit the circulation of leaflets and newspapers within their domain. The Golden Gateway Center and the Galaxy Towers are two examples of high-rise buildings that have exploited their spatial layout to ban leafletting and make sure that critical ideas did not circulate widely. Gated communities made up of detached houses have also outlawed the circulation of unsolicited materials. In *Laguna Publishing Company v. Golden Rain Foundation of Laguna Hills* a newspaper publisher in California challenged this practice on First Amendment grounds.[58] Leisure World, a residential community composed of over twenty thousand seniors, had a rule banning the delivery of unsolicited newspapers. Private security guards enforced the ban by preventing delivery people from entering the gated community. A local newspaper publisher challenged the policy, arguing that it reflected viewpoint discrimination because Leisure World did allow the unsolicited distribution of *Leisure World News*, its own house organ. The California Court of Appeals (Fourth District) agreed. According to the court, Golden Rain (the association administering Leisure World) "may certainly exclude *all* give-away, unsolicited newspapers from Leisure World, but once it chooses to admit one, where that decision is not made in concert with the residents, then the discriminatory exclusion of another such newspaper represents an abridgement of the free speech, free press rights…secured under our state Constitution."[59]

The legal rationale for this compromise is somewhat confusing. First, the court noted that *Marsh v. Alabama* (see Chapter 4 for a summary of this case) did not resolve the dispute because Leisure World did not have retail businesses and therefore did not fully resemble a company town. While acknowledging that the large scale and numerous amenities made Leisure World a distinctive hybrid, the court did not conclude that its governance structure established state action for the purposes of the First Amendment to the United States Constitution. The court also invoked *Pruneyard* and its more expansive protection of speech under the California State Constitution,[60] yet the justices emphasized that there was an important difference between a shopping mall and a gated community. Although both were private property, the shopping mall invited in the general public and the gated community was designed to exclude everyone but residents and their invited guests. Nevertheless, the court still relied on *Pruneyard* to establish that the protection of free speech in the California Constitution was more robust and did not necessarily apply only to state actors. In finally resolving the dispute, Justice McDaniel, writing for the majority, invoked a novel interpretation of the language of *Lloyd v. Tanner* (1972), one of the United States Supreme Court's shopping mall cases. According to *Lloyd v. Tanner*, the "First and 14th Amendments safeguard rights of free speech and assembly by limitations on state action, not on action by the (owners) of private property used non-discriminatorily for private purposes only."[61] Justice McDaniel took this to mean that private property owners could ban political speech but must do so in a nondiscriminatory matter. The bottom line was that Leisure World could exclude unsolicited newspapers altogether but once having admitted one newspaper, it could not prohibit another. Lest this be construed as an open invitation to leafletters of all types, the court emphasized that "The rule we announce as the basis for resolution of this phase of the case will not result in requiring unrestricted admittance to Leisure World of religious evangelists, political campaigners, assorted salespeople, signature solicitors, or any other uninvited persons of the like....The owners of this private property still remain in complete control of who shall enter Leisure World."[62]

PRIVATE GOVERNMENT

In the past two decades, courts have been reluctant to apply constitutional protections to private residential communities. The courts provide a twofold rationale for distinguishing between the company town in *Marsh v. Alabama* and Common Interest Developments like Leisure World. First, until the recent upsurge in mixed-use development inspired by the New Urbanism, private residential communities seldom included a business district. This meant that they did not meaningfully resemble company towns. Second, in *Marsh v. Alabama* nonresidents were implicitly invited into the town, which was traversed by a public highway. In contrast, many residential community associations or apartment complexes like the Golden Gateway Center are gated communities designed to exclude outsiders. Of course, throughout much of European history, the city was the paradigmatic gated community, designed to exclude outsiders. Cities often originated as fortresses or fortified castles; these safe spaces attracted artisans, peasants, and merchants seeking refuge from marauders, bandits, debts, and feudal obligations. Today walls do not cut off the city from the country so much as they separate neighborhoods from each other. The physical walls, however, should not become impermeable barriers between citizens. Nor should communities without brick and mortar walls create invisible ones by forbidding neighbors from distributing pamphlets or displaying political signs. Even if walls keep outsiders from entering a city or gated community, those living inside should still be able to express their political views to their neighbors.

Even without a "central business district"—a concept that today seems somewhat antiquated in an era of strip malls—neighborhoods are similar to cities and should therefore be treated like other state actors. A municipality has four distinctive characteristics: it is a territorially based unit in which membership is compulsory for everyone living in a geographically defined area; it collects resources by levying mandatory assessments on property; it uses the courts to enforce its rules; and it provides local services such as garbage collection, streetsweeping, and policing. RCAs share all four characteristics. Because RCAs function much like other components of local government, they should be treated as state actors for the purposes of the First Amendment.

The goal is not to judicialize local decision-making but to protect a space for politics. This space cannot be removed from everyday life, exiled from our neighborhoods, and excluded from polite conversation. If political space is a place that we inhabit on special occasions such as Election Day it will feel like our Sunday best—slightly uncomfortable and inauthentic. The alternative is to embrace a democratic polity constantly revitalized by a politics of everyday life.

ENDNOTES

1. Almost six percent live in communities surrounded by fences or walls; 3.4 percent live in communities where security systems and/or guards control entrance. This information comes from the 2001 American Housing Survey. Cited in Setha Low, *Behind the Gates; Life, Security, and the Pursuit of Happiness in Fortress America* (New York: Routledge, 2003), 15.
2. The most recent figures come from the Community Associations Institute website: www.caionline.org. Many Residential Community Associations, however, are not, strictly speaking, private communities because they do not own the streets.
3. Nancy Rosenblum, *Membership and Morals: The Personal Uses of Pluralism in America* (Princeton, NJ: Princeton University Press, 1998), 112.
4. See Clifford J. Treese, *1999 Community Associations Factbook* (Alexandria, VA: Community Associations Institute, 1999).
5. Wayne S. Hyatt, "Common Interest Communities: Evolution and Reinvention," *John Marshall Law Review* (Winter 1998), 305–394.
6. Evan McKenzie, *Privatopia* (New Haven, CT: Yale University Press, 1994), 122–149.
7. In *Gerber v. Longboat Harbour Condominium, Inc.* (1989) a federal court refused to enforce a provision banning the display of American flags. The court invoked *Shelley v. Kraemer* (the landmark civil rights case where the courts refused to enforce a racially restrictive covenant). The decision, however, was superseded by a statute passed by the Florida legislature guaranteeing that "Any [condominium] unit owner may display one portable, removable United States flag in a respectful way regardless of any declaration rules or requirements dealing with flags or decorations" [718.113(4)].
8. The most thorough and nuanced treatment of RCAs in political theory is found in Nancy Rosenblum's *Membership and Morals*, 112–157.
9. According to one study only eleven percent of members participated in association governance. Cited in Rosenblum, *Membership and Morals*, 135.

10. David Kennedy, "Residential Associations as State Actors: Regulating the Impact of Gated Communities on Non Members," *Yale Law Journal* 105 (December 1995), 761–793.

11. According to the *National Survey of Community Association Homeowner Satisfaction* (Alexandria, VA: Community Associations Research Foundation, 1999), members of community associations were significantly wealthier than nonmembers. For example, thirty-one percent of the general population has a household income of under $25,000 but only six percent of members do.

12. Steven Siegal, "The Constitution and Private Government: Toward the Recognition of Constitutional Rights in Private Residential Communities Fifty Years After *Marsh v. Alabama*," *William and Mary Bill of Rights Journal* 6 (Spring 1998), 526.

13. Over seventy-five percent of community associations with at least 150 units have swimming pools. The figure is slightly lower for smaller developments. See Treese, *1999 Community Associations Factbook.*

14. Robert Putnam, *Bowling Alone: The Collapse and Revival of Community* (New York: Simon and Schuster, 2000), 22–23.

15. Michael Walzer, "Michael Sandel's America," 1997; cited in Mark E. Warren, *Democracy and Association* (Princeton, NJ: Princeton University Press, 2001), 22.

16. Warren, *Democracy and Association.*

17. This claim is made on the Community Associations Institute website (www.caion-line.org/about/index.cfm). See also Robert Nelson, "The Privatization of Local Government: From Zoning to RCAs," in *Residential Community Associations: Private Governments in the Intergovernmental System?* (Washington, DC: Advisory Commission on Intergovernmental Relations, May 1989); Robert Jay Dilger, *Neighborhood Politics: Residential Community Associations in American Governance* (New York: New York University Press, 1992).

18. Jefferson outlined the concept of wards in his "Letter to John Cartwright," June 5, 1824. http://lachlan.bluehaze.au.com/lit/jeff20.htm.

19. "Letter to John Cartwright," June 5, 1824.

20. "Letter to Samuel Kercheval," July 12, 1816. http://lachlan.bluehaze.au.com/lit/jeff14.htm.

21. These figures come from the CAI website: www.caionline.org/about/facts99.cfm).

22. Hannah Arendt, *On Revolution* (New York: Penguin, 1990), 253.

23. Cited in Arendt, *On Revolution*, 253.

24. Mark E. Warren reaches a similar conclusion in *Democracy and Association* (Princeton, NJ: Princeton University Press, 2001). He argues that different types of associations promote different political outcomes. Associations such as gated communities that are made up of elite members and promote status are less likely to promote certain democratic effects.

25. The most influential work in this vein is Robert Putnam's *Making Democracy Work: Civic Traditions in Modern Italy* (Princeton, NJ: Princeton University Press, 1993).

26. For theorists such as John Stuart Mill and Alexis de Tocqueville, the conformism engendered by mass society was a constant threat to political liberty. Although the Bill of Rights prevents the federal and state governments from enforcing conformity, it does nothing to stop the private governments that rule neighborhoods from doing the same thing. The Bill of Rights was written in a period concerned with tyrannical government; a generation later theorists became concerned with the political consequences of powerful social structures.

27. Alexis de Tocqueville, *Democracy in America, Vol. II*, CD Rom, 213.

28. Tocqueville, *Democracy in America, Vol. II*, 214.

29. Although Tocqueville was writing about the threat posed by a centralized administrative state, the same logic applies to sublocal government. Homeowners associations are nominally democratic (they provide for the election of a board of directors), however, they often delegate authority to professional managers and lawyers who have the expertise to interpret the complex CC&Rs (covenants, codes, and restrictions). These CC&Rs require a greater deal of conformity than a local or national government would ever dream of demanding and most residents voluntarily obey these freely chosen constraints.

30. Tocqueville, *Democracy in America, Vol II.,* 214.

31. See McKenzie, *Privatopia.*

32. See, for example, Andrew Ross, *The Celebration Chronicles: Life, Liberty and the Pursuit of Property Values in Disney's New Town* (New York: Ballantine, 1999).

33. One survey of residents of gated communities found that the majority did not find their development friendly and did not feel a sense of community. See Georgeanna Wilson-Doenges, "An exploration of sense of community and fear of crime in gated communities," *Environment and Behavior* 32, no. 5 (2000), 597–611.

34. Edward J. Blakely and Mary Gail Snyder, *Gated Communities in the United States* (Washington DC: Brookings Institution, 1999), 35, 131–133.

35. Setha Low reaches a similar conclusion in *Behind the Gates.*

36. Richard Sennett, *The Uses of Disorder: Personal Identity and City Life* (New York: Norton, 1970).

37. According to the *National Survey of Community Association Homeowner Satisfaction* (1999), twenty-three percent of RCA residents earn over $100,000 compared to nine percent of nonresidents. (64)

38. Aida Hozic, *Hollyworld: Space, Power, and Fantasy in the American Economy* (Ithaca, NY: Cornell University Press, 2001), 30.

39. Benedict Anderson, *Imagined Communities* (London: Verso, 1991), 6–7.

40. Sennett, *The Uses of Disorder,* 33.

41. Sennett, *The Uses of Disorder,* 34.

42. Keally McBride, "Consuming Community," *Socialist Review* 3–4 (2001).

43. Michael Sorkin, "Acting Urban," *Some Assembly Required* (Minneapolis: University of Minnesota Press, 2001), 64–69.

44. For example, see Tyler Brule, "Once Upon a Time in America," *The Independent,* December 3, 1995, 4; Catherine Fox, "Disney Town, U.S.A: Going Back to the Future," *The Atlanta Constitution,* October 20, 1996.

45. See Keally McBride, "Consuming Community."

46. Congress for the New Urbanism, *Charter of the New Urbanism* (New York: McGraw-Hill, 1999).

47. Michael Sorkin uses this phrase to describe Disneyland in "See You in Disneyland," *Variations on a Theme Park: The New American City and the End of Public Space* (New York: Hill and Wang, 1992), 208.

48. Conversation with Diane Mahaffey, real estate agent, February 25, 2003.

49. This claim is based on an analysis of the retail structure of Haile Village Center and interviews with residents.

50. Housing prices for the Town of Tioga are current as of March 2003 and come from Tioga Realty. Median home prices for Gainesville come from the article "Florida Median Home Price Increases 8 Percent," *Naples Daily News,* May 5, 2002.

51. The figures are provided by the official Celebration website: www.celebrationfl.com (March 2003). The comparative figures for Orlando were published in the article "Florida Home Sales, Median Price Rise in September," *Naples Daily News,* November 3, 2002.

52. The initiation fee varies based on the level of membership. The lowest level (swimming pool use only) is $500. The full-service membership (including tennis courts and golf) costs $3000. Membership is by invitation only and new members must be sponsored by a current member. This information is current as of March 2003 and is provided by the Haile Plantation Golf and Country Club.

53. Interview with Carol Ann of the meeting hall staff, February 26, 2003.

54. "Letter to John Cartwright," June 5, 1824.

55. After the development is complete, management will be turned over to the Home-owners Association. According to Keally McBride, the CC&Rs stipulate that any decision reached by the association may be overridden by the majority of landowners. The Disney Corporation, however, will always be the majority landowner because it restricted development on the half of the property preserved as open space ("Consuming Community").

56. Most of the streets in the rest of Haile Plantation were dedicated to Alachua County.

57. Frank Askin, "Free Speech, Private Space, and the Constitution," *Rutgers Law Journal* (Summer 1998).

58. 182 Cal. App. 3d 816 (1982).

59. 131 Cal. App. 3d 843. Cited in Evan McKenzie, *Privatopia* (New Haven: Yale University Press, 1994), 159–160.

60. The California Constitution states, "Every person may freely speak, write and publish his or her sentiments on all subjects, being responsible for the abuse of this right. A law may not restrain or abridge liberty of speech or press." For a brief discussion of the significance of this wording, see Chapter 4.

61. 407 U.S. 551, 567.

62. 131 Cal. App. 3d 85.

7

BATTERY PARK CITY

Battery Park City provides an unparalleled view of New York City's utopian longings. From the waterfront one can see the Statue of Liberty and Ellis Island. And Battery Park City itself provides a certain insight into different unrealized, imagined futures. The history of the four billion dollar, ninety-two acre mixed-use development provides insight into the contradictory impulses that guide urban redevelopment. Originally proposed as a self-financing low- and middle-income neighborhood, it became a civic showpiece and playground of the rich. Tracing the production of this space illuminates changing assumptions about private and public and the meaning of the city.

EXCAVATING BATTERY PARK CITY

In the early 1960s New York was experiencing the transition from an industrial to a commercial economy. The decaying docks and wharves along the Hudson River, at the periphery of the financial district, were glaring signs of this transformation. More modern facilities in New Jersey had attracted cargo shipping, leaving the New York waterfront in decline.[1] A major new development in the Financial District—the gargantuan World Trade Center (proposed in 1964)—made the area appealing as a residential community for downtown workers. The Hudson River site also presented a solution to the dilemma of urban renewal: how to build high-quality new housing without displacing existing communities. Because the site was built on landfill excavated from the World Trade Center, it was an empty space, a *tabula rasa*, well suited to serve as a canvas on which different groups would paint their picture of an ideal city.

In 1966 Governor Nelson Rockefeller and New York City Mayor John Lindsay both proposed plans for waterfront revitalization. Their plans, however, reflected different ideas about the role of government in development. Lindsay favored luxury, market-rate housing for lawyers and financiers. Rockefeller, also a liberal Republican, proposed a parkland containing high-rise residential towers, with half the units commanding luxury prices, forty percent lightly subsidized for the middle classes, and ten percent reserved for low-income tenants. After two years of negotiations, during which Lindsay faced a contentious re-election campaign, the two political backers compromised on a formula which included extensive commercial and civic space as well as a large residential community.[2] The latter was made up of an equal number of units reserved for low-income, middle-income, and luxury residents.[3] This plan reflected the conviction, still dominant in the 1960s, that the government has an important role to play in providing affordable housing and that all neighborhoods should have a mix of different income groups. Yet by the time the residential phase of the development was flourishing in the 1990s, it included virtually no middle- or low-income housing with starting rents for studio apartments well over $2000.

The legal edifice created to oversee the project was a public benefit corporation, the Battery Park City Authority (BPCA).[4] In the agreement reached with the city, which owned the land, the BPCA received a 99 year lease and some financial support in exchange for a guarantee that all profits from the development would go to the city. The state authorized the BPCA to sell $200 million of bonds to pay for the initial site preparation and infrastructure.[5] The old docks were removed and replaced with landfill that was removed from excavation of the World Trade Center and sand dredged from the river. Out of the murky waters emerged prime real estate.

All subsequent construction was to be based on an ambitious Master Plan adopted in 1969.[6] Influenced by Le Corbusier's modernism, there were "no streets where kids could get into trouble, and formal landscapes…herald(ed)…a sense of order."[7] The development was to be composed of a massive, seven-story "spine" linking a series of high-rise towers. The spine included different levels for transportation, civic, and commercial infrastructure. The project featured a suspended people-mover. Roads were placed underground so that the circulation of traffic would not disrupt the park-like setting. Furthermore, by locating the highway underneath the development, there would be no barrier separating Battery Park City from the rest of lower Manhattan.

Other levels of the spine included schools, shops, restaurants, offices, utilities, and public recreational facilities. Seven pods (clusters of towers) were connected to the spine. They contained office space and apartments, based on the mixed-income model.[8]

Even though the Master Plan received support from architectural critics and planners, it was never built.[9] Several factors converged to delay implementation of the plan. First, timing was a crucial factor. The initial phase of development, creating the site through landfill, was completed in 1976, in the midst of a severe nationwide recession caused by the oil shocks. The decreased demand for retail and residential space due to the recession was compounded by a glut in the commercial real estate market caused by the completion of the World Trade Center. Between 1970 and 1973 the average Manhattan office rent fell from $13.00 per square foot to $7.00 and vacancy rates reached over twenty percent.[10] The city also lost 500,000 jobs in the 1970s.[11] The economic downturn coincided with a fiscal crisis in New York City. With record budget deficits, the city was not able to keep its commitment to finance improvements in the infrastructure of Battery Park City. Finally, changes in federal programs also had an impact on the development. Under President Nixon, funds for urban redevelopment and low-income housing dried up, leaving no federal support for construction of subsidized housing. By the late 1970s Battery Park City became a wasteland derisively referred to as "the beach."

Given the simultaneous crises in the government and the real estate market it is not surprising that the project ground to a standstill. There were elements of the design, however, that made it particularly difficult to attract private investment. The private part of the development (the high-rise towers) was literally built on top of a complex, innovative, and expensive public infrastructure. The viability of any building on the site was contingent upon the successful completion of the circulation and infrastructure system of the spine. During the recession, few developers were willing to work within the terms outlined in the Master Plan because it was financially risky and the complexity of the plan made it difficult to modify in response to changing circumstances.[12]

The economic downturn also coincided with both a political and aesthetic critique of urban renewal and modernist planning. Across the country, cities had demolished poor and working-class neighborhoods only to find themselves unable to attract alternative development. In Detroit, for example, urban renewal left a wasteland in the center of the city.[13] The dispossessed residents of these demolished neighborhoods were either abandoned to fend for themselves or were concentrated in new high-rise housing projects on the edge of the city. This segregation exacerbated existing problems and ruptured economic and social networks yielding more intense poverty and crime. These experiences left citizens very skeptical about the ability of planning bureaucracies to foresee the impact of their schemes and manage their unintended consequences. Although Battery Park City did not displace existing communities, it still seemed like a hubristic attempt to build a new city from scratch in order to accomplish social engineering.[14]

There was also an aesthetic dimension of the critique. Some found the futuristic style and massive scale of the Master Plan cold and forbidding. Others suggested that the implementation of Le Corbusier's "death of the street" would lead to disorientation and alienation and might also undermine the important social ties that emerge out of informal contact on street corners.[15]

The 1969 Master Plan was abandoned piecemeal during the 1970s. At least initially, what replaced it, however, was not a return to the mixed-use, street-oriented neighborhoods that Jane Jacobs so admired. After jettisoning the "spine" concept, the Battery Park City Authority sought out developers to build clusters or "pods" of high-rise apartment houses and office buildings linked by a more conventional, street-level circulation system. This scheme made it possible for the project to move forward despite the scaled-back commitment from public sources. Each "pod" could be built separately and incrementally, thereby providing greater flexibility for the developers. When completed, pedestrians would circulate between pods by walking on skyways and vehicular traffic would dominate at street level.

Only the Gateway Plaza, one of several proposed pods, was ever built; nevertheless, it represents an important stage in the production of urban space. The Gateway Plaza, built by the Lefrak Organization (the Levitt of urban construction), is composed of six high-rise buildings that form an enclosed quadrangle. At the center of the quadrangle is a small private park and swimming pool. Together the six buildings form a fortress-like enclosure that makes it possible to control access through one guarded entrance.[16] The goal was to create a self-contained compound that was completely separate from (yet convenient to) the rest of the city. The vogue in the 1970s was the concept of "defensible space."[17] The Gateway Plaza was the city's response to the fear of urban upheaval, ghetto riots, and suburban flight. It was an attempt to build a suburb in the city and was marketed to professionals seeking an economically homogeneous, sheltered, safe, and private environment without a long commute into work.

Both the unrealized megastructure of the 1969 Master Plan and the first pod were broadly modernist in style—concrete and glass buildings without historicist pretensions, arranged on the high-rise-in-a-park model—but this similarity hides more than it reveals. The earlier design was the unapologetic legacy of an era of big government: a monumental project with extensive public facilities and subsidized housing that was linked to the existing downtown core. The Gateway Plaza was a fortress-like, luxury residential development in a "public" park that was protected by a moat composed of the Hudson River on one side and a highway on the other. The 1960s were over.

By 1979 the project as a whole was in deep trouble. The original $200 million bond issue for the landfill was coming due and, with little interest from developers, the Battery Park City Authority was facing default. The only way to salvage the project was to obtain government guarantees for new bonds, but such support would only be forthcoming if the now much-maligned project could establish economic viability. As part of the bailout deal, ownership of the 92-acre site was transferred from the City of New York to the BPCA, increasing the agency's control and streamlining the permit process. In 1979, the BPCA approved a new Master Plan, prepared by architects Alexander Cooper and Stanton Eckstut. The new Master Plan was a repudiation of the principles of modernist planning and social policy that dominated a decade earlier. Whereas the 1969 plan envisioned spending $73.6 million on civic facilities, the new 1979 plan devoted only $3 million.[18] There was no provision for subsidized housing and the first priority (and geographic centerpiece) became a large commercial development. The World Financial Center, six million square feet of office space, was to be located at the core of the site, adjacent to the World Trade Center.

For the forty-two percent of the site now zoned for residential construction, the 1979 Master Plan emphasized a return to traditional forms of city planning. The gridiron, street-and-block system was adopted in order to reestablish greater continuity with existing urban forms. Traditional parcels also made the bidding and construction process more familiar to developers. By breaking up the site into 36 blocks rather than 7 pods, it became possible to involve a larger variety of developers.

Although the Gateway Plaza was marketed to upper-middle-class workers considering the suburbs, the new buildings targeted the market for high-end, luxury urban living. In order to achieve the goal of recreating, or at least alluding to existing elite New York neighborhoods, the plan included detailed design restrictions on the scale and height of buildings. The rules mandated brick exteriors, earth tones, varied ornamentation and materials, rooftops with terraces, parapets, and other decorative features. All metal elements had to be painted in black or dark green and reflective glass was prohibited. To complete the effect, the plan specified that all exterior illumination must come from lamps resembling those used in Central Park. In case builders had any doubt about the effect that the planners hoped to achieve, the design guidelines included pictures of elite New York neighborhoods such as Gramercy Park, Park Avenue, and Riverside Drive.[19]

BATTERY PARK CITY TODAY

Times architectural critic Herbert Muschamp wrote, "The New York City street is the social contract of modern democracy inscribed in space, the place where the Statue of Liberty's promise is fulfilled. In every street, public and private realms bump into one another a million times a minute. Thoughts explode. Emotions erupt. Inspiration comes. Despair is dispersed. Resolve is strengthened. Curiosity is rewarded."[20] But there is some debate about whether Battery Park City realizes or repudiates this social contract of the street. Boosters point out that Battery Park City (BPC) includes a public park and riverfront esplanade that attract New Yorkers from all over the island and visitors from all over the world.[21] At lunchtime the space is filled with office workers toting their brown bags and deli salads and evenings and weekends attract well-heeled visitors who frequent the outdoor summer concerts, the Museum of Jewish Heritage, and several high-end restaurants. For most commentators, Battery Park City is a poster child for the benefits of public–private partnership.[22] Not only is it a flourishing business and residential center, but it is also a kind of open-air museum featuring over a dozen works of public art, including stunning gardens and public spaces designed by prominent landscape artists. Initially Battery Park City appears to be a successful example of public-private collaboration to create high quality public amenities.

Although Battery Park City is scrupulously clean, safe, and aesthetically pleasing, the characteristic tensions of street life and diversity of other parks are lacking. In fact, notwithstanding the postcard-perfect view of the Statute of Liberty, the entire site seems eerily removed from New York.[23] Despite the design guidelines and architectural allusions to pre-war building practices, some have argued that Battery Park City feels more like a suburban gated community than a Park Avenue promenade.[24] Several architectural and design features contribute to this feeling. The site itself is protected by moat-like barriers and actual guardhouses. To one side is West Street, a 275 foot wide, ten lane, high-speed thoroughfare that functions as a formidable barrier to pedestrians.[25] The Hudson River and the harbor function as natural boundaries. This effect is intensified by a guardhouse that marks the south entrance. For anyone who has visited gated communities, the architecture will be immediately familiar.

There are other more subtle mechanisms that distinguish BPC from the surrounding areas. Despite the adoption of the grid system, the blocks in BPC are square, not rectangular as in the rest of the city. This undermines both the visual and kinesthetic continuity with lower Manhattan. According to Francis Russell, the historicist style of the residential buildings actually contributes to the disorienting alienating effect. Although the term Disneyfication has been overused, it captures the effect that is produced when the familiar iconography of "Main Street" is reproduced outside its geographical and historical context.[26] The multiple dimensions of urban life are distilled into a few characteristic signs that can be reproduced and isolated from the disturbing elements of actual cities. Through this strategy, Central Park-style lamps can suggest the atmosphere of Olmsted's great civic achievement while the staff at Battery Park City tells bag ladies to collect cans or rest elsewhere.

Although some visitors clearly appreciate the sanitized environment, others feel the sense of alienation and disorientation typical of the shopping mall. One commentator suggests that this sense of alienation results from the contradiction between the symbolic and functional dimensions of the architecture.[27] According to Christian Norberg-Schulz, the built environment usually tells the story of its own making. In stone and metal it expresses the historical circumstances under which it was produced. When the expressive dimension of a place disguises its own purpose and production, people will experience it cynically as a stage set rather than a real place.[28] This has happened in "historic" marketplaces like San Francisco's Cannery, Boston's Faneuil Hall, Baltimore's Harbor Place, and New York's South Street Seaport.[29] These places assert a sense of locality and history while eliminating diversity and substituting chain-store homogeneity. They trade on nostalgia for the sense of history and place that they obliterate.

Does Battery Park City (BPC) follow the same pattern of profiting from the nostalgia for a sanitized urban public life? Not exactly. First, despite the design guidelines, Battery Park City does not resemble existing New York neighborhoods but instead perfects a novel building genre: the luxury residential high-rise aesthetic. Second, Norberg-Schulz's theory of alienation presupposes a distinction between

Figure 7.1 Guardhouse, Battery Park City, New York. (Antonio Pietro Latini.)

authentic historical places and simulacra that is not viable. Many of the historic buildings admired today are composed of magnificent facades and modest interiors. Similarly, grand hotels often feature ornate lobbies and cramped, uniform rooms. Many of the turn-of-the-century landmarks that today inspire reproduction themselves imitated and modified styles from European capitals. Do these buildings insidiously hide the conditions of their own production or is display and simulation an intrinsic part of architectural meaning? Perhaps the label of authenticity is itself an indicator of nostalgia for an imagined past rather than something that meaningfully distinguishes older and newer places.

Although the appeal of Battery Park City is based on a certain dissimulation, the inauthenticity of some architectural references is not to blame. Instead, the operative dynamic is the way that public spaces and urbanity serve to mystify the essentially exclusive and elitist nature of the development. One example of this is the form that security and maintenance take in Battery Park City. The area is monitored by employees wearing uniforms of the Park Service. This gives the impression that they are public employees just like those in other city parks. In fact, they are paid by a private organization, the Battery Park City Parks Conservancy (public parks cannot afford Park Service employees and are maintained by workfare recipients).[30] BPC is usually promoted as a civic space, but at less cautious moments project developers acknowledge that the parks and gardens are essentially tools to increase the land's market value. Robert M. Serpico, president of the Battery Park City Parks Conservancy, explained the lavish budget for park maintenance: "I look at it as leveraged money. You're spending money to make money."[31] The interplay of public and private is not merely a matter of financing and governance, it is also a symbolic relationship whereby the site comes to connote a diversity and inclusivity that belies its true purpose.

The extensive work done on the psychology and semiotics of the shopping mall provides some clues about how this mystification works. The goal of sophisticated shopping mall designers is to promote consumption by stimulating a fantasy that masks the instrumental actions of buying and selling. This technique was pioneered in late nineteenth-century Europe when department stores began to stage fantastic scenes in order to stimulate mass consumption. Stores such as the Bon Marché in Paris would display exotic and flamboyant merchandise in exhibits reminiscent of the World Fairs.[32] The goal was to encourage the consumer to identify with a glamorous and lavish lifestyle rather than to focus on dollars and cents. The chaos and excess of the displays could promote a feeling of distraction or even hypnosis that might momentarily suspend the consumer's judgment and parsimony. A display might include hundreds of umbrellas that create a symphony of color. Another might be a harem scene with a profusion of hanging silk fabrics, lush carpets, oversized pillows, and bronze tea services. The variety and abundance were carefully calculated to disguise the underlying structure of the retail experience, which was increasingly based on standardized merchandise and prices. Today's malls have perfected this technique of using visual variation and sophisticated atmospherics in order to turn the instrumental experience of shopping into a spectacle, which incites consumer desires.[33]

The lavish gardens and public art of Battery Park City function in a similar way.[34] A pleasing aesthetic display creates an atmosphere that disguises the underlying function of the space. Take, for example, one of the most significant pieces of public art in Battery Park City, a "sculptural environment" by Ned Smyth. "The Upper Room" is a thirty-four by sixty-seven foot raised courtyard surrounded by colon-nades. The red pillars mark out the periphery of an open air, roofless platform, which is reminiscent of Roman or Greek ruins.[35] It also features mosaic decorations, a pergola, a long concrete table with a chess-board and twelve stools. The stylized and perhaps slightly ironic rendering of classical forms seems to suggest the agora of ancient Athens, the icon of public life and birthplace of democracy. Although the park does feature well-attended public events—mostly concerts and cultural performances—it is hardly an agora. Market stalls and street peddlers are carefully excluded and political gatherings are notably absent. The sculptural environment, located next to the Gateway Plaza, incites the fantasy of the *polis* as a way of mystifying the architecture of fear.

Does this mean that Battery Park City is a planning disaster? Not exactly. If the alternative is total decay, a gated community, or a strictly commercial space, then this fairly accessible waterfront Eden is a very appealing alternative. The view, the artwork, and the landscaping are quite striking and enrich the experience of New York. The point is not that Battery Park City is paradise or the inferno but instead that the particular configuration is the outcome of the struggle between com-mercial and public interests, popular and elite recreational styles. The public interest has been subordinated to the commercial interests, but this process has been obscured by the savvy design. Protecting existing public access and amenities is an on-going struggle but one that can only be fought effectively with a deeper understanding of the possibili-ties and meaning of public space.

WHAT LIES BENEATH

Battery Park City is the phoenix that emerged out of the bonfire of our idealism. Conspicuously missing in the mix of office space, restaurants, residences, and parkland is any subsidized housing. Recall that the Bat-tery Park City Authority (BPCA) originally planned to subsidize the construction of low- and middle-income housing through tax abate-ments and advantageous leases. This part of the project was abandoned during the slump of the 1970s. Although the BPCA did still provide tax abatements, these eventually went to reward commercial and luxury condo developers. The commitment to affordable housing, however, did not totally disappear.[36] Instead, city officials began to suggest that it made little economic sense to locate public housing on prime down-town real estate. Why should working-class people have river views

Figure 7.2 The Upper Room by Ned Smyth, Battery Park City, New York. (Courtesy of Project for Public Spaces.)

when the rich would pay a premium for this luxury and the extra revenue generated could be reinvested in public housing? According to a newspaper interview with BPCA president Sandy Frucher, minority leaders agreed that public dollars could be better spent in revitalizing deteriorating housing stock in Harlem and the Bronx.[37]

During the real estate boom of the 1980s when the financial success of BPC was secured, the Battery Park City Authority promised Governor Mario Cuomo that it would use surpluses to construct and renovate low-income housing in other parts of the city. Although this was a departure from the original vision of an economically and racially integrated lower Manhattan, it was a much-needed infusion of cash into the city's housing programs. The goal of the new plan was to renovate or build 60,000 units of subsidized housing by the late 1990s. In order to accomplish this, the state issued $400 million of bonds, to be paid off with Battery Park City revenues. The money was supposed to be used to renovate 24,000 units of subsidized housing. Battery Park City would also give New York an additional $600 million in direct payments for low-cost housing in other parts of the city.[38] According to the agreement signed by Mayor Edward Koch in 1989, the city could not use the $600 million dollar payment to cover the cost of regular city services; the money had to be earmarked for the construction and renovation of affordable housing.

Very little public housing was ever built. In the early 1990s, New York City used the money to renovate 1557 apartments in city-owned buildings in the South Bronx and Central Harlem. Under the administration of Democratic Mayor Dinkins, revenue from the Battery Park City project also financed a project to restore an additional 2128 units in the Bronx. But the rest of the money went into the city's general fund in order to cover deficits in operating expenses.

There has been some reciprocal finger pointing between the BPCA and city officials about who is to blame. The Giuliani administration argued that the revenue from Battery Park City was inadequate and unreliable because it was impossible to know in advance whether the project would be profitable in any given year. According to Jerilyn Perine, the commissioner of the Department of Housing Preservation and Development, this made it difficult to plan for large-scale construction projects or even to earmark the funds for a specific program.[39] The Giuliani administration claimed that it was not bound by the earlier agreement. Over the course of the 1990s, it cut the amount of money devoted to public housing by almost half and continued to use the Battery Park City funds for general city services, even at a time of budget surpluses.

The BPCA, on the other hand, claimed that as of 2000 it had provided New York City with $705 million, including $419 million specifically designated for subsidized housing.[40] Mr. Frucher, the former Battery Park City Authority president, called the city's diversion of the money "an abomination" and "a breach of faith."[41] This suggests that the problem with the public–private partnership fell squarely on the public side. The private developers paid their leases and the BPCA turned over the profits, but the Giuliani administration simply decided that public housing was not a priority.

The city could have made the argument that it was justified in using the profits from the Battery Park City project for the general fund because this windfall was actually money that was otherwise due the city as real estate taxes. If the city had simply sold the land to developers it would still have received significant revenue in the form of property taxes. But the city waived these taxes in order to jump-start the stalled project in the late 1970s. This becomes important if we are trying to decide whether the development was a savvy example of state capitalism or a subsidy for private developers and wealthy residents. The complexities of tax abatements make it extremely difficult to calculate the actual cost of the whole project. Even though Battery Park City is now a source of revenue for New York City, its actual impact on city finances is difficult to assess. Cost accounting is inaccurate because it includes the revenue from leases, subtracts operating expenses and debt service, and calls the difference profit. A more accurate assessment would need to take into account the costs incurred to the city in the form of revenue lost through tax abatements and tax-free municipal bonds. If these figures were on the ledger, the balance sheet would look very different.

The structure of the BPCA, a public benefit corporation, makes it possible to shield its finances from the vagaries of the city budget. This means that the parks located in Battery Park City are not affected by the fluctuations in tax revenues or shifting city priorities. The "public spaces" of Battery Park City are part of a distinctive and privileged economic zone, as is immediately clear from the first glance at the scrupulously manicured lawns and gardens. These high standards come at the cost of over four dollars per square foot, ten times what New York City, on average, spends on other parks.[42] Where does the lavish financing come from? Part comes from special assessments paid by property owners; in fact, one condominium association has sued the BPCA to lower its contribution.[43] The bulk of the funds, however, comes from the budget of the Authority itself. In 1998, for example, the BPCA collected $131 million in revenue; out of this $65 million was devoted to debt service and $21 million to operating expenses. According to Robert M. Serpico, one-quarter of the operating expenses goes to landscaping and maintenance of the public parks and promenades.[44] Unlike the Central Park Conservancy, which raises private donations to supplement tax revenue, the extra money spent on Battery Park City would otherwise become city revenue.

From one perspective, it looks like the city gets a well-maintained park without spending any tax money. This is the viewpoint that the BPCA and its supporters like to encourage. But another way of looking at it takes into account the fact that the entire 92 acre site is public land and all of the revenue it generates (after debt service) is public money. Yet over five million dollars of this money is devoted to beautifying the grounds of a single luxury neighborhood. One only need to compare Rockefeller Park in Battery Park City with a public park in the Bronx, say St. Mary's Park, to feel uneasy.

One weekday in July I walked through Rockefeller Park and noted that in addition to the manicured grounds and clean facilities there was a park attendant providing children with games, books, and activities. At first the crowd in the playground looked very diverse, until I realized that it was made up primarily of black and Latina women caring for white toddlers. In St. Mary's in the Bronx things look quite different. The Caribbean, Latina, and African-American women look after their own children but "(i)nstead of carefully tended flower beds…one finds a tired-looking place with an apparently unseeded lawn, green in some spots, brown in others…overflowing waste bins, 'rats as big as squirrels', 'long-abandoned sandboxes…knee deep with weeds'," no functioning drinking fountains, and a bathroom open a few days a month.[45]

The contrast sends the message that it is acceptable for public amenities in poor neighborhoods to be inadequate while public parks in rich neighborhoods are maintained in Versailles-like splendor. The problem with Battery Park City is not that the architecture or art is inauthentic, another manifestation of Disneyfication, but rather that it brings the troubling practice of differentiation and stratification to a new level of sophistication. Battery Park City, a project animated by the Federal Title VII project's goal of developing "good housing for all Americans without regard to race or creed" looks nothing like New York City.[46] It is an overwhelmingly wealthy, white enclave in an otherwise diverse city (see Table 7.1 and Table 7.2). Battery Park City is the spatialization of a new urban regime that has given up on values such as equity and integration and substituted economic efficiency and profitability. It is worth reflecting on the government's role in this process.

TABLE 7.1 Population Distribution by Race (1990 Census)[47]

	Battery Park City (%)	New York City (%)
White	80.64	43.41
Black	3.51	25.60
Asian	14.94	6.77
Hispanic	3.59	23.73
Other	.89	.48

TABLE 7.2 Household Income in Dollars[48]

	Battery Park City	New York City
Median	89,000	34,000
Mean	110,000	47,000

Walking along the Hudson River it is easy to forget that zones of safety like Battery Park City are deeply interlinked with the zones of danger that proliferate on their margins.[49] Battery Park City is a masterful example of the architecture of reassurance; it sends the signal that public life in the city is still rich and vibrant while undermining the political will necessary to maintain more than a few showplace public spaces. Why would a resident of Battery Park City vote for a city official who campaigned on a pledge to increase taxes to pay for public parks or police? After all, these things are generously funded out of assessments and revenues of the BPCA and impervious to shifting city government priorities. This makes it possible for residents to fund their own parks while supporting tax cuts that guarantee the deterioration of parks in less affluent parts of town. Jonathan Kozol calls this "another stage in the secession of the fortunate from common areas of shared democracy."[50]

Although the hybrid public–private structure of the Battery Park City Parks Conservancy makes it possible to provide an extremely high level of service and maintenance, it also opens up certain dilemmas. The BPCA is faced with conflicting mandates. It is torn between its civic responsibility to maintain an accessible, diverse, and desirable public place and its fiduciary responsibility to get top dollar for its assets, in this case the remaining waterfront parcels. The former would call for further investment in public housing or at least recreational and civic facilities for existing residents whereas the latter leads to additional luxury developments. This tension plays out every day, for example, in the conflict over an "interim" playing field in Battery Park. Whereas the residents of the small apartments wanted additional recreational facilities, the BPCA noted that such use would cost the city one hundred million dollars, the value of the land if fully developed. James Gill, the president of the BPCA, joked that forgoing this revenue would make it "the most expensive Little League field in the world."[51] The BPCA and residents reached a compromise that protected the field in exchange for more intensely developing other parcels, but it reveals why the language of profitability makes it difficult to defend nonpecuniary public priorities. Once each schoolyard, basketball court, and lawn is thought of in terms of millions of dollars of forgone revenue from commercial real estate development, then each of these alternative uses seems wasteful. Public or civic space will never seem like a rational choice from this perspective for the simple reason that such space does not generate a profit. Its benefits cannot easily be calculated in terms of dollars and cents.

The ballpark was protected because enough organized and politically powerful residents felt it was in their immediate self-interest to fight for recreational facilities for their community. This helps explain why other nonmarket based alternatives, say low-income housing, never became high priorities. Each of the 130,000 families on the waiting list for subsidized housing in New York City had a personal interest in access to an attractive, convenient, and safe development like Battery Park City, yet the chance of being placed in one of a few hundred low-rent units was extremely small. This made it less rational for any low-income individual to devote time and energy to mobilize on this issue. Geographically dispersed and without resources, those on the subsidized housing waiting-list had little chance of influencing politicians to include their needs in the final vision of Battery Park City.

THE BOUNDARY PROBLEM

The current ascendancy of market ideology makes it difficult to recognize the value of public space, however, this was not always the case. Central Park is a prime example of a public space that most people still agree should not be bought, sold, or fenced off for financial gain. Imagine for a moment a proposal to build a luxury condo development in Central Park and use the profits to finance park maintenance. I suspect that even today there would be an uproar. The attitude toward Central Park still reflects the influence of Frederick Olmsted, who envisioned the park as serving a civic purpose, uniting New Yorkers of different classes and neighborhoods by bringing them together in a natural area that temporarily erased urban hierarchies.[52] Olmsted was a reformer who had a transformative conception of public space. He insisted that Central Park should be neither a commercial fairground nor a highly manicured pleasure garden but instead a natural retreat for wholesome leisure activities.[53]

Today the public purpose that animated projects such as Central Park and Prospect Park in Brooklyn is disappearing. In the absence of a robust defense of public values, it is easy to fall back on the criteria of economic efficiency or profitability to make difficult decisions about collective resources and priorities. As David Bollier points out, in the age of market triumphalism the notion of a commonwealth—the idea that the demos should control collectively owned assets—seems anachronistic.[54] Although most people readily agree that markets are necessary in order to produce and distribute goods efficiently, they are less apt to be able to explain why the commons is also necessary. Bollier argues that the commons helps cultivate the "sense of trust and shared commitments that any society"—but especially a democratic one—must have.[55]

This sense of trust and shared commitment is undermined when a territory is carved up into zones of safety and zones of danger.[56] Creating and policing boundaries between these zones undermines the sense of citizenship that is crucial for a democratic polity. The "boundary problem" can be stated as follows: the creation of privileged places with special amenities, rules, and services for those inside the (metaphorical and sometimes literal) gates always affects (and often injures) those who are outside the gates.[57] This is true even when the boundary is not a private fence but a line separating different municipalities, sublocal governing bodies, or zones. This means that democratic processes can intensify the inequalities and exclusions that are usually associated with the term privatization.

Business Improvement Districts (BIDs) and Public Benefit Corporations such as the Battery Park City Authority are two different ways of creating such privileged zones by divesting city responsibilities to sublocal decision-making bodies.[58] Although they have often been successful in fostering a climate conducive to business and development, they are not necessarily the best mechanisms for solving urban problems. Due to their limited geographical boundaries and political mandate, they are only equipped to combat the signs, not the causes, of urban decay. Rather than reducing crime, poverty, and homelessness, they shift these problems to other less affluent, less organized neighborhoods. This intensifies existing disparities between neighborhoods in services and amenities. Finally, sublocal entities may encourage identification with a particular neighborhood at the expense of the city as a whole; this in turn may decrease support for solidaristic initiatives that aim to provide the same level of amenities and services for rich and poor neighborhoods.[59] Although NIMBYism (not-in-my-backyard) was the specter of the 1980s, the "only-in-my-backyard" attitude is also a threat. The legal form that this usually takes is (dis)incorporation: a large-scale luxury development or elite enclave decides to separate from the neighboring locality and incorporate as an independent municipality. This allows it autonomy in crucial matters of zoning and shields its tax base from the demands of less affluent neighbors.[60] When legal separation is impossible or undesirable, sublocal entities such as BIDs and homeowners' associations pursue similar goals.

Liberals often criticize these micro-municipalities and sublocal entities for exacerbating socioeconomic differentials, and conservatives celebrate them for increasing accountability by giving the citizen the power of consumer choice. The public choice school of economics has developed an influential argument that boundaries are beneficial because they make it possible for people to choose between different local communities based on various packages of services. According to

Charles Tiebout's seminal article "A Pure Theory of Local Expenditures," cities will be most efficient when they are forced to compete for residents.[61] Just as firms compete to attract customers by offering low prices or distinctive products, cities could attract residents by providing low taxation or premium amenities. As long as residents have the option of "exit" (relocation) they can exert sufficient pressure on cities to provide an advantageous mix of public goods.[62] With its emphasis on competition and choice, this theory has been very appealing to conservatives. It provides a convenient rationalization for people who choose to abandon diverse cities in favor of homogeneous enclaves. Furthermore, it implies that their flight actually improves cities by sending the necessary warning signals to local government.

One problem with Tiebout's model is that it assumes that families' decisions to relocate are based on different preferences when in fact they are often based on resources. Families cannot exercise consumer sovereignty if they do not have the money to relocate. It would be absurd to conclude that families living in dangerous, polluted areas with poor schools actually prefer these conditions. Economists have also pointed out that other assumptions underlying the model—that citizens are fully mobile, informed about the differences between cities, and that their decisions have no adverse impact on neighboring communities—are unrealistic.[63] Forty-five years after the publication of Tiebout's article we can use the historical record to judge whether the proliferation of micro-municipalities has improved city services. Even though some wealthy suburbs are certainly thriving, competition has done little to improve older industrial cities. Their residents have limited mobility and their municipal governments must try to provide services with revenue from a shrinking tax base.

The theory would predict that cities would improve amenities in order to attract affluent taxpayers, but in reality this is extremely difficult. Once the more affluent residents begin to leave, the city does not have the resources to provide even basic services let alone compete with wealthy suburbs. If the wealthiest people establish new communities, they avoid dealing with existing social problems such as poverty; moreover, they also escape responsibility for the social costs that are the side effects (externalities) of their own affluence, for example, polluted industrial sites and other environmental hazards.[64]

According to the theory of local expenditures, this problem would disappear as more needy citizens moved to the new suburbs to take advantage of the attractive amenities. But this is impossible for two related reasons. First, the affluent residents can erect contractual and statutory barriers protecting socioeconomic homogeneity.[65] By banning the construction of apartments and condos and mandating minimum lot and house sizes, localities effectively exclude those with moderate incomes. The political tactics work to intensify the effects of economic stratification. Simply put, the poor cannot exercise consumer choice if they do not have the resources to purchase products on the market. It is not that poor people do not want good schools, health care, or safe neighborhoods but simply that they do not have the money to buy them. Affluent families can move to the suburbs where they will receive a more attractive bundle of services; they enjoy parks with swimming pools and top-notch schools without having to share these things with others. The theory of public expenditures legitimizes the resulting inequalities in the name of choice and efficiency.

One consequence of this consumer-based approach to public goods is that it encourages people to think about parks, schools, and crime prevention as private privileges rather than public goods. This happened in San Marino, a wealthy suburb in Southern California. Lacy Park had always been accessible to the general public until Latino gardeners and nannies began to bring their own families, rather than just their young charges, to picnic on its lush lawns. Locals objected and the town council instituted a $12 weekend, nonresident user fee to reassert the exclusivity of the public park.[66] For residents of San Marino the park was a public place but for those who worked there during the week it was an exclusive, inaccessible retreat. This example once again highlights the difficulty in defining public and private space. Even though Lacy Park was owned by the government, not commodified, and freely accessible to residents (thereby meeting our definition of public space), the residents treated it as private property when they exercised their right to exclude outsiders. This raises the question of whether a space is public if it is surrounded by boundaries erected to exclude one's neighbors.

The $12 user fee is a particularly transparent illustration of such gatekeeping, but the same goal is often achieved with more subtle mechanisms. For example, Robert Moses used design features in order to keep working-class New Yorkers away from Jones Beach, the magnificent State Park on Long Island. At a time when only the affluent had private automobiles, he fought against a rail connection and built state-of-the-art parkway connections—with overpasses so low that buses could not access the beach.[67] Today affluent beach communities prevent their in-land neighbors from sharing what is supposedly a "public trust" by strictly enforcing resident-only parking and banning public transport.[68] These facially neutral restrictions are used to prevent stigmatized groups, usually minorities, from frequenting leisure spaces. Although minorities are no longer explicitly excluded from public accommodations (restaurants, parks, malls, etc.), there are still effective mechanisms that limit their access.

The presence or absence of public transportation is often a critical factor in establishing patterns of segregation.[69] One particularly tragic example of this deals with a shopping mall in Buffalo, New York. The No. 6 bus connected the inner city with the Walden Galleria, a suburban shopping mall. The owners of the mall refused to allow the transit authority to place a bus stop on mall property, presumably because they were not interested in the patronage of the predominately black and Latino inner-city residents. This meant that bus riders had to cross a seven-lane highway in order to reach mall property. In Buffalo, the snowiest city in the continental United States, crossing a highway on foot is particularly treacherous. On a cold day in December 1995, Cynthia Wiggins, a teen-aged mother employed at the mall, was killed by a dump truck while on her way to work.[70]

Many of these boundaries are invisible to those who are on the inside. After all, there are no signs at the beach saying "people of color not allowed." Instead, the barriers range from subtle architectural cues[71] to differential enforcement of rules to gates and guard towers.[72] One task of critical social theory is to identify these barriers so they can be acknowledged, debated, and, perhaps, dismantled. As long as groups live on different sides of enduring lines between zones of privilege and zones of deprivation, it will be difficult to sustain the communication and mutual recognition needed to act together as citizens. A dangerous situation emerges in which residents of cities and suburbs, affluent neighbors and poor ones, are bound together by economic ties and geographic proximity while separated by political and social barriers. One of the traditional purposes of public space was to provide a shared set of symbols, sites, and experiences that would counterbalance the centrifugal effect of private priorities. This goal becomes more elusive when the quality of public space is achieved by excluding pariah peoples.

DISCOVERING BATTERY PARK CITY

My first visit to Battery Park City forced me to think about the construction of zones of privilege in city space. One evening in the summer of 1998, I was walking in Historic Battery Park, a public park that was populated by homeless people lying on park benches. Continuing along the waterfront, I passed by a manned guardhouse and found myself in a different world that featured lush green lawns, manicured gardens, and striking sculptures along the promenades. Yuppie joggers and well-dressed workers strode by the yacht harbor. I wondered if I had accidentally been mistaken for a resident and allowed to enter some sort of urban gated community. But Battery Park City, as I soon discovered, was public property and three years later I returned to try to figure out why these two adjacent parks were so different.

During the hour or so that I strolled around Battery Park City on my second visit, I counted seven uniformed security guards patrolling an esplanade that was about a mile long. Several were on bicycle and others were equipped with modern, SUV-style patrol vehicles. The guards wore arm patches designating them as employees of the Parks Service. One explained to me that there were no homeless people because the area was carefully monitored by employees of the Battery Park City Authority, which he described as a city within a city with its own rules and regulations. If someone tried to lie down on one of the benches or caused other patrons to feel uncomfortable, that person would be asked to leave. The guard explained that the tenants of the luxury condos were demanding and insisted on high standards of cleanliness and safety.

Because the homeless transgress the line that separates public from private, they are a symbol of many people's anxieties about public space. The next chapter explores this issue of homelessness in more detail. Battery Park City, however, has solved this problem. During a half a dozen visits I never saw a homeless person but I did speak to Elmira, an elderly woman from Colombia who was collecting cans and bottles. She told me that the maintenance staff often told her to leave the area, insisting it was a private park. But she was skeptical of their claims and kept returning. Then she brought up the garbage problem in New York City (the city recycling program had just been severely curtailed because of budget problems). She was worried that so much garbage was being dumped in the oceans and the politicians did not care. By collecting bottles and cans, she was "helping herself and everyone else a little bit too." As she rinsed off her hands in the drinking fountain, she told me that she did not understand why the park staff did not want her to come back.

Where would someone who was asked to leave go? Right outside the confines of Battery Park City is Historic Battery Park. The security guard admitted, "it is a totally different world over there." Although the landscaping in Historic Battery Park is minimal, there is still something vital about the place. In the daytime, flocks of tourists pass through on their way to the ferry docks and street vendors sell snacks, drinks, and artwork. The summer afternoon that I observed the two adjacent parks there was a stark contrast in the racial diversity of the two spaces. Whereas Battery Park City was overwhelmingly white, Historical Battery Park was very diverse. In addition to tourists from Europe and Asia, there were kids from a Harlem summer camp playing jumprope and a group of half a dozen elderly African-American men gathered on benches telling stories.[73] At night, however, Historic Battery Park is much more desolate; grizzly bearded men and worn-out, unkempt women sit on a few old benches or lie on sparse grass.

In the next chapter, I will discuss the issue of homelessness in more detail and explore three theoretical rationales for criticizing the creation of homeless-free zones. This chapter tries to unravel the political story that explains how it is possible to segregate a public park into two zones, one a luxurious playland for upper-middle-class leisure and consumption and the other a rundown refuge for the downtrodden. Public–private partnerships between government and developers provide the flexibility necessary for such an arrangement. There are two New Yorks, right next to each other but separated by an invisible fence made up of unwritten rules and enforced by a private police force. Unable or unwilling to make the city safe for everyone, the solution is to separate it into zones of safety and zones of danger.

ENDNOTES

1. By the late 1960s only two of the seven miles of the Hudson waterfront remained devoted to shipping. M. Christine Boyer, *The City in Collective Memory: Its Historical Imagery and Architectural Entertainments* (Cambridge, MA: MIT Press, 1994), 452.
2. The 1969 Master Plan included 5,000,000 square feet of offices, 14,100 apartments, a 500,000 square foot shopping center, 27.5 acres of parks, schools, a library, fire and police stations, a health center, a cultural center, and a recreation center. David Gordon, *Battery Park City: Politics and Planning on the New York Waterfront* (New York and Amsterdam: Gordon and Breach, 1997), 33.
3. Martin Gottlieb, "Battery Park Project Reflects Changing City Priorities," *New York Times*, October 18, 1988, B1.
4. Dennis C. Muniak, "Housing New York: The Creation and Development of the Battery Park City Authority" in *Public Authorities and Public Policy: The Business of Government*, ed. Jerry Mitchell (New York: Praeger, 1992).
5. David Gordon, *Battery Park City.*
6. The Master Plan was a collaboration between Wallace K. Harrison and the firm of Conklin and Rossant.
7. Battery Park City Authority, *Battery Park City: Twenty-Five Years.* n.d.

8. For a brief description of the 1969 Master Plan (with drawings) see http://www.batteryparkcity.org/master_plan03.htm.

9. A. L. Huxtable, "Plan's Total Concept is Hailed," *New York Times*, April 17, 1969.

10. Gordon, *Battery Park City*, 51.

11. Gordon, *Battery Park City*, 52, 105.

12. Alexander Cooper Associates, *Battery Park City Draft Summary Report and 1979 Master Plan* (New York: Battery Park City Authority, 1979), 6.

13. Bernard J. Frieden and Lynne B. Sagalyn, *Downtown, Inc., How America Rebuilds Cities* (Cambridge, MA: MIT Press, 1989).

14. According to James Scott, high modernist planning often causes more harm than good because it substitutes the theoretical knowledge of centralized planners for the gradually acquired experience of local stakeholders. When backed by a strong state unchecked by processes of democratic accountability, centralized planning, he contends, often undermines the flexible, context-specific know-how necessary to make complex systems work. See *Seeing Like a State: How Certain Schemes to Improve the Human Condition Have Failed* (New Haven, CT: Yale University Press, 1998).

15. For an excellent discussion of the social consequences of modernist city planning see James Holston, *The Modernist City: An Anthropological Critique of Brasilia* (Chicago: University of Chicago Press, 1989). The classic argument outlining the benefits of traditional mixed-use neighborhoods is found in Jane Jacob's *The Death and Life of American Cities* (New York: Random House, 1961).

16. For information on the design of the Gateway Plaza, see http://www.lefrak.com/gateway.html.

17. Oscar Newman, *Defensible Space: Crime Prevention Through Urban Design* (New York: Collier, 1973). According to Newman, "'Defensible space' is a surrogate term for a range of mechanisms—real and symbolic barriers, strongly defined areas of influence, and improved opportunities for surveillance—that combine to bring an environment under the control of its residents." (3)

18. Gordon, *Battery Park City*, 74.

19. Francis P. Russell, "Battery Park City: An American Dream of Urbanism" in *Design Review: Challenging Urban Aesthetic Control*, eds. Brenda Case Scheer and Wolfgang Preiser (New York: Chapman and Hall, 1994).

20. Herbert Muschamp, "For Now Restricted Access: But What of the Future?" *New York Times*, October 7, 2001, sec. 2, 5.

21. J. M. Dixon, "The First 40 Years," *Progressive Architecture* (January 1993), 95–103.

22. According to Kirsten Hoffman, "A successful private-public development arrangement in which both sectors were flexible in accommodating the needs and practices of the other sector saved the Battery Park project, and made a significant contribution to the New York City waterfront." See "Waterfront Redevelopment as Urban Revitalization Tool: Boston's Waterfront Redevelopment Plan," *The Harvard Environmental Law Review* 23 (1999), 47. Paul Goldberg wrote, "Robert F. Wagner Park in Lower Manhattan is one of the finest public spaces the city has seen in at least a generation." See "A Small Park Proves That Size Isn't Everything," *New York Times*, November 24, 1996, sec. 2, 46, and *Architectural Digest* (November 1990), 143.

23. A newspaper article on Battery Park City (BPC) quoted Ms. Smith as saying, "This place is spectacular. I feel like I am in San Diego." Douglas Martin, "New Backyard in Lower Manhattan: Model Parks Along Hudson Prove Popular," *New York Times*, August 21, 1998, B1.

24. Abby Bussel, "Simulated City," *Progressive Architecture* (May 1994), 64–69.

25. Russell, "Battery Park City," 198–203.

26. See Michael Sorkin, ed., *Variations on a Theme Park: The New American City and the End of Public Space* (New York: Hill and Wang, 1992) and Karal Ann Marling, ed., *Designing Disney's Theme Parks: Architecture of Reassurance* (Montreal and Paris: Flammarion, 1997).

27. Russell, "Battery Park City," 198–203.

28. Christian Norberg-Schulz, *Architecture: Meaning and Place: Selected Essays* (New York: Rizzoli, 1988).

29. M. Christine Boyer, "Cities for Sale: Merchandising History at South Street Seaport," in ed. Michael Sorkin, *Variations on a Theme Park.*

30. In an otherwise well-researched book, David Gordon tries to refute charges of elitism by insisting that "the streets and parks are owned by the City, maintained by a public authority and policed by City park rangers" (*Battery Park City*, 113), when in fact the land is owned by a public benefit corporation (the BPCA) and maintained and policed by a private nonprofit, the Battery Park City Parks Conservancy, founded in 1989.

31. David Dunlap, "Filling in the Blanks at Battery Park City," *New York Times*, February 7, 1999, sec. 11, 1.

32. Rosalind H. Williams, *Mass Consumption in Late Nineteenth-Century France* (Berkeley: University of California Press, 1991), 67–69.

33. Margaret Crawford, "The World in a Shopping Mall," in ed. Michael Sorkin, *Variations on a Theme Park*, 3–30. See also eds. Chuihua Judy Chung, Jeffrey Inaba, Rem Koolhaas, and Sze Tsung Leong, *Harvard Design School Guide to Shopping* (Cologne: Taschen, 2001).

34. This same argument is made by Muschamp in "For Now, Restricted Access."

35. The catalogue description calls it a "contemporary reimagining of an Egyptian temple." See http://www.batteryparkcity.org/smyth.htm.

36. For an overview of the "social question," see Antonio Pietro Latini, *Battery Park City, New York: Principi e tecniche di Urban Design attraverso la storia di un modello* (Roma: Officina Edizioni, 2001), 276–298.

37. Gordon, *Battery Park City*, 91.

38. Eric Lipton, "Missing Element: Battery Park City Is Success Except Pledge to the Poor," *New York Times*, January 2, 2001, A1.

39. Quoted in Lipton, "Missing Element."

40. In the 1990s a few developers also chose to participate in a new 80–20 housing program that offered property tax abatements for developments that reserved twenty percent of units for families earning half the median income in New York City. Three hundred and twenty five affordable units have been built in Battery Park City so far (Lipton, "Missing Element"). David Gordon suggests that one reason that developers have shown interest in this program is the saturation of the luxury housing market. *Battery Park City*, 101.

41. Quoted in Lipton, "Missing Element." New York City spent $940 million on housing in 1991 and $535 million in 2000.

42. Douglas Martin, "New Backyard in Lower Manhattan: Model Parks Along Hudson Prove Popular (and Populous), *New York Times*, August 21, 1998, B1.

43. Gordon, *Battery Park City.*

44. David Dunlap, "Filling in the Blanks at Battery Park City," *New York Times*, February 7, 1999, sec. 11, 1.

45. Jonathan Kozol, *Amazing Grace: The Lives of Children and the Conscience of a Nation* (New York: Harper Perennial, 1996), 233–235. The quotations come from the article "St. Mary's Park," *New York Daily News*, July 18 and 19, 1994.

46. Although Battery Park City did not receive Title VII money (because the program was scaled back), it was inspired by the New City principles fostered by the legislation. See Mildred F. Schmertz, "Whatever Happened to Title VII," *Architectural Record* (December 1973), 96.

47. Richard Eric Boyers, *Cities Within a City: A Comparative Study of Roosevelt Island and Battery Park City, New York,* MA Thesis, Cornell University (1995), 41.

48. Boyers, *Cities Within a City,* 42.

49. See Aida Hozic, "Zoning or How to Govern (Cultural) Violence," *Cultural Values* 6: 1 (2002), 183–195.

50. Kozol, *Amazing Grace,* 109.

51. Cited in Dunlap, "Filling in the Blanks at Battery Park City."

52. See, generally, Galen Cranz, *The Politics of Park Design: A History of Urban Parks in America* (Cambridge, MA: MIT Press, 1982) and Roy Rosenzweig and Elizabeth Blackmar, *The Park and the People: A History of Central Park* (Ithaca, NY: Cornell University Press, 1992).

53. Thomas Bender, *Toward an Urban Vision: Ideas and Institutions in Nineteenth-Century America* (Lexington: University Press of Kentucky, 1975), 169–181; Geoffrey Blodgett, "Frederick Law Olmsted: Landscape Architecture as Conservative Reform," *Journal of American History* 62 (1976), 876–879.

54. David Bollier, *Silent Theft: The Private Plunder of Our Common Wealth* (New York and London: Routledge, 2002), 3.

55. Bollier, *Silent Theft,* 4.

56. Hozic, "Zoning or How to Govern (Cultural) Violence."

57. Richard Schragger, "The Limits of Localism," *Michigan Law Review* 100 (2001), 374. See also Richard Briffault, "Surveying Law and Borders: The Local Government Boundary Problem in Metropolitan Areas," *Stanford Law Review* 48 (1996), 1115–1171.

58. Richard Briffault, "The Rise of Sublocal Structures in Urban Governance," *Minnesota Law Review* 82 (December 1997), 503–534.

59. These are three of the four criticisms outlined in Briffault, "The Rise of Sublocal Structures in Urban Governance."

60. For a detailed description of this process in Los Angeles County, see Mike Davis, "Homegrown Revolution," *City of Quartz: Excavating the Future in Los Angeles* (New York: Vintage, 1992).

61. Charles Tiebout, "A Pure Theory of Local Expenditures," *Journal of Political Economy* 64 (1956), 416–434.

62. For an interesting critique of this position, see Gerald Frug, *City Making: Building Communities Without Walls* (Princeton, NJ: Princeton University Press, 1999).

63. For example, Truman F. Bewley, "A Critique of Tiebout's 'Theory of Local Public Expenditures'," *Econometrica* 49, no. 3 (1981), 713–740. For a survey of the extensive empirical literature on this topic, see Keith Dowding and Peter John, "Tiebout: A Survey of the Empirical Literature," *Urban Studies* 31, no. 4/5 (1994), 767–798.

64. Clayton Gillette, "Opting Out of Public Provision," *Denver University Law Review* 73 (1996), 1185–1219.

65. Bruce Hamilton, "Zoning and Property Taxation in a System of Local Governments," *Urban Studies* 12 (1975), 205–218. See also Frug, *City Making,* 168–170.

66. Mike Davis, *Magical Urbanism* (London and New York: Verso, 2000), 63.

67. Robert Caro, *The Power Broker: Robert Moses and the Fall of New York* (New York: Knopf, 1974), 318–319. See also Marshall Berman, *All That Is Solid Melts Into Air* (New York: Penguin, 1988).

68. Norimitsu Onishi, "Public Beach, Unspoiled by the Public," *New York Times,* August 24, 1996, 25 (about parking restrictions in Queens, New York). See, generally, Marc R. Poirier, "Environmental Justice and the Beach Access Movement of the 1970s in Connecticut and New Jersey: Stories of Property and Civil Rights," *Connecticut Law Review* 28 (1996), 719–811.

69. According to Benjamin Barber, many developers have agreements with municipal transportation systems not to permit stops near their malls. Trumbling Shopping Park in Connecticut fought to prevent Bridgeport Transit District buses from transporting passengers to the mall on Friday and Saturday nights. See "Civic Space," *Sprawl and Public Space: Redressing the Mall* (Cambridge, MA: MIT Press, 2002), 104. See also Jane Fritch, "Hanging Out with the Mall," *New York Times,* November 25, 1997.

70. Regina Austin, "Not Just For the Fun of It!: Governmental Restraints on Black Leisure, Social Inequality, and the Privatization of Public Space," *Southern California Law Review* (May 1998), 667–714.

71. See the chapter on "Fortress L.A." in Mike Davis, *City of Quartz.*

72. For example, the Morningside section of Miami voted to block off streets and put up two guard booths in order to prevent crime. This also restricted access to the attractive waterfront Morningside Park. John Lantigua, "Morningside Votes to Put Up Guard Booths," *Miami Herald,* July 3, 1997, B1. See also Peter Whoriskey, "Urban Barricades. What Do You Think? Gated Communities are Changing City Landscape," *Miami Herald,* August 17, 1997, L1.

73. During one afternoon visit (performed at 3 p.m. on a weekday in July 2002), the racial composition of Historic Battery Park was 42% black, 40% white, and 18% other (mostly Asian). Battery Park City was 83% white, 2% black (two women au pairs accompanying white children in the play area), 15% other. These figures do not include maintenance staff. The racial composition of Battery Park City may overestimate the black population because the Harlem summer camp (about 16 people) is included in the count.

8

HOMELESS-FREE ZONES: THREE CRITIQUES

LIVING IN PUBLIC

Homelessness is one of the most dramatic reminders of the interdependence of public and private. The homeless are those who have no private space, no dwelling where they can exercise sovereignty or perform the basic bodily functions that we think of as private: sleeping, washing, sexual activity, urinating, and defecating.[1]

Much of the aversion that people feel towards the homeless has to do with the transgression of these taboos about appropriate public behavior; many people feel disgust when they see someone sleeping, washing, or relieving themselves in a park or alley. Sometimes the aversion comes from the smell and appearance that is a logical consequence of the difficulty of maintaining hygiene when facilities for these activities are not accessible.[2]

When discussing the issue of homelessness, commentators often overlook the basic fact that "everything that is done has to be done somewhere."[3] If an individual has no private place to perform intimate bodily functions, these will have to be performed in public or they will not be performed at all. The latter, however, is not an option, because they are functions intrinsic to life itself. No amount of criminalization or harassment can prevent people from performing activities intrinsic to life itself, although policing strategies certainly can confine the homeless to certain limited zones of the city that are out of sight of the more affluent citizens.

This chapter explores the relationship between the experience of homelessness and the rules governing public and private space. In order to understand this topic, I contrast the positions taken by two

167

prominent political theorists, Jeremy Waldron and Robert Ellickson. Waldron argues that homelessness poses a serious problem for liberalism because it reveals the contradiction between two cherished liberal values: private property ownership and freedom. Insofar as the system of private ownership does not include everyone, then at least some individuals are denied the most basic freedom of having a place "where (they are) allowed to be."[4] Robert Ellickson also takes seriously the fact that the homeless must inhabit public spaces but concludes that cities should return to the old skid row model of social control. He argues that certain behaviors associated with transients, hobos, drunks, and homeless people should be confined to specific zones of the city so that other areas can enforce more rigorous quality of life ordinances against behaviors such as nonaggressive panhandling and bench sitting.

In this chapter I seek to expose the flaws in Ellickson's zoning strategy. His article is important because his proposal is a formalization and justification of the strategies currently being pursued (*de facto* if not *de jure*) in the United States today. In order to assess the problems with his proposal, I consider three lines of critique: the liberal, the romantic, and the democratic perspectives. Although all three can contribute to rethinking homelessness, the democratic critique is the most effective.

HOMELESS FREE ZONES

In "Controlling Chronic Misconduct in City Spaces," Robert Ellickson forcefully articulates a widely shared view.[5] He insists that "if city dwellers cannot enjoy a basic minimum of decorum in downtown public spaces, they will increasingly flee from these locations into cyberspace, suburban malls, and private walled communities."[6] He argues that the vitality of public space depends on the ability to exclude behavior that violates community norms of civility and appropriateness. Ellickson compares rules against non-aggressive panhandling to the rules of parliamentary procedure which function to ensure a small minority cannot disrupt the deliberation of a large group. Similarly, restrictions on certain behaviors enhance public spaces by eliminating the disturbances that cause others to flee into their homes or commercial spaces such as malls.

Ellickson advocates a system of zoning similar to the one that city governments use to restrict commercial development, but in this case panhandlers[7] rather than strip malls are the blight to be contained.[8] His schema is modeled on traffic lights with red signaling caution to the ordinary pedestrian, yellow, some caution, and green, a promise of safety.[9] Red zones would be composed of five percent of a city's downtown area; like the old skid rows, these areas would allow noise, public drunkenness, and prostitution. They would be "designed as safe harbors for people prone to engage in disorderly conduct." In yellow zones, ninety percent of downtown, chronic panhandling, bench squatting, and other "public nuisances" would be prohibited but some "flamboyant and eccentric conduct" would be allowed. In the remaining five percent of downtown, strict social controls would guarantee a sanitized environment for the most sensitive: the elderly, parents with toddlers, and unaccompanied children. In these areas, even mildly disruptive activities such as street performances, leafletting, and dog walking would be prohibited.

Although Ellickson's highly structured schema is put forth as a proposal, it is actually a codification of existing practices. As Mike Davis documents in *City of Quartz*, Los Angeles has long maintained the practice of excluding street people from the downtown core of Bunker Hill and containing them in a Skid Row along Fifth Street, east of Broadway.[10] The contrast between Battery Park City and Historic Battery Park provides another dramatic example. Most cities and small towns have de facto red light districts where prostitutes ply their trade without police interference. Times Square in New York City, until its recent and controversial rebirth as a tourist mecca, was the best known icon of zoned transgression.[11] No one who has ever taken the 4, 5, or 6 train from the Upper East Side of Manhattan to the Bronx could doubt that social zoning (segregation) is already well developed in the United States. In different zones, vastly different levels of government service, poverty, and policing prevail.

Ellickson argues that this informal system should be formalized and strengthened because chronic street nuisances are a serious harm that must be prevented. Whereas other proponents of strict laws against begging usually focus on aggressive panhandling, Ellickson targets nonaggressive panhandling and the menace of "chronic bench squatting." It seems clear that he would also object to camping in parks and public urination, which, although not aggressive or intimidating, are annoying to most people. For Ellickson, panhandling causes harm by disturbing the privacy of passersby. He suggests that people may fear violence, resent the fact that the panhandler thrusts his problems on the public rather than social service agencies, or become annoyed that someone has shirked his moral duty to be self-supporting. Chronic bench squatting, although less offensive than begging, may still disturb others by monopolizing space in prime tourist destinations; more likely, the smell or appearance of street people may discourage others from sharing public space.

A proponent of law and economics, Ellickson relies on a utilitarian calculation to advance his proposal. After quickly dismissing the alleged benefits of begging (such as the pleasures of altruism) and non-utilitarian considerations (religious legitimization of begging and constitutional protections) he concludes that the harms of street nuisances justify the zoning system. A full treatment of the issue, however, requires that we also consider possible harms that arise from the proposed zoning system.

This zoning proposal formalizes existing patterns of marginalization and exacerbates social problems. One consequence of confining street people to five percent of downtown (significantly less than one percent of a metropolitan area) is creating an extremely high concentration of the most troubled, impoverished people. Describing skid row in Los Angeles, Mike Davis noted that "by condensing the mass of desperate and helpless together in such a small space, and denying adequate housing, official policy has transformed skid row into probably the most dangerous ten square blocks in the world."[12] Under these conditions it seems particularly unlikely that those with problems such as alcohol or drug addiction will receive treatment. Those in recovery or fighting addiction will be in constant contact with dealers, dangers, and indulgers, making it almost impossible to stay clean. The environment seems guaranteed to exacerbate rather than solve the conditions that often cause and/or accompany homelessness not to mention the fact that, surrounded by the most poor, they will have little chance to receive the alms they rely on for survival.

Another problem is that these isolated areas are often far from adequate schools and medical facilities. One mother living in subsidized housing in the South Bronx suggested that life in a homeless shelter in Manhattan had been preferable because "at least we were close to better hospitals and we were in the middle of an area of normal life, normal activity and you could walk along Fifth Avenue and take your kids to Central Park."[13] But Ellickson is unconcerned with the plight of the homeless (he suggests they choose the lifestyle) and therefore sees the discomfort of seeing street people (rather than being one) as the serious harm.

It is dubious whether such discomfort should even be counted as a harm in the first place. My subjective discomfort is not necessarily a legitimate reason for prohibiting otherwise acceptable behavior. I may feel a certain class rage when I see a Prada bag, a Rolex watch, or a Lexus SUV but that does not mean that such objects are objectively harmful and should be banned or even excluded from ninety-five percent of the city center. Or to take a more serious example, major social transformations such as the civil rights movement would have been impossible if we had taken racist whites' feelings of resentment, hatred, and fear into account when deciding if equal treatment of minorities was legitimate.[14] Even utilitarians such as John Stuart Mill recognized that perverse outcomes would result if an evaluation of moral worth were based on a simple calculation of pleasure over pain. Instead, Mill suggested that we make decisions based on utility "in the largest sense, grounded on the permanent interests of man as a progressive being."[15]

Is the discomfort that some feel when confronted with a panhandler a serious harm? In a survey carried out by the New York Transit Authority, two-thirds of respondents had felt intimidated by panhandlers in the subway.[16] But it is possible that these fears are unwarranted or exaggerated.[17] In San Francisco, the police undertook a sting operation in which undercover cops sought to arrest homeless people engaged in aggressive, intimidating behavior. After a few days, the operation had to be called off because there were so few arrests.[18] Undoubtedly there are cases of street people, especially those who are mentally ill, who become aggressive and violent. The question is whether the overwhelming majority who sit passively next to a sign "will work for food," sell homeless advocacy newspapers, or call out "spare a smile" should be banned from ninety-five percent of downtown and all of the surrounding residential areas too. It is hard to imagine a law prohibiting all sales of stocks because some brokers have deceived or defrauded clients. Similarly, we should not prohibit peaceful bench squatting and panhandling because of isolated incidents of violence.

It is also debatable whether the discomfort that passersby feel when they see street people is a harm at all. It is possible to imagine that some people, say tourists from wealthy suburbs or small rural areas, may not have been aware of the extent of poverty and homelessness in cities. Upon seeing the suffering of someone sleeping on the street in brutal weather or going through a garbage can for food, they may feel shock, anger, and discomfort. Although these feelings are aroused by seeing the homeless person, the anger might actually be aimed at a government that cuts social welfare or an economy that cannot provide affordable housing. The "harm" of discomfort might also be a benefit, the benefit of becoming better informed about existing social conditions. This knowledge might make one a more informed citizen, better able to evaluate priorities on government programs. If a voter has never seen a homeless person urinate in the park, it is unlikely that she would recognize the necessity of using tax money to provide public toilets.

Although it is true that witnessing suffering can and should cause dismay, the moral consequences of this depend very much on whether we believe the harm comes from the suffering itself or from the act of witnessing. If the problem lies in the act of viewing, then it makes sense to banish those who suffer out of sight. But if the problem lies in the suffering itself, then the appropriate response is to take action to mitigate the suffering.

Public opinion on this issue is somewhat difficult to gauge. Although 53.5% of people in one survey agreed that the homeless are more violent and dangerous than other people, 85.8% also felt compassion for the homeless and/or felt anger that homelessness existed in a country as rich as the United States.[19] Large majorities favored prohibitions on panhandling and sleeping on the street (69%), but even more favored providing additional public housing (79%), drug treatment (83%), and higher wages (70%). These results reflect the deep ambivalence about homelessness in our society. Perhaps more systematic reflections on the political, moral, and legal implications of homelessness will help us evaluate these different strategies for solving the problem of homelessness. The next section looks at three different rationales for rejecting criminalization or marginalization of the homeless: the liberal, the romantic, and the democratic.

THE LIBERAL POSITION: HOMELESSNESS AND FREEDOM

In "Homelessness and the Issue of Freedom," Jeremy Waldron articulates a distinctively liberal case against the criminalization of homelessness. He argues that prohibiting certain behaviors associated with homelessness is an attack on the most cherished value of freedom. Waldron seeks to expose the tension between the universality of freedom and the unequal distribution of private property that prevents the enjoyment of freedom.

A liberal society is structured in order to protect the individual's prepolitical rights and for many theorists, private property is foremost among these rights. Property, insofar as it means control over access to land, is essential to our very existence. As embodied beings, everything we do has to be done somewhere. No one is free to perform an action unless there is some place where she can perform it.[20] The Wobblies claimed that the "right" to free speech was meaningless when they were prohibited from speaking or selling their newspapers on the downtown street corners where their target audience congregated. For the homeless, restrictions on living in public (e.g., bench squatting, sleeping in parks) are more burdensome, inasmuch as they prohibit basic life functions.

Waldron argues that if all property were private then the homeless would not have the right to be; everywhere they went they would be subject to arrest and expulsion for trespassing.[21] Most people who live in homes or apartments have access to many other spaces that they legitimately enter and share with others: workplaces, restaurants and bars, gyms, and shopping centers. Most of these places, however, are commercial establishments that are only accessible to paying guests. Although a charitable individual or group could give a homeless person a place to rest, sleep, or clean himself, most people and businesses tend to take the opposite tack.[22] As the ubiquitous "restrooms for customers only" signs suggest, even businesses that serve the general public still try to exclude the homeless.

According to Jeremy Waldron, "(the homeless) are allowed to be in our society only to the extent that our society is communist."[23] Waldron, a well-known liberal, is polemically making the point that a regime of private property rights becomes oppressive if there is no public or common property that the dispossessed can inhabit. Finally, it is tyrannical that the majority of North Americans who have the luxury of disposing over private space would also restrict public spaces so that over one million homeless people would have no place to perform primal human functions.[24]

Waldron's argument, unlike Ellickson's, does not rely on a utilitarian calculation. He does not try to weigh the suffering of a million homeless people against the annoyance and discomfort of the majority who bear witness. His argument is based on rights and is therefore meant to trump the (possibly selfish or tyrannical) desires of the majority.

A critic might object that the claim that "homelessness is unfreedom"[25] employs the term freedom in a manner inconsistent with the liberal tradition. For liberals, freedom is the ability to live as one chooses as long as one's actions do not impinge on the freedom of others. The role of government is to enforce the law and administer justice in order to guarantee individual freedom. Insofar as government is not responsible for an individual becoming homeless by destroying or expropriating his dwelling (actions that did occur on a large scale during the so-called urban renewal movement of the late 1960s and 1970s[26]), then no one's freedom has been violated. According to this critique, Waldron's position diverges from the typical liberal defense of negative freedom to embrace the more expansive and problematic notion of positive freedom, for example, that the government has the obligation to fight social inequalities in order to foster each individual's potential for autonomous thought and action.[27]

Despite Waldron's polemical invocation of "communism," his solution does not involve abandoning private property altogether. The one concrete proposal that he makes is that localities should provide public toilets. The guiding principle seems to be that a society based on exclusive private property is morally required to maintain a commons provisioned with adequate facilities and governed by fair rules. As long as the dispossessed can glean a living in the commons, then the system of private property is still legitimate.

Which rules are fair? Waldron distinguishes three categories of prohibitions on conduct in public places. The first category includes conduct that is illegal no matter where it happens, crimes like murder or rape. The second category is made up of restrictions specific to public places that "provide the basis of their commonality" and "can be justified as rules of fairness."[28] Interestingly, he chooses park curfews, jaywalking, and obstruction of the street as examples. The final category covers activities such as making love and urinating that are only illegal when they are performed in public. Waldron convincingly argues that such measures are intentionally adopted to drive street people out of public places in order to make such spaces feel safer and more attractive to other users. The problem, however, is how to distinguish between the second and the third categories. Which rules are fair bases for sharing public space and which are punitive restrictions aimed at the homeless? It is puzzling that Waldron uses park curfews as an example of fair rules when curfews are among the strategies most commonly employed to ensure that homeless people cannot sleep in parks. It would be perfectly acceptable to sleep in one's own garden, therefore it seems as though this restriction should be in category three.

There is a lot of disagreement about what rules are necessary to accommodate different users of public space. Should activities such as walking a dog off the leash, playing a radio, or skateboarding be allowed? These activities are permissible in private but restricted in public, yet it seems likely that these would count as reasonable restrictions designed to make sure that some people's use does not preclude the use of others. Why can park authorities prohibit these activities or restrict them to certain areas of the park? Some people, especially small children or the elderly, might be afraid of unleashed dogs; loud radios make it difficult to converse or read; fast-moving skateboards are hard to control and pose a risk to pedestrians. So park administrators often decide to create special zones where these otherwise legitimate activities are prohibited.

Communitarians who favor stricter rules governing conduct in public space argue that restrictions aimed at the homeless are fair measures designed to balance the interests of different users. In other words, they claim that prohibiting sleeping on a park bench is like prohibiting radio playing. One weakness of Waldron's otherwise well-constructed essay is that he does not explain how to distinguish between "fair rules" that make sure that some uses of public space don't foreclose others (category two) and unfair restrictions (category three). Ellickson believes that his own proposed rules zoning out chronic panhandling and bench squatting are similar to traffic lights or other rules of the road.

The only way that Waldron can distinguish between fair and unfair restrictions is to rely upon the argument that certain types of restrictions effectively prohibit bare biological life for homeless people. Waldron claims that society can legitimately regulate conduct in public space only insofar as such regulations do not make the most basic functions of life impossible for homeless people. Despite the rhetoric of freedom, Waldron's argument ultimately protects homeless people's right to bare life. Although this is undoubtedly an advance over the criminalization of basic life functions, it has certain unintended consequences. According to Leonard Feldman, "Paradoxically this reduction—of the homeless to bare, biological life and its compulsions (eating, sleeping, breathing)—reinstates and criminalizes the agency of the homeless."[29] If the rights of the homeless only extend to the basic functions of survival, then they have no legitimate grounds for turning down a shelter space or leaving the confines of an area like skid row. Once constructed as "bare life," rejecting any basic provision that ensures survival becomes a volitional and therefore punishable act. A homeless person who has access to a shelter, even one that is filthy, dangerous, or separates families, cannot claim to have no "place to be" and therefore has no right to live on the streets. As Feldman puts it, "Once the homeless have been reduced to bare life in the legal imagination, the shelter becomes a legitimized space of confinement and resistance to it becomes constitutionally punishable."[30]

The problem with Waldron's liberal position is that it does not actually provide the philosophical or legal basis for refuting Ellickson's zoning scheme. In response to Ellickson, Waldron makes a convincing argument that it is philosophically wrong to count moral distress as a harm for the purposes of utilitarian calculation. But nowhere does he specifically object to the idea of creating a small restrictive zone where "street nuisances" are permissible. As long as the homeless have some zone of the city where they can perform basic life functions, then their right to exist is not infringed. An analogy with property rights explains why this is so. Imagine that a poor family lives in a cockroach, lead paint infested apartment in a dangerous neighborhood. These unappealing living conditions do not give the family the right to move into the more sanitary, safe accommodations in an affluent neighboring suburb. Similarly, the fact that areas zoned for street sleeping and bench squatting are dangerous, squalid, and remote from basic facilities does not give the homeless the right to enter "yellow" or "green" areas of the city.

Waldron is convincing when he argues that as long as homelessness exists we must construct rules for public space that take the needs of street people into account. But a defense of bare life is not robust enough to combat the trend towards criminalization and punitive treatment. This became apparent in *Love v. City of Chicago* (1996), a case that challenged the city's policy of confiscating the belongings of homeless people. A group of homeless petitioners claimed that Chicago's policy of removing and destroying the property of homeless people during street cleaning violated the Fourth, Fifth, and Fourteenth Amendments of the United States Constitution. The federal district court judge who decided the case emphasized the voluntary nature of homelessness and concluded that the loss of private property was the unavoidable consequence of a lifestyle choice. In a later iteration of the same case, the court spelled out that the homeless petitioners lost their entitlement to protection because they accumulated possessions ("chairs, boxes, sofas, computers, keyboards, potted plants, box springs, and extra mattresses") beyond what was essential for physical survival.[31] According to the court, their rights only extended to a sleeping bag and several blankets, items indispensable for survival on the street. The minimalist defense of the right to bare life does not foster freedom.

Even cases that strike down punitive sanctions against the homeless sometimes unwittingly reinforce the same dehumanizing logic. In *Pottinger v. Miami* and *Johnson City v. the City of Dallas*, the courts concluded that statutes prohibiting sleeping in public constituted cruel and unusual punishment. Noting that Miami had some 6000 homeless people and only 700 shelter beds, the judge pointed out that the homeless "truly have nowhere to go." Under such circumstances, the judge concluded that the statute in question was unconstitutional because it effectively criminalized "involuntary status." But what if a homeless person chose to live on the streets because she did not want to be separated from her partner or pet, or feared theft or disease? According to this decision, if shelter existed, no matter how inadequate, living on the streets would be a lifestyle choice that was not constitutionally protected. This opens up the possibility of implementing schemes such as those proposed in New York City and Los Angeles to confine the homeless in fenced encampments on the periphery of town. In order to combat such proposals we need an approach to homelessness that treats the homeless as more than passive victims with a right to primal survival.

THE ROMANTIC AND THE DEMOCRATIC VIEWS

The romantic view of street life is much less common in theoretical and legal treatises but it does play a role, albeit a marginal one, in the popular imagination. The texts that provide a window into this perspective are often films, literature, and essays. By calling this approach romantic I do not mean to imply that it necessarily looks at the plight of the homeless through rose-colored glasses. Instead, I use the term romantic in a manner indebted to Northrop Frye.[32] According to Frye, a romance is a literary genre in which the hero goes through a series of adventures (often including much suffering) before ultimately triumphing over evil. Throughout the story, the viewer or reader is encouraged to identify with the values of the hero. The romantic view treats homeless people as heroic individuals, urban nomads or victims-turned-rebels, who symbolize a principled rejection of the materialistic values and competitive ethos that dominate capitalist society. This picture first emerged in the early twentieth century in IWW folk songs such as "Mysteries of a Hobo's Life" in which leaving a job and riding the rails was depicted as an act of rebellion against abusive labor practices.[33] Although the figure of the hobo is often assimilated to the "bum" or "derelict," it can also signify an alternative set of values that provides the basis of critique or insight into the corruption of capitalist society.

In the Great Depression, films and stories sometimes had itinerant workers, homeless families, or hobos as protagonists. Perhaps the most famous and critically acclaimed example was John Ford's film of John Steinbeck's *The Grapes of Wrath* (1940). The film and novel tell the story of the Joads, a family of sharecroppers that is turned off its farm and seeks work in California only to have their dreams of plenty destroyed by the crushing poverty of the migrant camps. Throughout the narrative, the hero Tom Joad, an ex-convict and itinerant worker, challenges the policies and practices that seem designed to dehumanize and defeat the common man's struggle for survival and dignity. The film, unlike the book, tries to provide a happy ending. Driving out of camp in their old jalopy, Ma Joad insists that the poor will ultimately be triumphant. But nothing in the film suggests that her optimism is likely to be rewarded.

The Grapes of Wrath is not really an example of the genre of romance because the ending is ambivalent at best. The audience identifies with the values of the hero as he fights the dragon of soulless agribusiness, but the more cynical viewers might note that the dragon is not slain in the end. Although the film clearly ennobles the struggle of the Joads to maintain integrity and morality in the face of suffering and exploitation, it does not valorize "homelessness" or "nomadism" in the same way that poststructuralist theorists such as Deleuze and Guatarri do. The film mourns the loss of a kind of American pastoralism, where families were rooted to each other and to the land. The film captures the transition from agrarian America to a rootless society with new values and new heroes. At the beginning of the film, John Casey, the preacher, is traveling around the abandoned countryside alone, sleeping in the open. An outsider and hobo, he is welcomed by the Joads on their trip out West. He immediately recognizes that the family values of the old world have become anachronistic and is the first to fight for a more class-based solidarity. For Tom and others, Casey becomes a Christ figure and a source of enlightenment and inspiration.

This "romantic" image of the marginal and dispossessed as the carriers of authentic American values emerged in the Great Depression. It was rediscovered and transformed in the 1960s when books such as Jack Kerouac's *On the Road* valorized a certain kind of urban nomadism as the realization of human freedom. This equation of homelessness or nomadism with freedom finds echoes today in the work of political theorist Thomas Dumm, who wrote, "If the material conditions that enable…any one of us to be homeless disappear, the spiritual possibility of homelessness as the open road, as a possible path of freedom, disappears as well."[34] Another recent example is French filmmaker Agnes Varda's *The Gleaners and I* (2001). Varda takes Jean-Francois Millet's famous painting *Les Glaneuses* (1867) as inspiration to explore the survival strategies of modern-day urban and rural gleaners who gather food and objects left behind after the harvest or in the garbage. Her subjects include the rural poor and urban homeless as well as artists and resourceful bohemians who find freedom at the margins. Living on the street is figured as a refuge from the constraints of bourgeois society and a source of alternative values and meanings.

The romantic view of the homeless is a useful corrective to the more common depiction of the homeless as victims or threats. It humanizes the homeless person by emphasizing his agency when confronting structural constraints beyond his control. From the romantic point of view, the hobo or migrant is not someone who failed in terms of bourgeois standards of success but someone who has embraced a different set of values even at great material cost to himself. The romantic perspective makes it possible to see nomadism and gleaning as heterotopic practices,[35] which create spaces on the margins of society that preserve a way of thinking and living differently.

The problem with the romantic perspective is that it aestheticizes homelessness. This has two disadvantages. First of all, most homeless people are not urban nomads who choose life on the street because of the freedom that it provides.[36] To the degree that this understanding of the problem came to predominate it could probably lead to counterproductive government policies. Second, the romantic view of homelessness does not provide convincing reasons to elicit the support of those who do not share the antisystem values. If homelessness is framed as the consequence of the existing social and economic structures, then it is possible to argue that it is a requirement of justice that those who disproportionately benefit from those structures help those who disproportionately suffer. If homelessness is perceived as a lifestyle choice, however, it is unclear why taxpayers should subsidize this choice by providing safe shelters, facilities, or outreach programs. Many voters believe that they should not be obliged to support someone who chooses not to work if he or she is capable of doing so. Although the romantic view does not adequately explain why others have an obligation to aid the homeless or resist criminalization, it does make an important contribution by counteracting the tendency to dehumanize the homeless and view them as abject.

Both Waldron's liberal perspective and romantic perspective offer arguments against the criminalization of homelessness, but neither one provides a complete critique of the zoning strategy that is employed today in areas like Battery Park City. A proponent of zoning could always argue that the homeless could subsist or even create their hobo heterotopia in nearby Historic Battery Park where few unwilling New Yorkers would be forced to see them. The difficulty with this solution is that it has consequences for democratic decision making. How can citizens make informed decisions about social programs if they don't grasp the full extent of social problems? If bench squatting and nonaggressive panhandling are confined to five percent of downtown (and excluded from residential areas) then most people will probably never see a homeless person. The suffering caused by homelessness and extreme poverty will not go away but most citizens will simply become less aware of it. Or their awareness will not come through the personal experience of occasionally chatting with the woman selling the *Street Sheet* but rather through news reports of sporadic acts of extreme violence that take place in forbidden, terrifying, unfamiliar parts of the city. The racial and socioeconomic segregation of American cities is already far advanced and exacerbating it through new antivagrancy laws will only intensify the tendency of different groups to live in wholly separate and unequal worlds.

Of course, citizens can learn about the phenomenon of homelessness through newspaper articles that document the growing numbers of families seeking shelter or perhaps an occasional piece featuring some individual's hard luck story. But the reality is that even a well-researched fact piece or sympathetic feature does very little to overcome the enormous gap between each person's individual experience and the abstract remote reality that happens elsewhere. This is particularly true of international news, where suffering and atrocities happen in places so far away that it is impossible, for most people, to identify with the victims. The deaths of thousands of remote foreigners seldom elicit even passing interest. Restricting street people to danger zones on the wrong side of town turns fellow citizens into the equivalent of Ethiopian famine victims or Liberian child soldiers. They become slightly exotic, unfamiliar, and easy to dismiss from individual consciousness and policy-making priorities.

Zoning is motivated by the desire to create a veil of ignorance that is the reverse of the one developed by moral philosopher John Rawls. Rather than imagining that we do not know our individual characteristics and life situation in order to develop principles of justice, this veil of ignorance ensures that we make political decisions without ever having to think about how they might affect differently situated persons. Reverend Overall, a pastor serving a poor congregation in the Bronx, made a similar point when commenting on the ban on panhandling in the New York subway. She rejected the MTA's (Metropolitan Transit Authority) suggestion of giving to organized charities instead of individuals, explaining, "I don't think that the point is charity but self-protection. I mean emotional self-protection. Looking into the eyes of a poor person is upsetting because normal people have a conscience. Touching the beggar's hand, meeting his gaze, makes a connection. It locks you in. It makes it hard to sleep, or hard to pray. If that happened, you might be profoundly changed, the way that Paul was changed. Writing a check to the Red Cross or some other charity can't do that. What this card is really telling us is 'Do not open up your heart. Don't take a chance! Send a check and we will do the touching for you.' That is why I think it is sacrilegious."[37]

Of course, there is no guarantee that encountering a panhandler on the street will elicit sympathy. As Ellickson points out, many encounters evoke judgment and scorn rather than compassion. Democracy does not guarantee that society will advance specific values such as the recognition and celebration of difference or heterogeneity. Some people, perhaps the majority, may feel nothing more than aversion when confronted with a panhandler or bench squatter. They may choose neither to give alms nor to support programs to provide subsidized housing or shelters. Nevertheless, as a society we cannot make decisions about how to solve the problem of homelessness if most citizens are unaware of the nature and scope of the problem. This means that the solutions we adopt should not permanently block the flow of relevant information.

Some might say that citizens have decided how they want to deal with the problem of homelessness and the solution that they have chosen is criminalization. The rationale behind this policy is that individuals choose homelessness over less appealing options such as working low-wage jobs, therefore laws against panhandling and sleeping in parks "solve" the problem of homelessness by providing a disincentive for choosing this lifestyle. It is beyond the scope of this essay to try to resolve the debate about whether homelessness is a choice, but it seems fairly uncontroversial to assume that for some significant proportion, for example, the 12,800 homeless children in New York City, it is not voluntary.[38] Furthermore, a recent report put out by the National Coalition for the Homeless studied 80 rural and urban communities in 37 states and found that 100% lacked an adequate number of shelter beds to meet demand.[39] Regardless of the precise causes of homelessness, a zoning system like the one proposed by Ellickson is inconsistent with liberal-democratic principles. Today many political theorists argue that democracy is more than a set of procedures; it is also a culture of equality and solidarity. Although I am sympathetic to this view, the "democratic" argument against the criminalization of homelessness does not depend on this more expansive definition. The case can also be made by relying on the mainstream definition of representative democracy articulated by pluralist Robert Dahl.

Democracy is not simply government based on majority rule. In *Democracy and Its Critics*, Robert Dahl argues that there are several procedural elements that must be in place before a decision-making process is democratic. The first condition is what he calls "*effective par-*

ticipation." Citizens must have an adequate opportunity to express their preferences about the final outcome, place items on the agenda, and convince others of their views. They must also have the same impact on the outcome as other citizens at the decisive stage. Another crucial precondition is the *"opportunity for informed choice."*[40] Each citizen must be able to gather information on how a given decision affects her interests and the public good. From this principle, Dahl derives well-established rights such as freedom of speech and the press. But the principle of informed choice is also a reason to be skeptical of other government policies that would leave citizens ignorant about the basic structures of society and the consequences of their own decisions. The democratic case against zoning is that it effectively shields citizens from crucial knowledge about the way their society and economy work. The democratic perspective provides an important supplement to the liberal, rights-based view that the government cannot criminalize the basic life functions of a certain class of people.

A critic might respond that the democratic argument instrumentalizes the homeless as carriers of a certain social critique rather than treating them as human beings with a right to housing. Or, to put the objection more starkly, there is a danger of turning the homeless into a spectacle of pathos. Insofar as the privileged viewer actually experiences a certain pleasure in viewing the suffering of others, the encounter simply reinforces the distance between subject and object, privileged viewer and abject. Furthermore, if the homeless person's right to inhabit public space is justified exclusively in terms of the pedagogical benefit it gives to the middle classes, then it is precarious indeed.

The homeless are not simply a text for citizen-readers to learn from and interpret. They are political agents who initiate and take part in a societal conversation about poverty, marginalization, work, and responsibility, both individual and collective. The ubiquitous homeless advocacy newspapers capture this position well; they provide street people with a source of income while also describing the experience of homelessness through poetry and prose and translating this experience into a political program.

It is worth emphasizing that the preferred solution to homelessness is not legalizing begging but providing more housing. The right to housing and the right to inhabit public space, however, are not mutually exclusive and the latter may help strengthen the former.[41] I support redistributive programs, including public housing, but I also recognize that the amount of funding devoted to social programs depends on the priorities of citizens and their representatives. A theory of justice may provide a compelling reason in favor of redistributive programs, but it does not explain why citizens should take the standpoint of justice rather than self-interest. To examine a question from the standpoint of the other person requires more than mere reflection or mere feeling. It requires an act of imagination.[42] To imagine the standpoint of someone else is difficult when they are made invisible by laws that are meant to exclude them from the city.

The democratic argument strengthens the legal construction of the homeless as political agents, participants in a certain kind of civic conversation, rather than treating them as criminals or recipients of government largesse. When federal courts have struck down anti-homeless statutes or policing tactics, they have done so based on two different rationales. Some courts have found that statutes that criminalize the status of homelessness violate the cruel and unusual punishment clause of the Eighth Amendment.[43] As Leonard Feldman pointed out, this outcome may be laudable but it also unwittingly reinforces the legal construction of the homeless as bare life, for example, deserving of pity but bereft of agency and humanity. Looking at a different set of court cases, however, reveals another legal construction of homelessness, one more akin to the democratic perspective. The jurisprudence protecting panhandling as political speech treats the homeless as citizens and bearers of a legitimate social critique.[44] In cases such as *Blair v. Shanahan* (1991) and *Loper v. New York City Police Department* (1992), the federal courts have held that "begging gives the speaker an opportunity to spread his views and ideas on, among other things, the way our society treats its poor and disenfranchised."[45] The homeless plaintiffs in these cases were not portrayed merely as victims but also as citizens with an important message to communicate.

Those who reject panhandlers' First Amendment claims argue that begging is conduct not speech.[46] The courts have faced this issue in the past when they have had to decide whether flag burning or wearing symbolic clothing constituted protected expressive conduct or prohibitable behavior. In *Spence v. Washington* (1974), the court established a two-part test to decide whether conduct contains enough communicative content to invite constitutional protection. First, there must be the intent to convey a particularized message. Second, there must be sufficient likelihood that it will be understood.[47]

Panhandlers rely on a variety of communicative strategies. Some "sell" a homeless advocacy newspaper filled with well-researched articles and editorials; others display a simple sign such as the one I saw the other day stating, "Lost my lease to co-op conversion. Please help"; some simply chant, "Spare some change." Are these forms of speech?

Are they saying something that we need to hear? Do these three examples meet the criteria outlined in the Spence test? The person distributing the *Street Sheet* most obviously conveys a very clearly articulated and easily comprehensible critique.[48] The cardboard sign also makes a definite political statement and most New Yorkers would understand that it is trying to show the consequences of using condo and co-op conversion to make more profit from rent-controlled apartments. Robert Teir has argued that it is possible to prohibit begging (the solicitation of money) while still allowing discussions about poverty or criticisms of existing welfare provisions. But to allow a sign saying "Lost my lease to co-op conversion" while prohibiting "Help me" is to eviscerate the core of the message. The homeless person is not primarily making an abstract point about real estate speculation but rather drawing attention to the painful personal costs. The communicative goal of the sign-holder (and the person repeating, "Spare some change?") is a plea for individual help. If the goal is to prevent violence and intimidation, it would make more sense, as the court in *Loper* suggested, to enforce existing laws against aggressive behavior (e.g., it is already illegal to intimidate someone into giving money, to follow them, or to block their passage on the street) without targeting peaceful speech.

In a culture of individualism and achievement, many people, perhaps the majority, may be unsympathetic to the homeless person's message, regardless of the manner in which it is communicated. But if there is one basic rule of democratic governance, it is that the minority has a fair chance to become the majority. If the homeless do not have the opportunity to be visible in public space, if they cannot communicate their needs, then there is no chance that they will convince others to make the social changes necessary to meet these needs.

CONCLUSION: THE EYES OF THE POOR

In *Paris Spleen* (1869) Baudelaire included a short vignette called "The Eyes of the Poor." The narrator of the prose poem recounts the events of the previous day in order to explain to his beloved why he "hates" her. After spending the afternoon together, feeling "two souls would be as one," the couple rested in a café situated on a boulevard that was "already displaying uncompleted splendor." The café was "dazzling," a celebration of "gluttony," "lighted with all its might the blinding whiteness of the walls, the expanse of mirrors, the gold cornices and moldings...." Outside this splendid palace stood three figures, a man and his two small children "dressed in rags." The narrator was moved by the "six eyes" staring admiringly at the splendor. He explains to his beloved, "Not only was I touched by this family of eyes, but I was even a little ashamed of our glasses and decanters too big for our thirst. I turned my eyes to look into yours, dear love, to read my thoughts in them; and as I plunged my eyes into your eyes, home of Caprice and governed by the Moon, you said: 'Those people are insufferable with their great saucer eyes. Can't you tell the proprietor to send them away?'"[49]

Marshall Berman has described this encounter as one of the primal scenes of modernity. "The Eyes of the Poor" captures the tension between opposites, rich and poor, sympathy and contempt, played out against the background of the changing metropolis. In this period, Paris was undergoing major renovations to transform its crowded medieval quarters and confusing streets into a modern capital city with wide, luxurious promenades. Under the guidance of Baron Haussmann, the project was meant to improve the flow of traffic and make workers' neighborhoods more accessible to the military. The restructuring that opened up space for brilliant new street cafés also destroyed neighborhoods, displacing thousands of poor people from the center of Paris. These new promenades brought people together and made the contradictions of urban life more apparent. For Berman, these ur-encounters, between the petit-bourgeois clerk and the soldier-aristocrat or the lovers and the poor family, were manifestations of a latent class struggle that would come to shape the urban environment and polity.[50]

Today's metropolis is designed to limit the possibility of such encounters. Those dressed in rags stay in areas like Historic Battery Park while their affluent counterparts promenade along the riverfront in Battery Park City. Lovers seldom need to confront the unpleasant discovery that one partner feels sympathy while the other feels only disgust when faced with the eyes of the poor. We have built ourselves a Garden of Eden and sacrificed the knowledge of good and evil.

ENDNOTES

1. The definition of homelessness most commonly employed is the definition adopted by the 1987 McKinney Homeless Assistance Act: "(a homeless person is) an individual who lacks a fixed, regular, adequate nighttime residence or an individual who has a primary nighttime residence that is a) a supervised publicly or privately operated shelter designed to provide temporary living accommodation; b) a public or private place that provides temporary residence for individuals intended to be institutionalized; c) a public or private place not designed for or ordinarily used as regular sleeping accommodations for human beings."

2. New York City, for example, has no public toilets. Most of the toilets in the subway were closed in 1982 and only 138 out of 266 "comfort stations" in parks were open. Reported in the *New York Times*, May 30, 1992, 22. As of summer 2002, no public toilets had been opened in New York City. In some cases, planners intentionally do not provide public toilets because they feel that such facilities will attract homeless people and other users of public space can use "semi-public" toilets in restaurants and shops. See Mike Davis, *City of Quartz* (New York: Vintage 1992), 232–233.
3. Jeremy Waldron, "Homelessness and the Issue of Freedom," *UCLA Law Review* (December 1991), 296.
4. Waldron, "Homelessness and the Issue of Freedom," 299.
5. Other examples of the position include Robert Teir, "Maintaining Safety and Civility in Public Spaces: A Constitutional Approach to Aggressive Begging," *Louisiana Law Review* 54 (1993), 285–338 and Williams L. Mitchell, "'Secondary Effects' Analysis: A Balanced Approach to the Problem of Prohibitions on Aggressive Panhandling," *University of Baltimore Law Review* 24 (1995).
6. Robert Ellickson, "Controlling Chronic Misconduct in City Spaces: Of Panhandlers, Skid Rows, and Public-Space Zoning," *Yale Law Journal* 105 (March 1996), 1172.
7. Ellickson resists using the term homeless to describe the population targeted by his proposed ordinance. He suggests that many panhandlers are not homeless and few of the most disadvantaged actually beg. The empirical evidence on this is mixed. In the footnotes he cites a study done in Manhattan that found that 81% of panhandlers surveyed had been homeless the night before. A study of homeless people in Chicago found that 20.6% had received handouts during the prior month. See Peter Rossi, *Down and Out in America: The Origins of Homelessness* (Chicago: University of Chicago Press, 1989). This article deals both with the homeless (people who must sleep on the street or in shelters), street people (people who spend most of their time on the street because of inadequate private space or who work in the informal economy on the streets, e.g., collecting cans), and panhandlers (people who support themselves by requesting alms). When it seems appropriate I use the terms interchangeably.
8. Ellickson, "Controlling Chronic Misconduct in City Spaces," 1172.
9. Ellickson, "Controlling Chronic Misconduct in City Spaces," 1120.
10. Mike Davis, *City of Quartz*, 232.
11. Samuel R. Delany, *Times Square Red, Times Square Blue* (New York: New York University Press, 1999).
12. Davis, *City of Quartz*, 232–233. In a footnote he adds that at one point skid row had a murder rate of one per week.
13. Jonathan Kozol, *Amazing Grace: The Lives of Children and the Conscience of a Nation* (New York: Harper Perennial, 1995), 52. See also Jonathan Kozol, *Rachel and Her Children: Homeless Families in America* (New York: Crown, 1988).
14. See also Jeremy Waldron, "Homelessness and Community," *University of Toronto Law Journal* 50 (2000).
15. Cited in Waldron, "Homelessness and Community," 381. See also Jeremy Waldron, "Mill and the Value of Moral Distress," *Political Studies* 35, (1987), 410–423.
16. Evidence presented by Peter Harris in *Young v. New York Transit Authority*, United States Circuit Court of Appeals, 903 F.2d 146; 1990 U.S. at 10.
17. See David Snow and Leon Anderson, *Down on Their Luck: A Study of Homeless Streetpeople* (Berkeley: University of California Press, 1993).
18. National Law Center on Homelessness and Poverty, report entitled "The Right to Remain Nowhere" (1993). On the issue of homelessness and criminality more generally, studies have found that the homeless do commit more crimes than the general population but most of these crimes are nonviolent offenses that are part of survival strategies, for example, trespassing in abandoned buildings or violating "quality of life" ordinances. See David M. Smith, "A Theoretical and Legal Challenge to Homeless Criminalization as Public Policy," *Yale Law and Policy Review* 12 (1994), 487–517.

19. Cited in Wes Daniels, "'Derelicts,' Recurring Misfortune, Economic Hard Times and Lifestyle Choices: Judicial Images of Homeless Litigants and Implications for Legal Advocates," *Buffalo Law Review* 45 (1997), 720.
20. Waldron, "Homelessness and the Issue of Freedom," 296.
21. Waldron, "Homelessness and the Issue of Freedom."
22. New York City filed suit against the Fifth Avenue Presbyterian Church, trying to prevent the church from allowing homeless people to sleep on the steps ("Ruling Favors Churches Camp," *New York Times*, June 14, 2002).
23. Waldron, "Homelessness and the Issue of Freedom," 301.
24. Estimates of the number of homeless vary widely, from 250,000 to over 2,000,000. Part of the discrepancy depends on whether you count the number of homeless on any given night or the total number of people who were homeless at any point in a given year. Eighty percent of those registered in New York City shelters were categorized as "transitional" (needed shelter for a few weeks and did not return). The dramatic increase in housing prices in the 1990s, however, exacerbated the problem. In New York City alone there are 130,000 families on the waiting list for subsidized housing. (Source: "Housing a Growing City," report issued by the Coalition for the Homeless (2000); based on data from the Housing and Vacancy Survey of the United States Census Bureau.) In 2002 the number of homeless families increased by 22%; on a single day in June (usually low season for shelters) there were 33,840 people in the New York City shelter system, the highest figure since the city started tracking homelessness figures in the 1980s. (Source: "Bloomberg Plans More Housing for the Homeless: First Increase Since '95," *New York Times*, June 18, 2002, 1.) The lack of shelter beds and lack of affordable housing are among the reasons why so many people are forced to eke out an existence on streets and in parks. I am not making an argument about the controversial issue of what causes homelessness, whether it is individual pathology, addiction, deindustrialization, deinstitutionalization, changing family structure, or lack of government programs. My point is simply that many people do not have permanent shelter and given that temporary shelter is often unavailable, homelessness is the inevitable result. To explain why so many people in industrialized countries do not have permanent shelter would involve another study.
25. Waldron, "Homelessness and the Issue of Freedom," 306.
26. Federally funded urban renewal programs based on a strategy of "downtown revitalization" led to the destruction of 400,000 low-income dwellings, displacing over one million people, half of them black. See Gerald Frug, *Citymaking: Building Communities Without Building Walls* (Princeton, NJ: Princeton University Press, 1999), 146. Bernard Frieden and Lynne Sagalyn, *Downtown Inc.: How America Rebuilds Cities* (Cambridge, MA: MIT Press, 1989).
27. The original distinction between positive and negative freedom comes from Isaiah Berlin, *Four Essays on Liberty* (Oxford: Oxford University Press, 1969). This use of the terminology, however, is slightly different than Berlin's. Positive freedom does not mean that there is a specific set of actions that are free or unfree; instead, it captures the position widely held by egalitarian liberals that the state can and should actively intervene in order to rectify social inequalities.
28. Waldron, "Homelessness and the Issue of Freedom," 312.
29. Leonard Feldman, *Citizens without Shelter: Homelessness, Democracy, and Political Exclusion* (Ithaca, NY: Cornell University Press, 2004).
30. Ibid.
31. *Love v. Chicago* No. 96-C-0396 (1998) at 36. Cited in Feldman, *Homeless Politics*.
32. Northrop Frye, *Anatomy of Criticism: Four Essays* (Princeton, NJ: Princeton University Press, 1957).
33. Credited to T-Bone Slim, *Little Red Songbook*, 1920.
34. Thomas Dumm, *United States* (Ithaca, NY: Cornell University Press, 1994), 169.

35. The term heterotopia comes from the work of Michel Foucault and designates an actually existing utopia, a space that actually exists yet allows people to live differently. See "of other spaces," *Diacritics*.

36. The majority of people in shelters have lost their private dwelling due to some sort of financial crisis and many of the long-term homeless (the ones usually associated with the label "street people") have problems with addiction or mental illness.

37. Kozol, *Amazing Grace*, 223.

38. This number only includes children in the New York City Shelter system, as of June 2002. This number represents a 55% increase since 1998. These figures come from the Coalition for the Homeless website, page entitled "Basic Facts." http://www.coalition-forthehomeless.org.

39. Press release from the National Law Center on Homelessness and Poverty. www.nlchp.org.

40. Robert Dahl, *Democracy and Its Critics* (New Haven, CT: Yale University Press, 1989).

41. Furthermore, providing public housing would diminish but not resolve the problem of regulating conduct in public places. It is always possible that recipients of social programs, even fairly generous ones, may turn to begging during a crisis or sell the *Street Sheet* in order to push for more suitable programs. Shelter residents may also want to engage in "chronic bench-squatting" in order to sustain social ties with other homeless people.

42. This phrase comes from Hannah Arendt, "Understanding and Politics," *Partisan Review* 20 (1953), 392.

43. *Robinson v. California* 370 U.S. 660 (1972) deemed criminalization of a status (drug addiction) cruel and unusual punishment. Some courts have applied this precedent to the criminalization of homelessness.

44. See Helen Hershkoff and Adam S. Cohen, "Begging to Differ: The First Amendment and the Right to Beg," *Harvard Law Review* 104 (1991), 896–942.

45. *Blair v. Shanahan* 775 F. Supp 1315 (N.D. Cal 1991) at 322–323.

46. Robert Teir, "Maintaining Safety and Civility in Public Spaces: A Constitutional Approach to Aggressive Begging," *Louisiana Law Review* 54 (1993), 285–338; Williams L. Mitchell, "'Secondary Effects' Analysis: A Balanced Approach to the Problem of Prohibitions on Aggressive Panhandling," *University of Baltimore Law Review* 24 (1995).

47. Peter A. Barta, "Giuliani, Broken Windows, and the Right to Beg," *Georgetown Journal on Law and Policy* 6 (Summer 1999), 165–190.

48. The *Street Sheet* is the name of the paper distributed in San Francisco. Many cities have something similar. The newspaper usually contains articles and editorials on social policy as well as some personal accounts or poetry written by homeless people. Vendors receive a supply to sell, keeping the proceeds for their own needs.

49. Charles Baudelaire, "The Eyes of the Poor," *Paris Spleen* (http://www.scils.rutgers.edu/~favretto/eyesofthepoor.html)

50. Marshall Berman, *All That Is Solid Melts Into Air* (New York: Penguin, 1988).

9

CONCLUSION: THREE RATIONALES FOR THE PROVISION OF PUBLIC GOODS

One of the motifs that runs throughout this book is the suggestion that vibrant public space fosters other public goods. Most notably, it facilitates the diffusion of political information, especially marginal or dissenting views that are underrepresented in the corporate-dominated media. Otherwise invisible points of view—that universities exploit the Third World by allowing their lucrative athletic wear to be manufactured in sweatshops or the reasons for abolishing the federal income tax—can be disseminated in the less competitive arena of public space. Leafletting, bell-ringing, demonstrating, and petitioning are still among the core tactics of grassroots campaigns. Some of these groups' ideas, such as the benefits of school prayer and the dark side of globalization, circulate at the margins until grass-roots mobilization, marketing savvy, or political opportunity propels them into the mainstream media.

Public space plays an important role in fostering democracy by preserving opportunities for political speech and dissent. The Wobblies first made this claim forcefully during the Free Speech Fights in the early twentieth century. Standing on soap boxes perched on street corners, they articulated controversial ideas that challenged the truisms repeated from the church pulpit or university lectern. Although many people initially rejected the idea that marginal groups had an equal right to trumpet their views on public streets and plazas, a more expansive embrace of political speech gradually came to dominate the courts and public opinion.

Rights consciousness is far more diffuse now than it was in the era of the IWW soap box orators. Today few North Americans would say

189

that democracy implies the right of the majority to silence the minority. At least in the abstract, the consensus in favor of basic political rights is fairly robust. This book takes such a consensus as its point of departure. Rather than providing another theoretical defense of free speech guarantees, it explores the ruse by which citizens continue to defend the concepts of free speech and assembly while protecting themselves from the discomforts of politics. This book shows how the privatization of public space makes it possible for citizens to pay homage to democratic values while shielding themselves from contact with ideas and people they find disturbing. Unwilling to reject liberal democratic ideals such as equality, toleration, and civil liberties, many citizens retreat from the public spaces where these ideals are realized.

In defending public space as a locus of confrontation and transgression, however, I fear that I might leave readers with the impression that entering public space is like eating your vegetables: something you do because it is good for you. In fact, public spaces can be attractive, vital, and fun. They are desirable places that most people cannot afford to provide for themselves or places that they prefer to share with others.

In my experience, public space does help build social capital.[1] During the year I lived in Toronto, most of my friends were people I met in public places: the neighborhood park, community center, and drop-in center (a kind of indoor playground for children supported by the City of Toronto). The neighborhood park provided a balance of sameness and difference. The friends that I made were all English-speaking parents with young children but sharing space also encouraged a sense of sympathy with other users: dog walkers, skateboarders, a Falun Da group, teenagers, and street people. These experiences encouraged me to identify as a part of the city and neighborhood. These contacts pointed me toward other local resources and motivated me to support a similar web of services for others.

Public parks and community centers provide important collective amenities but even less elaborate and more accidental public spaces such as the street have something to offer. Despite or perhaps because of its anonymity, a crowded street can serve as a distraction from one's own worries and private concerns. Petula Clark put it best in her hit song *Downtown:*

> When you're alone and life is making you lonely
> You can always go…Downtown
> When you've got worries all the noise and the hurry
> Seems to help I know…Downtown.

It is worth reflecting on why this is the case. Part of it is probably the visual stimulation provided by the confluence of alluring window displays, varieties of people, perhaps street art, cafes, and advertisements. Or, as the song suggests, "You may find somebody kind to help and understand you." But even if you remain alone, the presence of others tends to diminish your own self-regard and thus the intensity of your problems. Adam Smith explained this dynamic in the *Theory of Moral Sentiments*. The presence of others encourages the individual to look at his or her problems through the eyes of others, who take a more distanced point of view.

COMMUNITY AND CONSUMERISM

For many people, going to the mall is the equivalent of going downtown. The popularity of shopping malls and gated communities is a complex phenomenon because it reflects both an embrace and rejection of public life. A visit to the mall is often motivated by more than the need for a particular product. For seniors and stay-at-home parents, a trip to the mall is the opportunity to overcome the isolation of the home and neighborhood. Surrounded by soothing lighting, stimulating images, enticing products, movement, controlled crowds, and unthreatening strangers, the mall-goers experience some of the pleasures of public space. Even the decision to purchase a home in a Common Interest Development is often motivated by the desire for community.[2] The current vogue for New Urbanist design, with its front porches, parks, and playgrounds, reflects dissatisfaction with suburban anomie and an appetite for informal social encounters. Even though the New Urbanism would be more appropriately labeled the New Suburbanism, its popularity does reflect the desire for a more fulfilling balance between privacy and social life.

Although shopping malls and Common Interest Developments realize one of the quintessential dimensions of public life—the desire to see and be seen by acquaintances and strangers—they preclude other dimensions. Public spaces are characterized by general accessibility, collective ownership, and a tendency to foster interaction between individuals. The proliferation of places like shopping malls makes it apparent that it is anachronistic to divide the world into public and private, because there are many spaces that fall into neither category. There is a vast gray zone made up of "social spaces" that are privately owned but do facilitate contact with strangers. Many social spaces are also commercial spaces that simulate public life in order to sell goods and services. Gated communities materialize their exclusivity in stone and steel. Shopping malls, on the other hand, are designed to entice potential consumers, therefore they appear more accessible and inviting. Some malls achieve exclusivity using more subtle means: choosing locations in affluent suburbs, keeping out public transportation, and including only the most expensive stores. Most malls also rely on security guards to expel nonconsumers: chronic bench squatters, groups of teenagers, and political activists. Although shopping creates the illusion of freedom, choice, and individuality, the mall often fosters conformity.

The case of Battery Park City illustrates how even government-owned property can come to resemble private commercial space. The logic of the market played a crucial role. Once the Battery Park City Authority began to feel that its mandate was to obtain the highest possible lease payments for the reclaimed waterfront land, then it made sense to treat "public spaces" (the waterfront promenade, plazas, and gardens) as marketing tools for selling the adjacent real estate. Inevitably tension arose between the Battery Park City Authority's goal of turning a profit and the project's public functions, such as providing low-cost housing and recreational opportunities to all New Yorkers. It is not surprising that the ubiquitous "Parks Service employees" tell gleaners (e.g., people who gather and recycle cans) to go elsewhere, claiming that the public park is private property.[3]

The concepts of public and private coexist uneasily alongside "community," a term that is both a bridge and a rival. Community suggests a level of association beyond the intimate/family/household yet not as remote and formal as the state. It evokes a group that is linked together by shared values and identity. Ever since the path-breaking work of Ferdinand Tonnies, scholars have distinguished between *gemeinschaft* and *gesellschaft*, community and society.[4] Community, the category that Tonnies favored, was an idealization of the qualities of small-town life: family values, interdependence, shared social life, absence of conflict, and homogeneity. In contrast, the term society was an elaboration of the characteristics of city life: anonymity, alterity, mobility, heterogeneity, and alienation.

Over one hundred years later, the images and concepts of community and society have not lost their power. This study suggests that the characteristics of *gesellschaft*, its diversity and fluidity, are positive qualities that public space should foster. Some scholars have argued that the longing for community (*gemeinschaft*) is motivated by a nostalgia for a past that never existed.[5] According to this position, nostalgia artfully conceals forms of violence and exclusions that existed in the past and makes them harder to recognize in the present.[6] For example, New Urbanist communities in the South sometimes employ references to plantation architecture in order to evoke a feeling of grace, hospitality, and charm, a set of associations hardly shared by the descendants of slaves.

Advertising and marketing take advantage of this nostalgia for community and reproduce it. As Keally McBride puts it, "Visions of sociality pervade consumer images—families, small towns, friendly neighbors. The model of consumption allows us to desire these images or find them pleasurable at the same time that we might, for example, flee family gatherings in tears, find small towns provincial, or be bothered by nosy neighbors."[7] This is part of the allure of New Urbanist residential developments, festival marketplaces, and small-town-shopping-district-style malls. People are not deceived into believing that these stylized reproductions are "real" communities or "authentic" remnants of the past. They are savvy consumers who prefer the representation to the original, the image to the reality, the appearance to the essence.[8]

One illustration of this marketing of community is the appeal of Starbucks. A Los Angeles-based advertising agency interviewed Starbucks customers in focus groups and discovered that a recurrent theme in their comments was the "community feeling" or "social atmosphere" of Starbucks. Yet the agency found that only ten percent of customers actually talked to other patrons. "Most customers waited in line silently and spoke only to the cashier to order a drink."[9] According to Howard Schulz, the chairman and chief global strategist of Starbucks, his customers do not want the genuine community of a Milan coffee bar. They want "upscale, vaguely European ambience in which contemporary culture has been decontextualized, wrapped in a blanket of the dim past, made cozy, comfy, secure, palatable, and attractive to the business class."[10]

This does not mean that community is simply created by advertising. The selling of community is successful because it appeals to a widely shared longing for sociability.[11] Community, at least in its incarnation as *gemeinschaft*, collapses the distinction between public and private. It fulfills people's longing for sociability in a context that incorporates the appeals of private life: security, familiarity, identity, and (for some) control.

THREE RATIONALES FOR THE PROVISION OF PUBLIC GOODS

Community is an appealing alternative to public life. It promises to provide the pleasures of sociability without the discomforts of the unfamiliar. It offers the fellowship of a shared world without demanding the sacrifices of sharing with those who have less to offer. Although the desire for community is legitimate, it must be supplemented by public spiritedness. According to the logic of community, we share with others who are similar to ourselves. Public spiritedness, in contrast, involves sharing with those who are different. When I use the term public spiritedness I have three things in mind: sharing, solidarity, and diversity. *Res publicae*, public things, are not for the exclusive use of an individual or group. They are shared solidaristically, in other words without regard to what each person can contribute. Public schools, public parks, and public health (in Canada) are goods that are provided to residents based on their needs, not on their ability to pay. They are things that society recognizes as priorities and decides to finance in a way that does not unduly burden those with greater needs (e.g., the chronically ill) or fewer resources. Public spiritedness involves sharing with those who are different as well as those who are similar. Amoral familialism, the opposite of public spiritedness, also involves subordinating self-interest to the common good but the group is conceived in an excessively narrow fashion. The term public, in contrast, comes from the Latin *pubes* meaning adult and describes the population as a whole without distinction. In a heterogeneous polity, this means public spiritedness embraces those who are different.

There are three different ways of making the case for public goods: the economic, the normative, and the political. The economic argument comes from rational choice theory and emphasizes that certain types of goods and services cannot be effectively supplied by the market. The normative argument suggests that the provision of public goods is a requirement of justice. After discussing the strengths and weaknesses of these two alternatives, I briefly introduce the alternative that I find most compelling: the claim that public goods and public space are essential to the formation of civic-minded citizens.

When economists write about public goods they mean things such as national defense that one person can enjoy without diminishing someone else's ability to do so (these are "nonrival" goods). Public goods also include things such as clean air that cannot easily be allocated based on the individual ability to pay ("nonexcludable").[12] Civic leaders such as Frederick Law Olmsted treated parks and plazas as public goods. These places are not consumed or diminished when others enjoy them. In fact, in many public places, their value actually increases when a critical mass of strangers congregates. Unlike the tragedy of the commons, which describes the tendency of individuals to overexploit shared resources, we could call this the carnival of the commons. When large numbers mass in one place, visitors are more likely to encounter acquaintances, young people can meet possible romantic partners, and older people feel the safety that is absent in isolated areas. Since the reforms of the progressive era, Americans have taken for granted that streets, plazas, and parks are provided by the government.

The paradigmatic examples of public goods include national defense and clean water, things that everyone benefits from regardless of whether they contribute. Because each individual has the incentive to free ride, to benefit without paying, it is almost impossible to provide these goods without some sort of mandatory assessment. The government often provides goods that are nonseverable, things that cannot easily be easily sold on the market because they cannot be divided into individual proprietary parcels.

Economists have argued that there are two reasons why certain goods cannot be efficiently provided by the market.[13] First, some goods are nonexcludable. These are things such as national defense that are enjoyed by everyone regardless of whether they pay for them. They are called nonexcludable because it is impossible to prevent noncontributors from sharing the beneficial effects. Second, the market cannot provide goods with high transaction costs. For example, if the cost of collecting the toll on a road is higher than the utility of the road for drivers, then it will not be cost effective for an entrepreneur to build a road. It may be that the drivers want the road and would be willing to pay for it, but they are unwilling to pay the much higher cost of the road plus the toll-collector's salary. From the perspective of rational choice theory, it may make sense for government to build roads (and parks and plazas) if the high cost of gatekeeping makes it unprofitable for entrepreneurs to furnish them.

This economic rationale helps explain why government provides certain goods and services, particularly things with high transaction costs such as sidewalks and roads. But it fails to explain why government should provide other public spaces, such as community centers, parks, and plazas.[14] It is perfectly feasible to build a gate and charge an entrance fee. Amusement parks such as Disney World illustrate that parks do not necessarily fall into the category of nonexcludable goods. There are many other examples of private enterprises financing collective leisure amenities by requiring membership or charging an entrance fee, such as country clubs, health clubs, and vacation resorts.

The market has also proved effective at providing plazas. Shopping malls are ubiquitous and they traditionally provide a large open space where friends and strangers can see and be seen. Shopping malls overcome the free-rider problem and produce a collective good through "site rents." The attractive social spaces of the shopping mall entice consumers and increase stores' profits. The mall management passes on the cost of maintaining these spaces to the tenants as rent, and the retailers choose to pay it because a location in the mall is more profitable than one outside.

As Fred Foldvary points out in *Public Goods and Private Communities,* there is evidence that far from failing, markets have been successful at supplying parks, roads, and recreational amenities. Drawing upon the experiences of private territorial governments (examples include Disneyland and residential community associations), he argues that private entities are adept at providing what he calls civic goods. But what exactly are civic goods? Foldvary uses the term *public goods* as a synonym for *collective goods,* which refers to things that cannot be divided ("nonseverable"). *Civic goods* refer to those public goods that are traditionally supplied by government.[15] His claim is that private entities such as the Walt Disney Corporation can provide parks, plazas, and community centers more efficiently than governments.

This argument seems plausible to someone who has been taken in by Disney's effective imagineering. But Disney World's Main Street, with its colorful facades and scaled-down architecture,[16] is an imaginative rendering of the fantasy of small-town life, not a public space. Public space belongs to the citizens at large and is open to general use. The example of Disneyland illustrates that the private sector is very effective at providing entertainment and amenities to those who can afford it. But with an average cost of $391 per day for a family of four, it is inaccessible for many people.[17] Unlike real Main Streets, it is not part of everyday life but something set apart as an escape and fantasy.

The private sector may be able to provide *social spaces* but it is unable to provide *public spaces,* for example, places where *all* citizens can come together. The reason is simple. As long as entrepreneurs sell collective goods at market prices there will be market segmentation based on ability to pay. Wealthy consumers will choose places with particularly luxurious amenities. Middle-class consumers will choose more modest alternatives. And poor people will have no access to collective goods at all. This market segmentation is already far advanced in the residential housing sector, where high-end gated communities boast walking trails, security staff, golf courses, and swimming pools. Middle-class condos might feature a party room or weight room, and the poor are lucky to have housing at all. One purpose of public space is to overcome this stratification and provide an occasion for contact between people from different subcultures, residential enclaves, and social classes. As long as social space remains segregated, then it cannot foster a sense of solidarity.

Rational choice theory cannot provide an adequate rationale for protecting public space. Libertarians are right when they argue that markets can provide collective amenities such as parks and plazas. The problem is that they cannot provide these amenities to all people, only those with the ability to pay. If inviting spaces are to be accessible to the entire public, including the poor, then they must be subsidized by those with more resources. This brings us back to the question of why should the government devote resources to providing public space. The second way to answer it is by drawing upon normative theory. Liberal-egalitarian theory provides one way to explain why justice requires the provision of public amenities. The argument for the public (as opposed to market-based) provision of collective goods is basically redistributive. Just rules are those that you would agree to if you did not know whether they would benefit you personally. John Rawls hypothesizes that individuals behind the "veil of ignorance"—a hypothetical condition in which people do not know if they will be born rich or poor—would only agree to inequalities insofar as those inequalities benefit the least well-off. He calls this thesis "the difference principle." This principle is supposed to guide citizens when making decisions about public policy.

Does the difference principle require a fairly extensive provision of public amenities including parks, swimming pools, and community centers? The answer depends on how actual citizens prioritize public space vis-à-vis other goods such as health care, defense, childcare, and transportation. But if we assume that people do desire parks, plazas, and playgrounds, then they should not be the exclusive privilege of the rich. Public goods are a way to counterbalance the inequalities that result from morally arbitrary factors such as differences in talent and marketability of skills. If individuals did not know whether they could procure parks and swimming pools for themselves on the open market, they would prefer public provision, which would minimize the risk of having no access at all.[18] The heuristic device of the veil of ignorance helps legitimize the concept of redistributive public goods, even if it cannot predict exactly how a given society would allocate scarce resources.

In his book *Sovereign Virtue: The Theory and Practice of Equality*, Ronald Dworkin develops a similar heuristic device. He suggests that we imagine a system in which individuals who don't know their life situations (socioeconomic status or health) buy insurance against a series of misfortunes such as unemployment or sickness. The premiums would be proportional to one's income. Following this logic, we could imagine public space as a kind of insurance scheme.[19] If people did not know whether they would be able to afford a landscaped garden or country club membership, they might be more likely to support parks and playgrounds available to everyone. The "insurance" scheme takes into account the fact that different communities might rank various priorities (public space among them) in different ways. The funding of public amenities would vary according to the preferences of citizens, but it would still meet the requirements of justice insofar as it provided shared public amenities for everyone regardless of ability to pay.

The normative rationale for supporting public goods differs from the economic rationale because it is based on justice rather than self-interest. According to the economic rationale, the individual acts as a consumer who purchases the collective goods that he desires and can afford. In most cases these collective goods will be provided by private entrepreneurs such as the Walt Disney Corporation but, in exceptional cases of market failure, they may be provided by the government. The normative point of view recognizes that public space is not public if it is only available to those who can pay an admission charge. It acknowledges that creating public spaces involves some government subsidy. Both the original position and the hypothetical insurance scheme are based on the conviction that justice requires that we imagine a fair social structure and commit to building it regardless of whether our individual contribution will be less or more than the collective goods that we receive. If attractive social spaces are part of this imagined world, then we must provide them for everyone.

The normative position provides theoretical reasons why citizens should support funding for public amenities. Public space, however, is not exclusively a redistributive issue. The argument against the privatization of neighborhoods is not simply that poor people need parks or swimming pools. If this were the case it would be possible to accommodate low-income individuals in segregated facilities or provide subsidies so that they could patronize commercial recreational facilities. The normative argument sketched above also fails to explain why citizens should prioritize public space over other goods and services. By treating public space as yet another resource to be distributed, it overlooks the distinctive character of public space. Public space symbolizes and fosters social relations between residents. It also plays a political role by providing a place where different viewpoints can be expressed. Plazas have traditionally been sites where citizens assemble to petition their government. The government has also used public plazas to orchestrate ritual displays of power, unity, or ideology. When sidewalks double as forums for political activity, no particular expense is incurred, and therefore redistributive arguments are beside the point.

There are also some conceptual difficulties with the normative view. First of all, a heuristic device that requires that people abstract from their own self-interest in order to make decisions and allocate priorities has certain limitations. Even if people agree on a general principle of justice, they will still disagree about how to apply the principle to particular cases. According to the difference principle (one of Rawls' two basic principles of justice) people behind the veil of ignorance would only agree to economic inequalities insofar as those differences benefited the least well off. What this means in practice depends on whether one is convinced by the theory of "trickle-down" economics. A wealthy person might believe that a rising tide lifts all boats or that economic inequalities motivate the poor to strive, thereby becoming more productive for themselves and society. An individual's experiences and self-interest, in part, determine how he or she thinks that the economic and social realms operate. Behind the veil of ignorance, without this information, individuals could not make determinate choices about principles of justice because they would lack the basic understanding of the social and economic world. If they did have the type of understanding that one gradually acquires through experience, then they would see the world from a situated, self-interested point of view and would fail to agree on general principles.

A second problem with the normative defense of public goods is one of motivation. This is similar to Hegel's famous critique of Kant. According to Hegel, abstract theories of justice require that people act in a certain way but fail to provide the training that will motivate them to do so. Hegel uses the term ethical life to describe the social structures that inculcate specific values and dispositions. Without the type of character that is fostered through ethical life, the individual has no reason to forgo self-interest for the sake of justice.[20] This criticism is relevant to the discussion of public goods. The normative position explains why citizens should support public goods but does not pay enough attention to the type of experiences or identities that would motivate them to do so once they knew whether specific policies would benefit them personally.

Progressive era reformers made a political as well as a normative case in favor of the public provision of social space. They argued that citizens who were unmoved by the spirit of altruism or duty still had pragmatic reasons for resisting the privatization of public space. Progressive era reformers saw public space as a vehicle for preventing social disorder and fostering a civic identity on the part of new immigrants.

In the early twentieth century, progressives established a system of urban parks and playgrounds as a way of improving the living conditions of the urban poor. Large families lived in crowded, rundown tenements and children had nowhere to play but the streets. Because real tenement reform would have required massive government funding, reformers focused on something more feasible, creating public amenities, mostly parks and playgrounds, where children and adults could enjoy the benefits of leisure and play.

There were several motivations driving this movement. Parks and playgrounds were thought to improve health by bringing sunlight and air into dank, overcrowded neighborhoods. More importantly, progressive era reformers believed that public spaces could help solve urban social problems and prevent vice. Paul Boyer called this ideology "positive environmentalism."[21] Its proponents thought that the character of urban dwellers, especially children, could be improved by the elevating influences of wholesome leisure, nature, and inspiring civic monuments. Thus the movement was motivated by altruism combined with an interest in developing benign forms of social control.[22] The basic premise of the movement was that society was like an organism, and therefore the living conditions of one group affected the others. Jane Addams, founder of Hull House, argued that improving the mental and physical health of the largely immigrant working class would benefit everyone by decreasing crime and disorder. According to the ideology of "positive environmentalism" public spaces could encourage virtues and temper vices by fostering identification with the polity.

I call the progressive's case for parks and playgrounds *political* because its proponents were motivated by a concern for social order rather than a sense of justice. Similar concerns animate a modern-day variant of the playground movement: the "midnight basketball" initiative that tries to keep school gyms and playgrounds open at night in order to provide an alternative to gang activity. Support for public recreation programs, however, has generally been declining. On the left, the ideology of positive environmentalism has fallen out of vogue. There is no longer such confidence in the power of charity or government to improve the lives or lifestyles of individuals. Furthermore, the disciplinary character of some of these efforts—the playgrounds with trained supervisors, stringent rules, and tight schedules—is now perceived as paternalistic: an attempt to encourage working-class children to adopt middle-class behavior and abandon their own more exuberant styles of play. Many elites have come to question the political rationale behind the expansion of public spaces in the early twentieth century.

For many people today public space is not a microcosm of a more perfect social order but rather a site of relative disorder. What then could motivate people to embrace the risks and uncertainties of public life? Throughout this book I have argued that public space strengthens a democratic polity by providing a forum for dissenting views. But public space has another equally significant, albeit more illusive, effect. It influences the way that we are constituted as subjects and the way we identify with others. The privatization of public space narrows our sensibility by diminishing the opportunities to encounter difference. Given this book's focus on the legal and political dimensions of privatization, this phenomenological claim is merely suggestive. Rather than attempting to provide a systematic argument, I introduce (in a suggestive manner) some theories that explain how the public realm fosters politically salient capacities and identities. In a sense this is "positive environmentalism" turned upside down. Rather than building monuments and playgrounds that encourage the urban poor to assimilate middle-class values, the goal is also to create public places where the middle classes may also question their own values.

The basic premise of this contemporary variant of positive environmentalism is that the individual is constituted as a subject through interactions with other people. The built environment facilitates interactions with certain people and limits contact with others. The most frequent interactions are with family and friends, people who usually look and act very much like we do. In public space, the individual encounters a more diverse range of others, which potentially expands the community of people with whom she identifies. By encountering the unfamiliar, he or she becomes more adept at accepting difference.

According to Adam Smith, the basis for ethical judgment is rooted in a human propensity that he calls sympathy. Sympathy comes from a feeling of identification evoked by the experiences of others. When we see the suffering of others, we imagine ourselves suffering in the same way, which elicits the emotion of sympathy. Of course it is easier to sympathize with people who are similar to us because we already identify with them. Smith explains,

> The spectator must, first of all, endeavor as much as he can, to put himself in the situation of the other, and to bring home to himself every little circumstance of distress which can possibly occur to the sufferer. He must adopt the whole case of his companion with all its minutest incidents; and strive to render as perfect as possible, that imaginary change of situation....[23]

This is very difficult to do when the other person who is suffering is someone who looks and acts very different from ourselves. Unethical behavior, or at least ethical indifference, is often the result of a failure of imagination, the inability to recognize the shared humanity that interests us in another's suffering.

Sympathy has two sides. It is not only the psychological mechanism whereby the spectator assimilates the suffering of the other but also the way that the sufferer internalizes the viewpoint of the spectator. By looking at his own experiences through the eyes of others, the individual learns to put his suffering in perspective and control his emotions. Ethical life emerges from this habit of evaluating our own actions from the viewpoint of an imaginary spectator. Because of sympathy, we care what others think of us. This desire for approval motivates us to evaluate our actions based on the imagined judgment of an impartial spectator, thereby internalizing social norms.

If Smith is right and ethical judgment comes from assuming the viewpoint of the impartial spectator, which he calls "the man within," then it is worthwhile to ask: What does the man within look like? Writing in a homogeneous, aristocratic society, Smith was pessimistic about the possibility of sympathy and identification across class and cultural barriers.[24] For Smith it was not problematic if the impartial spectator looked very much like the self. But today we have come to recognize that the imaginary spectator is not really impartial if he represents the values of a narrow, privileged social milieu. If the impartial spectator is an idealization of our social milieu, then taking the viewpoint of the impartial spectator helps correct the problem of excessive self-regard but not the equally serious problem of group privilege.

The theory of moral sentiments is thus beset by the following limitation: the capacity for judgment comes from internalizing what the impartial spectator thinks of our actions but this impartial spectator is the idealization of ourselves. Imagining the impartial spectator corrects our desire to exempt ourselves from general rules that we apply to others, but it does not force us to think about how these general rules might themselves unfairly favor people like us. The problem is that we can know the other only through sympathy, in other words, by projecting our own dispositions and feelings onto the other. The public realm is a way of correcting this limitation.

According to Hannah Arendt, one of the characteristics of the public realm is that public actions can be seen by everyone.[25] This means that acting in public expands the range of spectators who view and, potentially, judge my actions. Not only am I observed by those who are similar to me (the people who I frequent in private life) but I am also visible to, and in some sense, accountable to, those who are different. The public realm can provide an alternative to the hierarchies and exclusions that characterize private space. By facilitating encounters with concrete others, it makes it possible for the subject to look at herself from another perspective. The diversity and heterogeneity of the public realm can potentially motivate one to pose the question, "Who is the man within?"

This possibility was illustrated in Baudelaire's poem "The Eyes of the Poor" (see Chapter 8 for a fuller discussion). The narrator describes his encounter with an impoverished family standing on the street. While sitting in a luxurious new sidewalk café, he notices that a man and his two children are staring at the forbidden splendor. Seeing himself through their eyes, he considers for the first time that perhaps there is something excessive about such abundance in the face of such poverty. Confronted with the "eyes of the poor," the standards that he had hitherto used to judge his own actions were questioned.

The narrator's companion reacts very differently to the same experience. She wishes that the proprietor would send away those people who disturbed her aesthetic pleasure and ease. She fails to recognize the far greater discomfort of the family's need (and perhaps her own complicity in it). "Eyes of the Poor" illustrates two opposite reactions to the same encounter. It captures the fact that exposure to suffering does not necessarily evoke a feeling of sympathy. But it does open up the *possibility* of expanding the circle of people with whom we sympathize. There is no guarantee that enlarging public space will lead to an enlargement of social imagination but the alternative is to live in a world of private spaces where the proprietor has already sent the street people away. The encounter described in the poem takes place in a sidewalk café, a site that transgresses the border between the public and private realms. In the fully privatized world of the shopping mall it would be impossible.

Public space facilitates the mutual recognition of strangers. Strangers are not merely individuals who have not yet become acquainted with one another but rather people who are disturbing to one another because they bear markers of difference: race, age, poverty, or culture. Public space provides a context in which such people can become familiar, not intimate, with one another. This familiarity potentially has two salutary effects. This shared world-in-common can help individuals sympathize with the suffering (and the joys) of others. More important, it can help us see ourselves through the eyes of others so that when we look to the "man within" to provide a moral compass we are not simply looking in the mirror.

In *The Theory of Moral Sentiments*, Adam Smith wrote, "How selfish soever man may be supposed, there are evidently some principles in his nature, which interest him in the fortune of others, and render their happiness necessary to him, though he derives nothing from it except the pleasure in seeing it." According to Smith, the spectator receives one benefit from the happiness of others, and that is the pleasure of *seeing* it. In public we witness the happiness (or suffering) of others and, to some small degree, share it. The capacity for sympathy is one of the psychological propensities that make political life possible because it motivates individuals to consider the needs of others. It is the basis of a modest degree of solidarity and reciprocity, which are two of the basic components of citizenship.

In political theory in the past decade there has been much interest in the politics of recognition.[26] Usually the term recognition implies the formal acknowledgment of a group's autonomy, identity, or claims. According to Nancy Fraser, a politics of recognition targets injustices that are cultural, in other words, rooted in patterns of representation, interpretation, and communication.[27] Recognition requires a tenuous balance between respecting difference and perceiving commonality. But there is also a more basic meaning of the term. To recognize is "to know again, to perceive a person previously known." Recognition, then, is dependent upon prior familiarity with or exposure to diverse others. In order to recognize the claims of others we must first know them as both different from and similar to ourselves. Herein lies part of the significance of public space. In private we choose our companions according to our preferences and in public we learn to share the world with those who are different.

According to Hannah Arendt, "the term 'public' signifies the world itself, insofar as it is common to all of us and distinguished from our own privately owned place in it."[28] It is this world that both brings us together and separates us from each other. For Arendt the public realm is constituted by diverse points of view and characterized by "the simultaneous presence of innumerable perspectives and aspects in which the common world presents itself."[29] Although Arendt did not believe that the public realm was a physical place, it is still worthwhile to think of public space in terms of her concept of publicness. Public space may seldom realize this ideal, but it nevertheless captures the spirit that animates it and makes it worth protecting.

Democratic solidarity depends upon a shared public realm, a "public good," that allows individuals to counterbalance their ethnic, religious, and economic differences. Public space promotes contact: the sociability that bridges the divisions between people and makes it possible for them to imagine one another as citizens.[30] Even though opportunities for contact may tend to decrease in an age of television,

Internet, consumerism, suburbs, and long commutes, this is no reason to give up the public realm as an ideal. Only this ideal can challenge the reality of today's metropolis, which is designed to limit the possibility of contact. We are faced with two different ways of relating to strangers. One is marginalization. This is the strategy pursued by many shopping malls, gated communities, and business improvement districts, which are structured to prevent unsettling encounters with people who cast doubt upon our favored narratives of community and equality. The other is understanding, the capacity that "makes it bearable for us to live with other people, strangers forever, in the same world, and makes it possible for them to bear with us."[31]

ENDNOTES

1. Robert Putnam, *Making Democracy Work: Civic Traditions in Modern Italy* (Princeton, NJ: Princeton University Press, 1993).
2. See, for example, Setha Low, *Behind the Gates: Life, Security, and the Pursuit of Happiness in Fortress America* (New York: Routledge, 2003); Andrew Ross, *The Celebration Chronicles: Life, Liberty, and the Pursuit of Property Value in Disney's New Town* (New York: Ballantine, 1999).
3. This claim is based on an interview with "Elmira," Battery Park City, July 29, 2002.
4. Ferdinand Tonnies, *Community and Society*, trans. Charles Loomis (New York: Harper and Row, 1957).
5. Gerald Suttles, *The Social Construction of Communities* (Chicago: University of Chicago Press, 1972).
6. William E. Connolly, "Democracy and Territoriality," *Millennium: Journal of International Studies* 20, no. 3 (1991), 464.
7. Keally McBride, *Social Imagineering: Producing and Consuming Ideals of Community*, unpublished manuscript.
8. This argument is made by Guy DeBord, *The Society of the Spectacle*, trans. Donald Nicholson-Smith (New York: Zone, 1994).
9. Howard Schultz, *Pour Your Heart Into It: How Starbucks Built a Company One Cup at a Time* (New York: Hyperion, 1997).
10. David Shields, "The Capitalist Communitarian," *New York Times*, March 24, 2002, section 6, page 28.
11. This term comes from Hannah Arendt's *On Revolution* (New York: Penguin Books, 1990). See below for a fuller discussion of the concept.
12. Frug, *City Making*, 167–168.
13. See for example Robert L. Heilbroner and Lester C. Thurow, *Economics Explained* (New York: Simon and Schuster, 1987).
14. Fred Foldvary, *Public Goods and Private Communities: The Market Provision of Social Services* (Brookfield, VT: Edward Elgar, 1994).
15. Foldvary, *Public Goods and Private Communities*, 13.
16. Most buildings are five-eighths to seven-eighths in size in order to scale things down for children and create a memory-landscape for adults. See Robert Stern, *Pride of Place* (New York: Houghton Mifflin, 1986), 211.

17. According to Bob Sehlinger's *The Unofficial Guide to Walt Disney World 2002* (New York: Wiley, 2002) the average cost of a day at Disney for a family of four was $391 (not including transportation to Orlando).

18. This is an over-simplification of the Rawlsian model. In *Theory of Justice*, he recognizes that individuals behind the veil of ignorance would only decide general principles of justice, such as the difference principle. In order to apply this principle to actual policy decisions, they would have to have more concrete and complete knowledge and experience. (Cambridge, MA: Harvard University Press, 1971).

19. Ronald Dworkin, *Sovereign Virtue: The Theory and Practice of Equality* (Cambridge, MA: Harvard University Press, 2000), 65–119.

20. G.W.F. Hegel, *The Philosophy of Right*, trans. H.B. Nisbet (Cambridge, UK: Cambridge University Press, 1991).

21. Paul Boyer, *Urban Masses and Moral Order in America, 1820–1920* (Cambridge, MA: Harvard University Press, 1978).

22. See, for example, Frederick Law Olmsted, *Civilizing America's Cities: A Selection of Frederick Law Olmsted's Writings on City Landscapes*, ed. S. B. Sutton (Cambridge, MA: MIT Press, 1971). Jane Addams, *Twenty Years at Hull House* (Urbana and Chicago: University of Illinois Press, 1990).

23. Adam Smith, *The Theory of Moral Sentiments* (1759), Part I, Section I, Chapter IV.

24. Smith was concerned with the inculcation of morality in the lower classes after they left village society. He felt that religious sects such as Methodism had a positive effect because they recreated small communities in which members would be observed by others and therefore more likely to internalize ethical norms.

25. Hannah Arendt, *The Human Condition* (Chicago: University of Chicago Press, 1958), 50.

26. See, for example, Charles Taylor, *Multiculturalism and the Politics of Recognition* (Princeton, NJ: Princeton University Press, 1992); Axel Honneth, *The Struggle for Recognition: The Moral Grammar of Social Conflicts*, trans. Joel Anderson (Cambridge, MA: MIT Press, 1996).

27. Nancy Fraser, *Justice Interruptus: Critical Reflections on the 'Postsocialist' Condition* (New York: Routledge, 1997), 6.

28. Arendt, *The Human Condition*, 52.

29. Arendt, *The Human Condition*, 57; Dana Villa, "Postmodernism and the Public Sphere," *American Political Science Review* 86, vol. 3 (1992), 712–721; Bickford, "Constructing Inequality," 257.

30. Richard Sennett, *The Uses of Disorder* (New York: Knopf, 1970).

31. Hannah Arendt, "Understanding and Politics," *Partisan Review* 20 (1953), 391.

10

AFTERWORD: NO CENTRAL PARK IN CYBERSPACE

The objection that I encounter most frequently when presenting this work is that physical space is irrelevant in the age of the Internet. According to this argument, cyberspace is becoming a favored site of encounter and the need for physical gathering places correspondingly diminishes. Sitting here writing in Tango Palace, my neighborhood café, surrounded by other regulars who are reading newspapers or chatting in groups, this objection intuitively seems incorrect or at least exaggerated. We may all have checked our email this morning, but email is not a substitute for the diffuse sociality of the café.[1] Nevertheless, cyberspace does provide a powerful means of communication that challenges us to reassess the importance of public space. Cyber-romantics have argued that the World Wide Web is a utopia of free speech where individuals can publicize their views and reach vast numbers of potential sympathizers.[2] They claim that the Web, by radically decreasing the cost of publication and undermining the power of intermediaries (publishers and distributors), provides a public forum that is much more effective than public space.

This final chapter is more tentative and exploratory than the rest of the book, in part because the Internet is rapidly changing. My impression, however, is that the balance between commercial and noncommercial uses of the Internet is shifting and this transformation, although much more rapid, parallels the commodification of public space. If that is true, then a close analysis of the structure and function of cyberspace strengthens rather than weakens the case for protecting public space. More importantly, perhaps, this book's defense of public space also has lessons for debates about the architecture and regulation of cyberspace. Many of the arguments in favor of public space are also reasons for building some sort of equivalents in cyberspace, such as public e-gateways and virtual public forums.[3] The increasingly commercial character of the Web comes into focus when we consider that the architecture of the Web often looks similar to a shopping mall. Privately owned portal sites attract customers in order to entice them to follow links to online stores and advertisements provided by corporate partners. These portal sites such as Yahoo! and AOL are the new gathering places on the Web and they do not usually provide places where dissenters can set up their soap boxes. Instead of diminishing the need for public space, the growth of the Internet illustrates the importance of the concept of "public space" and the need to think about the development of virtual public spaces on the Web.

During the euphoria of the late 1990s, many people thought that the Internet would provide a powerful alternative mode of communication that would make the face-to-face politics of public space anachronistic. In fact, the Internet has become an important tool for political mobilization. Most readers of this book probably receive petitions and updates about political causes via email. New social movements have been quick to take advantage of technology to facilitate communication between sympathizers, to organize demonstrations, and to lobby decision-makers.[4] The Internet can link local movements with supporters in other places, including those with vastly greater resources or international influence. The success of the Zapatistas' Web campaign is a much-cited, if somewhat outdated, example.[5]

Even sympathetic accounts of the efficacy of the Internet, however, recognize that organizing in cyberspace complements rather than replaces other forms of activism. Email, listserves, and Web pages played an important role in organizing large-scale demonstrations such as the anti-globalization protests. They were also crucial for coordinating timely actions against the war in Iraq. But despite the critical contribution of Internet-based organizing, these were still fundamentally traditional demonstrations where protesters came together in public space in order to publicize their point of view and convince politicians of their strength and determination. One reason why protesters gather together is to exchange information about their cause and to listen to speeches by influential dissenters whose views are underrepresented in the mainstream media. It is worth considering why such protests continue to be a widely employed tactic in the repertoire of collective action even though the Internet provides alternative forums for communication. Instead of organizing a demonstration, a political group could simply post the speeches, pamphlets, and chants on its website and "demonstrators" could log on to access the information and to record their presence. I suspect that neither allies nor adversaries, however, would find this to be a particularly convincing form of protest. One reason is that demonstrations are not only about communication, at least not in the rationalistic sense of sharing arguments and evidence. They are also opportunities for forging solidarity through shared rituals (marching, chanting) and these rituals are intensified by sensory experiences. Demonstrations often function as secularized pilgrimages in which participants leave their normal routines and converge on a place where all stimuli tend to encourage identification with the cause.

There are several other features that distinguish demonstrations from their cyber-equivalents. In a demonstration, organizers exercise some control over the context, which shapes participants' and spectators' interpretation of the event. In the age of mechanical and digital reproduction (the age of both television and the Internet), it is easy to remove images, ideas, and actions from their context and assign different meanings to them. For example, a television report might focus on an isolated incident of violence that was only a marginal element of the event. A visitor to a "cyber-demonstration" Website might choose links to certain speeches while skipping others that explore different points of view. The Internet strengthens the individual's control over information, but this filtering can have negative as well as positive consequences. If even a sympathizer may quickly skip over the speeches at a cyber-demonstration, it is even easier for the apathetic to ignore them. Traditional demonstrations encourage sympathizers to identify with the cause but they also target unwilling listeners. By parading through downtown and gathering in front of an important building (city hall, the embassy, etc.) participants hope to get the attention of precisely those citizens and especially decision-makers who would never voluntarily log on to their Website. By becoming visible in public space, demonstrators have a chance to expose nonparticipants to their cause and their message. Often this exposure is magnified by the effect of television and newspaper coverage, but the media usually cover a dissenting political viewpoint only when it is expressed as part of an event. An event involves something out of the ordinary, for example, the presence of celebrities, the disruption of routines, violence, mockery of power, or crowds. The Internet is not particularly suited to the staging of events because it provides little of the thrill of co-presence and none of the drama of confrontation. A demonstration in cyberspace would be easy for both politicians and passersby to avoid simply by turning off the screen, deleting an email, or leaving a site. As Andrew Shapiro put it, "though the Net empowers us as speakers, it empowers us as listeners even more. We need never be 'captives' subject to speech we don't want to hear."[6]

DISINTERMEDIATION

In the literature on the Internet, there are two lines of criticism, which are somewhat at cross purposes. One focuses on the way that the Internet decreases individual agency because it is dominated by large corporations that tend to stifle innovation and expression (for a summary of this argument see the section below entitled "Communications and Control"). The second focuses on the way that the Internet facilitates excessive individual control, by undermining the role of traditional institutional intermediaries. The latter argument is made by cyber-skeptics, who regret the gradual eclipse of print journalism, especially the local daily newspaper, which they suggest used to provide a common lens for viewing events and a common language for evaluating them. According to this position, the Internet provides extensive choice but little direction; it offers exhaustive information but little synthesis. By making it easier to read news and analysis produced by like-minded people, the Internet reinforces rather than challenges our parochial world views.

Recently, cyber-skeptics have become concerned with the issue of personalization, in other words, the way that the Web allows the individual to exercise greater control over the information that she receives. For example, technology makes it possible to create a personalized newspaper with the local weather, stock quotes, and favored news categories prominently displayed. The Net also facilitates access to a variety of specialized new sources tailored to one's ideological orientation and interests. This has certain advantages. It allows people to draw upon a much broader range of information and decreases reliance on the gatekeeping function of the mainstream media. Those with alternative viewpoints are easily able to contact a geographically dispersed community of sympathizers.

Recently I had an experience that illustrates the potential pitfalls of the hyper-specialization made possible by the Internet. My seven-month old son was diagnosed with a medical condition that the pediatrician assured me was not too serious. I did some research on the condition and joined a list-serve devoted to it. Over the next few days, as I read the old postings, I became increasingly anxious and worried about the most dire possible side effects that some list-serve postings mentioned. Friends and relatives thought it was nothing to worry about and I began to suspect that through the Internet I had come into contact with the dozen people in the country most obsessed with the condition.

This experience reminded me of Adam Smith's point that we learn to moderate our fears, anger, self-pity, and excessive self-regard by learning to look at our own experiences through the eyes of the impartial spectator, a member of the community who will sympathize with our predicament but only to a reasonable degree.[7] If we want to continue to receive sympathy, respect, and admiration, we must attempt to modify our feelings and actions in accordance with community norms. But this moderating effect takes place only when the relevant community is composed of people with diverse interests, tastes, and experiences so that they are unlikely to share an individual's idiosyncratic obsessions. This moderating influence disappears when the community from which I conjure my impartial spectator is made up of others who are similarly obsessed with a particular experience. The Internet brings us in contact with just such a narrowly focused community. If there is no Archimedean point from which to objectively evaluate our judgments, then we are very dependent upon communities of meaning for guidance. Internet communities, to the degree that they are based on hyper-specialization, may be more likely to inflame rather than moderate our passions.

Several commentators have recently noted that this increased capacity for customization may have negative consequences for political community and solidarity. According to Cass Sunstein, the ability to filter out alternative viewpoints may potentially balkanize citizens according to different ideologies and identities.[8] In *Republic.com*, he documents how Websites usually link to other sites with a similar point of view, creating a solipsistic effect. Sunstein worries that the ideological polarization that computer technology facilitates will impoverish the diverse experiences that sustain a pluralistic culture.

It is far from clear, however, whether the cyber-skeptic position is correct. Many people have told me that they are more likely to peruse a wide range of sources on the Internet. A conservative who would never subscribe to the *Nation* might look at it online in order to see what progressives are writing about. Or a lefty who would never spend $3.00 on the *Weekly Standard* might glance at a headline online and be intrigued (or outraged) enough to read the article. The Internet makes accessing information much less costly (in terms of time as well as money) and therefore may encourage people to be more experimental in choosing diverse sources of information. The widespread use of search engines on the Web can also facilitate exposure to unfamiliar (and ideologically unsympathetic) points of view. Before the Internet, people usually chose a newspaper or television program, which provided content. Most information was accessed through a filtering mechanism that generally reflected (and reinforced) the readers' point of view. Now, the reader can identify the topic that he or she is interested in and then receive information from a vast range of sources. Under the old system, the typical businessperson would buy the *Wall Street Journal* and see what it had to say about tax cuts. Now, she might search for "tax cuts" on Google and receive a list of articles from right-wing and left-wing, urban and rural, mainstream and fringe publications.

By directly connecting writers and readers, the Internet undermines the intermediation provided by media organizations. There are both advantages and disadvantages arising from this change. It becomes easier for a wide range of citizens, including those with highly idiosyncratic views, to circulate their ideas. Some people may find it difficult to evaluate this vast array of information, given that the unstructured context provides very few tools for assessing its credibility. The reputation of a certain information source, say the *New York Times* versus the *National Inquirer*, provides cues that help the reader interpret the stories. Search engines make it easier to access articles from a wide range of publications, but the results are displayed by topic, which makes the interpretive clues provided by the source hard to recognize. For example, the facts about affirmative action in a white-supremacist newspaper would be interpreted differently than the information provided in the *Wall Street Journal*. More generally, how would a New Yorker know whether the *Small Town X Tribune* is a well-respected local paper or the rantings of discredited conspiracy theorists? Furthermore, many articles are simply posted without any editing or peer review and are therefore more likely to contain inaccuracies that the casual reader cannot identify.

Search engines provide the Web surfer with the serendipity of the chance encounter. My Web search for the term "new urbanism" led me to commercial sites promoting new developments, a lecture by the prominent critic Michael Sorkin, a real estate agency in Seaside, Florida, and a nonprofit newspaper. One link leads to the other and suddenly I am exploring possibilities for a beach vacation rather than researching my book. Cyber-skeptics exaggerate the degree to which the Internet fosters tunnel vision and hyper-specialization. But the serendipitous character of the Web is decreasing under the impetus of commercialization. Search engines now typically list the sites of paid sponsors before other results and some do not distinguish between the two categories. Pop-up ads are the most frequent chance encounters. Furthermore, the architecture of the Web makes it difficult for non-commercial interests (such as political groups) to be visible to people moving between commercial sites.

This is an important difference between physical space and cyberspace. In physical space there is the opportunity for people to congregate in public places such as markets, plazas, parks, and passageways. Many vital places have a strong commercial component—think of a favorite shopping street or a plaza with a sidewalk café—but the commercial activities are (or were) linked together by public spaces. This makes them accessible for a variety of noncommercial uses, including political activity, as well as social activities such as hanging out, eating, chatting, people watching, listening to or performing music, or playing cards or sports. On the Internet, the places to hang out are privately owned and this means that their commercial orientation is not counterbalanced by public alternatives. There is no Central Park in cyberspace.[9] And this has consequences for political life, particularly for the dissenter whose strategy is to take advantage of existing gathering places in order to find a potential audience for his message. There are few public gathering places on the Web where political activists are free to post their signs and hand out their leaflets. There are important differences between physical space and cyberspace. The information superhighway takes us from site to site without even a glimpse at the landscape, villages, and crossroads that we pass on the way to our destination. This forecloses a certain kind of serendipity, or to be more precise, the unsought stimuli are usually in the form of paid advertisements for consumer goods and services.

Several commentators have championed the idea of a digital public forum as an alternative to the proliferation of cybermalls. This would be an online space called "PublicNet" where community groups, artists, and activists might have the opportunity to confront their fellow citizens.[10] One way to do this would be to require that Internet service providers display an icon that would take the user to a forum that linked together Websites and chat rooms created by nonprofit organizations devoted to politics, culture, and science.[11] Another idea that has already proved successful is community-based networks and gateways. These gateways integrate forums devoted to local issues with access to the World Wide Web; they can be designed to facilitate communication among local residents, to sustain links between cyber and physical space, to highlight local resources, to encourage citizens to produce as well as consume content, and to reflect the distinctiveness of a particular area.[12] But it seems that these initiatives have been weakening rather than growing in strength. In the early days of the Internet, computer cognoscenti built innovative portals and multiuser domains (MUDs) with civic, social, or aesthetic goals. Although some continue to flourish as real alternatives, the more successful ones were purchased by large Internet companies and others suffered from competition with well-funded, growth-oriented alternatives such as AOL.[13]

But perhaps this is painting an excessively bleak and one-sided picture of the Web. Despite the increasing commercialization, one could claim that the entire Internet is a big speaker's corner, where speech is cheap and easily accessible.[14] As the Supreme Court put it, any Internet user can be "a town crier with a voice that resonates farther than it could from any soapbox."[15] But is it really true that the Internet effectively amplifies the voice of the political dissenter? In some ways, a website is more like a clubhouse than a soap box. Before the Internet, a citizen who was interested in a particular political group could visit its headquarters in order to receive pamphlets and literature. Today, websites make it much easier for interested individuals to receive this information. But the purpose of the soap box was quite different. For the Wobblies, street speaking was meant to expose potential allies to information that they would never think to seek and to confront adversaries with their anger. Moreover, the Wobblies set up their soap boxes in front of the labor recruiters' ("sharks") storefronts because this was the most effective place to reach vulnerable workers and to disrupt the sharks' activities. On the Web, it is nearly impossible to set up a soap box on public property outside a business that engages in unfair labor practices, discriminates against minorities, or violates environmental standards. This has important consequences for consumer and labor activists in particular. If the workers at Amazon.com go on strike for better working conditions, how could they inform customers about their cause and try to elicit sympathy and support? Perhaps they could create their own Website outlining their grievances, but it seems unlikely that even a small fraction of Amazon customers would even be aware of it let alone look at it. [16] Customers entering a bricks-and-mortar bookstore, on the other hand, would be forced to see a picket line and then make a decision about whether to ignore it.

Cyberactivists have been savvy about finding alternative ways to challenge commercial interests. Because it is impossible to set up soap boxes in front of online retailers, protesters cannot rely on physical proximity to establish the connection between corporation and critique. Instead, some have tried to subvert the semiotic system of corporate power. For example, Kieron Dwyer, a cartoonist in San Francisco featured a parody of the Starbucks logo on his Website. The image was similar to Starbucks' mermaid, but she was topless, pierced, and displayed the message "consumer whore." Starbucks' lawyers were not amused and filed a suit for trademark infringement. U.S. District Judge Maxine M. Chesney found that Dwyer's parody did tarnish Starbucks' corporate image and forbade him from profiting from it.[17] As part of the settlement of a related civil suit, Dwyer agreed to remove the parody from his website.[18]

In many ways this altered logo was a typical example of culture jamming. Culture jams are countermessages that make use of a corporation's own method of communication to send a message starkly at odds with the intended one.[19] The tactic was pioneered by artists and activists who transformed billboards and other ads through creative edits. With just a magic marker Virginia Slims can become "Virginia Slime" and the hollowed-out faces of fashion models can look like skulls.[20] Dwyer's parody of the Starbucks logo was clearly in this spirit but whereas many incidents of cultural jamming are untraceable acts of aesthetic-political resistance in the tradition of graffiti, a Website is fairly easy to trace. Technology is Janus-faced. Desktop publishing has proved an effective tool for cultural jammers because it has made it easier to produce slick parodies that might be confused with the original advertisements. The Internet facilitates the diffusion of subversive images but it also makes it easier for corporations to identify and prosecute individuals who infringe on trademarks by parodying them online. The Internet may furnish resources for creative new forms of dissent but it also provides technological tools for increasing corporate control of communications.

COMMUNICATIONS AND CONTROL

In the early days of the Internet there was much euphoria about the revolutionary nature of the Net. The structure of a network—a decentered, rhizomatic form of communication—seemed to undermine any attempt at hierarchical modes of control. In the past few years, however, scholars have begun to point out ways that the Internet increases corporate control over the exchange of ideas, cultural products, and consumer goods. It is a Faustian bargain; individuals voluntarily embrace the new technology that gives the illusion of greater speed, efficiency, and autonomy and in the process they become dependent upon corporations that can subtly control what they see and do on the Web.[21] In *The Future of Ideas*, law professor Lawrence Lessig explains the basic logic of this process. Communications systems that rely on complex and costly technology require an investment of capital. The corporations that make this investment try to maintain as much control as possible in order to maximize their own profits. This means they will prevent innovative new technologies and products that threaten their market position.[22] Lessig, a former law clerk for Justice Scalia, recognizes that corporations must have some return on their investment but the thrust of his argument is that they should not be allowed to set up permanent barriers to future creativity and innovation.

Lessig artfully explains how the increase in creativity and communication in the early days of the Internet is being undermined. In order to illustrate this process, he suggests that communication technologies are made up of different layers that can be either free or controlled.[23] By free he means that access is not conditional on permission granted by someone else (even though a modest and neutrally applied fee may be charged).[24] In any communications system, there are three layers, each of which could be free or controlled: the physical layer, the code layer, and the content layer. Lessig presents several illustrations to clarify the nature of these different layers.

The first one is the Hyde Park speakers' corner, a place in London with a tradition of public oratory dating back to the mid-nineteenth century (see Table 10.1). Political activists, religious zealots, comedians, and crazies stand on soap boxes and try to attract a crowd of listeners. Hyde Park is also the site of political demonstrations, including one against the war in Iraq, which was one of the largest demonstrations in British history.[25] According to Lessig, the physical layer (the park), the code (speech), and the content (the text of the speeches) are all free. Speakers at Hyde Park do not need permission from the government and no one demands a royalty for the use of the English language.

The second example is Madison Square Garden, a sports/concert venue where the code layer (speech) is free and the content layer (what gets uttered) is mixed (some material may be copyrighted and other material may be in the public domain) but the physical layer is controlled. Madison Square Garden L.P., the owner of the venue, decides who may enter and charges a significant fee. The next two examples, the telephone system and cable television, are even more restrictive. Both the physical infrastructure (the wires) and the logical infrastruc-

TABLE 10.1

	Hyde Park	Concert Hall	Telephone System	Cable TV	World Wide Web
Content	Free	Mixed	Free	Controlled	Mixed
Code	Free	Free	Controlled	Controlled	In Transition
Physical	Free	Controlled	Controlled	Controlled	Controlled

Adapted from Lawrence Lessig, *The Future of Ideas*, 25.

ture or code (the principles of connectivity) of the telephone system are privately owned, but the content (the conversation) is free. Cable television is an example of a totally closed system in which the physical infrastructure and code (the cable and signal) are used to provide content that is protected by copyright.

According to Lessig, the Internet mixes freedom and control at different levels. The physical layer is controlled. Computers are privately owned by individuals or organizations that limit access. The code layer, written by people in government and academia in order to facilitate the exchange of data, was initially free but is potentially becoming more controlled as cable companies and other Internet service providers begin to act as gatekeepers, filter information, exclude certain applications, and privilege others.[26] The content layer includes both free (public domain) and controlled (copyrighted) material, but here too the trend is towards greater control. Although many people initially assumed that the ease of digital reproduction on the Web would weaken the protections of copyright, Lessig suggests that the Web may actually strengthen copyright. By creating a set of potentially liable deep pockets, the Internet service providers, copyright can be enforced more effectively. Internet service providers have a strong financial incentive to refuse to host the Website of anyone even suspected of copyright violation. When individuals in real space share music, images, or text no one is likely to find out but when they do so over the Web, it is easy to identify and penalize them.[27]

The concept of layers is particularly helpful in illustrating the continued importance of public spaces such as the Hyde Park speakers' corner. According to Lessig's schema, it is the only system of communication in which all three levels are "free." The other communication systems may be more powerful, but they are all controlled on at least one level. As the example of Madison Square Garden illustrates, control at even one level, the physical level, is enough to make a communication system unsuited to many types of political communication. As long as a venue is privately owned, the goal of profit maximization means it will usually be used for commercial rather than civic or political purposes. The private control over the physical layer also makes it easy to censor controversial views. Even when the Wobblies could afford the costs of a meeting hall, the owners often refused to rent to them because they objected to the Wobblies' doctrine or feared vigilante action.

Control over the physical layer—computers and modems—is also an issue in access to the Internet. As of 2000, about sixty percent of Americans had access to the Internet.[28] Despite efforts to make computers accessible through public schools and libraries, there is still a digital divide that separates Internet users (who tend to be young, white, educated, and affluent) from other Americans.[29] According to surveys done in 2000, lack of physical access to computers (particularly the high cost of equipment and service) was one of the major obstacles to the majority of nonusers.[30] The digital divide is even starker internationally. For example, less than one percent of Africans have Internet service.[31] This suggests that the Internet, although an effective tool for reaching educated and affluent consumers in developed countries, may not currently be effective for communication among other groups, particularly the elderly, poor, illiterate, and those living in less industrialized countries. Private ownership of the physical layer is part of the reason for the digital divide.

Community groups, academics, and government have experimented with different ways to expand access to the Internet. In addition to providing computers in libraries and public schools, some localities have equipped community centers with Internet terminals and offered courses to train people to become more savvy consumers (and sometimes even producers) of Web-based content.[32] Known as e-gateways, these are real places that provide access to the virtual world.[33] Public e-gateways (and to a lesser degree commercial Internet cafés) make the Internet more accessible by decreasing the cost of access and providing guidance to those unfamiliar with the new technology, which is another significant barrier to usage. If such public e-gateways were to proliferate, then it might make sense to modify Lessig's schema and designate the physical layer of the Internet as "mixed" rather than controlled. Of course, public e-gateways are still controlled by the government agencies that own the computers and provide the Internet connection. These government bureaucracies—libraries, schools, or community centers—can establish rules, for example, limiting time slots or requiring a library card. These restrictions are a form of control but it is control exercised in order to distribute a scarce resource fairly.

It is important to remember that physical spaces, even public places such as parks and streets, are not intrinsically free. Their accessibility is the product of cultural norms and legal guarantees. There are reasons why streets and parks became public and we should consider whether these same reasons apply to cyberspace.[34] In physical space most of the roads that link houses and businesses are public. This is partially due to the fact that many streets were originally pathways that developed gradually through general usage over time. Streets are usually owned and maintained by the government because history has shown that private control exacts excessive costs for the individual and the community as a whole. In feudal and early modern Europe, bandits and lords collected tolls from travelers and merchants, making the movement of goods and people an excessively costly enterprise. By socializing the cost of securing and maintaining the roads, each user paid less and the community benefited from the growth of markets and productivity. Far from supplanting private enterprise, this form of public property made private property more efficient.

The Internet is much like a system of public roads. Most Websites (just like most businesses) are privately owned. Some sites allow access only to members or subscribers and many others are open to everyone, but the protocol for moving around the Web is not controlled. It was pioneered by scientists, supported by the government, and extended by countless anonymous users over time. No one exacts a toll when Web surfers move from site to site and the entire Web profits from increased circulation. With new technologies, however, it may be possible to collect such a toll or at least to privilege certain sites as Internet providers begin routing some sites more directly than others.[35] One reason to think about the virtues of public space is that it reminds us why Internet users and regulators should resist excessive privatization of cyberspace. As consumers and citizens we must think about whether we want cyberspace to look like a shopping mall, a flea market, or a vibrant downtown center.

ENDNOTES

1. For a good discussion of the social function of the café and other third places, see Ray Oldenburg, *The Great Good Place: Cafés, Coffee Shops, Community Centers, Beauty Parlors, General Stores, Bars, Hangouts and How They Get You Through the Day* (New York: Paragon House, 1989).
2. For a good overview of both the utopian and dystopian positions on the Web, see David Bell, *An Introduction to Cybercultures* (New York: Routledge, 2001). One particularly influential early work in the genre was Howard Rheingold, *The Virtual Community: Homesteading on the Electronic Frontier* (New York: Harper Perennial, 1994).

3. Andrew L. Shapiro, *The Control Revolution: How the Internet is Putting Individuals in Charge and Changing the World We Know* (New York: Public Affairs, 1999).
4. See the essays in eds. Martha McCaughy and Michael D. Ayers, *Cyberactivism: Online Activism in Theory and Practice* (New York: Routledge, 2003); Mark Poster "Cyberdemocracy: Internet and the Public Sphere," in *Internet Culture*, ed. D. Porter (London: Routledge, 1997), 201–217. For some other examples of net campaigns against corporate power, see Naomi Klein, *No Logo* (New York: Picador, 2000), 393–396.
5. Manuel Castells, *The Power of Identity* (Cambridge, MA: Blackwell, 1997); D. Ronfeldt and A. Martinez, "A Comment on the Zapatista 'Netwar,'" in *Athena's Camp: Preparing for Conflict in the Information Age*, eds. J. Arquilla and D. Ronfeldt (Washington, DC: Rand Corporation, 1997), 369–391.
6. Shapiro, *The Control Revolution*, 128.
7. Adam Smith, *The Theory of Moral Sentiments* (New York: Cambridge University Press, 2002).
8. Cass Sunstein, *Republic.com* (Princeton, NJ: Princeton University Press, 2001).
9. Beth Simone Noveck, "Designing Deliberative Democracy in Cyberspace: The Role of the Cyber-Lawyer," *Boston University Journal of Science and Technology* 9 (Winter 2003), 25.
10. James Boyle, "The Second Enclosure Movement and the Construction of the Public Domain," *Law and Contemporary Problems* 66 (Winter/Spring 2003); Shapiro, *The Control Revolution*, 205.
11. Shapiro, *The Control Revolution*, 205.
12. Shapiro gives the Blacksburg Electronic Village, a local e-gateway with a participation rate of 60%, as an example. Shapiro, *The Control Revolution*, 210, 214.
13. The literature on the Internet as a site of community has focused on MUDs. See, for example, L. Cherny, *Conversation and Community: Discourse in a Social MUD* (New York: Cambridge University Press, 1999).
14. Noveck, "Designing Deliberative Democracy in Cyberspace," 27.
15. Cited in Shapiro, *Control Revolution*, 204.
16. There are some interesting alternatives; for example, critical groups have registered domain names that are similar to well-known corporate sites in order to mock or disparage them (e.g., starbuckssucks.com). Some targets have tried to shut down these critiques by suing for trademark infringement.
17. See also Paul Brandus, "Hot Water: Starbucks Sues a Citizen. How a San Francisco Cartoonist Ticked off the Seattle Java Giant," *salon.com*, June 1, 2000.
18. According to Dwyer's Website, Dwyer claims that he is not allowed to disclose the terms of his settlement with Starbucks, but that it requires that he remove the logo. http://members.tripod.com/`LowestComicD/GREED.htm
19. Naomi Klein, *No Logo*, 281.
20. Klein, *No Logo*, 285–286.
21. For example, search engines are increasingly sorting information to funnel users to paid corporate partners and advertisers. It is beyond the scope of this book to document the new forms of control that are emerging on the Internet. Lawrence Lessig provides an excellent discussion of this issue, including an overview of the government's case against Microsoft. He explains Microsoft's motives for trying to destroy the Netscape browser. The core idea is that Microsoft used its dominance over the operating system market to force computer manufacturers to adopt its own browser. Its motive was the desire to maintain a near monopoly on the operating system market, which would have been imperiled by innovative uses of Netscape. See Lawrence Lessig, *The Future of Ideas* (New York: Random House, 2001), 61–68.
22. Lessig, *The Future of Ideas*.

23. Lessig, *The Future of Ideas,* 23–25. He credits Yochai Benkler with the schema. See "From Consumers to Users: Shifting the Deeper Structures of Regulation," *Federal Communications Law Journal* 52 (2000), 561–563.
24. Lessig, *The Future of Ideas,* 20.
25. Police estimated the crowd at 500,000; organizers claimed there were over 1,000,000 participants.
26. Lessig, *The Future of Ideas,* 156–158.
27. Lessig notes that a student in his dorm room might have a photocopy of a cartoon from *The New Yorker,* a poster of Bart Simpson, and a rock song playing without any fear of prosecution for copyright infringement, but should he put those on a Website—even a Website that will probably not be visited by more people than come to his dorm room—his Internet service provider will close down the site to prevent liability under the due diligence doctrine. Ibid. 177–183.
28. A study by the University of California at Los Angeles (November 2000) reported that 66.9% of Americas used the Internet. A December 2000 poll of the Pew Institute found that 56% of the population (over age 18) had Internet access. For a discussion of these studies, see James E. Katz and Ronald E. Rice, *Social Consequences of Internet Use: Access, Involvement, and Interaction* (Cambridge, MA: MIT Press, 2002).
29. Katz and Rice, *Social Consequences,* 35–65. On the digital divide, see Lisa J. Servon, *Bridging the Digital Divide: Technology, Community, Public Policy* (Malden, MA: Blackwell, 2002); ed. Benjamin Compaine, *The Digital Divide: Facing a Crisis or Creating a Myth* (Cambridge, MA: MIT Press, 2001).
30. Katz and Rice, *Social Consequences,* 75. According to one 2000 study, the most commonly cited reason for "dropping out" of Internet usage was difficulty (65.5%) followed by cost (54.5%) and loss of access (48.2%).
31. According to the United Nations Commission for Africa, only one in 250 people in Africa have Internet access and two-thirds of these are in South Africa. (Reported in *The Australian,* June 4, 2002, C02). Some have challenged these figures, noting that although few people have individual Internet service at home, more have shared access through Internet cafés or workplaces.
32. Sonia Liff, Fred Steward, and Peter Watts, "New Public Places for Internet Access: Networks for Practice-Based Learning and Social Inclusion," in *The Virtual Society: Technology, Cyberspace, Reality,* ed. Steve Woolgar (Oxford: Oxford University Press, 2002).
33. Liff, Steward, and Watts, "New Public Places," 97.
34. Carol M. Rose, "The Public Domain: Romans, Roads, and Romantic Creators: Traditions of Public Property in the Information Age," *Law and Contemporary Problems* 66 (Winter/Spring 2003), 89–100.
35. Lessig, *The Future of Ideas.*

INDEX

A

abolitionists, 23–24
abortion clinics, 42, 59–63
Abortion Services Act (1996), 60
Abrams v. United States, 23
accessibility, 11, 13, 15, 21, 25, 28, 38, 79, 191, 218
Addams, Jane, 200, 206
affirmative action, 53, 212
agora, 12, 21, 57, 150
Airplane, 47
airport, 47–48, 51–52, 54–57, 59, 60, 62, 66
Alexander Cooper Associates, *See also* Cooper, Alexander,163
Alexander, Mark, 89
alienation, 147
Amana, 99–100, 112
Amazon, 214
American Civil Liberties Union (ACLU), 38, 53, 64, 79, 96, 111
American Federation of Labor (AFL), 25
American Revolution, 44
Amish, 97, 99, 106, 112
amoral familialism, 194
Anderson, Benedict, 125, 139
Anderson, Rocky, 95
animal rights protesters, 76, 78
anti-abortion protesters, 42, 51, 59–65
antiglobalization protesters, 37, 39, 208
AOL, 208, 214
Appleby, Joyce, 45
Arendt, Hannah, 10, 21, 120, 138, 188, 202–203, 205–206
Aristotle, 103
Arkes, Hadley 19
Askin, Frank, 140
Austin, Regina, 166

authenticity, 148, 193
automobile, 52–53, 78, 129, 159
Avery v. Midland County, 85, 91, 112

B

bad tendency doctrine, 23
balkanization, 10, 107, 119, 211
Barber, Benjamin, 20, 79, 90, 166
Barney, Darin, 20
Barta, Peter A., 67, 188
Battery Park City, 18, 141–166, 169, 179, 185, 192, 205
    Authority (BPCA), 142–166, 192
    master plan, 142–145, 162–163
    Parks Conservancy, 149, 155, 161, 192
    Upper Room, 149–150
Baudelaire, Charles, 188, 203
Beadle, J. H., 98, 112
begging, 3, 170, 182–184, 188
Bell, David, 219
Bender, Thomas, 165
Benkler, Yochai, 221
Berlin, Isaiah, 173
Berman, Marshall, 165, 185, 188
Bickford, Susan, 19–20, 206
Bill of Rights, 1, 16, 33, 73, 88, 95–97, 109, 138
    eighth amendment, 183
    fifth amendment, 73, 176
    first amendment, 1, 17, 19–20, 23, 42, 48, 50–51, 53, 55, 57–58, 60, 70–74, 81, 89, 94–97, 115, 135, 183
    fourteenth amendment, 71, 135, 176
    fourth amendment, 176
Bimeler, Levi, 100, 112
Black, Justice, 71, 72